D0394448

POPE JOHN PAUL II

An Intimate Life

POPE JOHN PAUL II

An Intimate Life

THE POPE I KNEW SO WELL

CAROLINE PIGOZZI

New York Boston Nashvile

FaithWords
Hachette Book Group USA
237 Park Avenue
New York, NY 10017

Visit our Web site at www.faithwords.com.

Printed in the United States of America

First Edition: September 2008
10 9 8 7 6 5 4 3 2 1

FaithWords is a division of Hachette Book Group USA, Inc.
The FaithWords name and logo are trademarks of Hachette Book Group USA, Inc.

Library of Congress Cataloging-in-Publication Data

Pigozzi, Caroline.
Pope John Paul II : An Intimate Life / Caroline Pigozzi.—1st ed.
p. cm.
ISBN-13: 978-0-446-50550-5
ISBN-10: 0-446-50550-1
1. John Paul II, Pope, 1920-2005. 2. Popes—Biography. I. Title.
BX1378.5.P578 2008
282.092—dc22
[B] 2007047219

To Marina and Cosima

In memory of my mother,
my father, Henri Théodore Pigozzi,
and Roger Thérond, my professional mentor

And in memory of my years of study
at Saint-Dominique

CONTENTS

POPE JOHN PAUL II

An Intimate Life

Chapter One

A FORMER DOMINICAN PUPIL SETS HER SIGHTS ON THE VATICAN

One evening, John Paul II was due to leave the Hôtel de Ville dock in Paris aboard a *bateau-mouche* riverboat on his way to the Nunciature. I was then living in an attic apartment opposite the Hôtel de Ville on the Quai aux Fleurs. It was June 1980, and the Pope was in Paris on a pastoral trip. A few hours before the Holy Father's appearance, a squad of marksmen armed with binoculars and telescopic-sight rifles invaded my apartment. A ballistics specialist accompanied members of the anti-terrorist squad, who were hooded and clad in midnight-blue coveralls. It was feared that the jubilant city of Paris could be the scene of an assassination attempt on the Eastern European Pope. I was 28 years old, and the event revived my curiosity and passion for the history of the Roman Church, a subject that I was already fascinated with when I was a pupil at the Dominican convent in the Via Cassia. I was now getting closer to Saint Peter's Square . . .

I had once met a Supreme Pontiff during an audience granted to junior and senior pupils. Hieratic and majestic, Paul VI corresponded perfectly to the holy image that a young girl from an austere boarding school would have of the Patriarch of the West. I will never forget that extraordinary morning. The Vatican seemed to me so mysterious, especially when, a few weeks later, Mother Superior Marie Johannès sent me with a group of other pupils to represent our establishment at Saint-Louis-des-Français, the French national church in Rome, at a mass celebrated by Cardinal Tisserant. She inspected our dark-colored uniforms and checked that we had remembered our black mantillas before telling us in an authoritative tone that she counted on us to do credit to our institution, since the Frenchman who was celebrating mass was the senior member of the Sacred College—in other words, the second most important person at the Vatican after the Pope. In addition to his prestigious post, this eminent native of the Lorraine region had an imposing air, a serious gaze and a gray beard trimmed in the style of a Renaissance cardinal, in short, a panache that struck me from the very first. When I saw him arrive in his scarlet cape, his pectoral cross attached to a heavy gold chain, his right hand bearing an Episcopal ring set with a gleaming purple amethyst that covered a third of his finger, I was, then and forever after, intrigued and dazzled by the princes of the Church and everything to do with them.

Since then, and having become a journalist, I have been haunted endlessly by the desire to penetrate the mysteries and life of the Vatican and the Pope, just as others dream of gaining access to the Kremlin or the White House. But on that day back in 1980 in Paris, I vowed I would force open the doors of Saint Peter's. I was driven by passion and by the challenge it represented: by passion, since the Pope who had set the Lutetia on fire was Slavic, and I myself, through my mother, had Slavic blood in my veins, and by the challenge it represented, because it seemed far from easy for a female journalist to approach Karol Wojtyla, the charismatic shepherd to more than 1 billion 71 million Catholics, or 17.2% of the planet's population.

The idea of writing a report on the Holy Father—and, later on, a book—took firm root in my mind and stayed there. I thus spent many years, each time I found myself in Rome, going to Saint Peter's Square to breathe in the air of the Vatican while trying to catch sight of the Pope during the Sunday Angelus. At midday, I was blessed along with the crowd of pilgrims and tourists, all applauding and chanting "*Viva il papa!*" before leaving once again, filled with emotion and enthusiasm. His powerful voice invariably resonated in me. I was deeply moved, beyond the realm of words, and I told myself that it would bring me luck and that the happy day would come when I would finally bring my plan to fruition—although, in reality, this challenge seemed to be insurmountable, demanding as it did a fund of patience, diplomacy and persistence. I did finally succeed, and, excluding the birth of my two daughters, Marina and Cosima, nothing else has given me as much happiness as coming into such close contact with John Paul II. Thanks to this Pope, I enjoyed many years' worth of exceptional moments and marvelous discussions with him and his close entourage, first within the Vatican and then in the intimacy of his private apartments, where he received me on several occasions. I also accompanied him as a reporter during his pastoral visits throughout the world. It is thanks to him that I discovered the real meaning of the famous words that had, in my eyes, long been an abstract concept from my childhood catechism: "Go forth and teach all nations." I was also able, sadly, to observe the slow transformation of his triumphant apostolate into a long, hard, sorrowful road.

Outside of his close colleagues and friends, who encouraged me and helped me to appreciate him, few people have had the chance to share the things I saw and learned—unforgettable moments of respite from an existence which, when the melancholy of journalism descends, continue to comfort me when I am assailed by the endless doubts and fears inherent to my profession. These memories, as moving as they are astonishing, allow me today to paint a faithful, frank portrait of John Paul II in his daily life without, I hope, allowing myself to be too carried away by my feelings.

The Vatican was, in principle, open to everyone, since every Wednesday the Pope gave a general audience to the faithful. But they observed him from afar: until 2000, some people could just about manage, by jostling and shoving, to touch his cassock as he passed through the rows, without, however, managing to talk to him. But I wanted more than that: I would never be content with the holy image and distant views of the Supreme Pontiff. My ambition was to read the story of his life. I did not want to merely skim the surface of the man in white; I dreamed of entering his mythical, secret universe. However, that universe, the Vatican, was a fortress, and over the centuries many imposing barriers, invisible gulfs and prohibitions have built up around the Popes.

During John Paul II's era, the first barrier for a journalist was the director of the pressroom, Dottore Joaquin Navarro-Valls. This handsome Spaniard was a psychiatrist trained at America's famed Harvard University, a former correspondent for Iberian newspapers and an influential member of Opus Dei, the powerful and highly structured international organization for Catholic propaganda created in Spain and comprising a secretive elite of laymen, priests and even cardinals whose official object is to attain holiness through work. With his psychiatrist's reflexes, he analyzed every visitor and suspected French journalists in particular—a major drawback since Rousseau and Voltaire—of religious disrespect or even insolence; excluded from this suspicion were certain colleagues who kept him happy by taking such measures as giving their front page articles obliging titles like, "Navarro-Valls: a key man at the pontificate." For the rest of us, he represented the unavoidable obstacle that French reporters had to overcome. Reaching him on the telephone was impossible for anyone he didn't know. Élisabeth Fouquet Cucchia, his omnipresent, gruff French secretary (whose career in the Holy See press room began under Paul VI), was ruthlessly daunting in blocking access to him. And if, miracle of miracles, you did succeed in getting an interview, there was always a considerable waiting period—coincidentally, longer than the duration of your stay! The princes of the Church have, in any event, a relationship with time similar to the one they have with eternity. For example, when I asked for an audience in October 1999 with the new nuncio to Paris, Msgr. Fortunato Baldelli, the adroit papal ambassador in France, he suggested that I call back in October 2000 since his schedule was too full!

Another barrier that has historically hindered access to the Holy See is language. Cardinals and *monsignori* always express themselves in such a diplomatic fashion, with such subtle nuances and playful airs, that those not familiar with Machiavelli and Talleyrand are thrown off balance. Their manner is smooth, oblique, solemn and deceptively gentle, and even though they give the impression that they are whispering in Church Latin, they are in fact speaking Italian! Communication is therefore difficult for the barbaric foreigner. With no knowledge of the language, rites and rhythm of the life lived in this little world—holy and remote, traversing the centuries, confined to majestic, hushed palaces—it is almost impossible to penetrate this universe, in others words, to find some charitable soul who will initiate you into the secrets of the keys and locks that open the doors to Saint Peter's.

With the Italian blood inherited from my father, maybe I was better equipped than many to infiltrate the heart of this strategic circle and decipher the codes that governed it, thanks to my childhood years with the Dominican nuns in the Via Cassia. In the library there, between missals bound in bottle green or burgundy and the *Lives of the Saints*, you could still find a weekly publication called *Bernadette, l'illustré catholique des fillettes (Bernadette, the Catholic Illustrated Magazine for Girls)*. An efficient group of Dominicans ran a large religious boarding school whose pupils included Italian girls from the Black Nobility—the Roman aristocracy that has produced so many Popes and palaces—as well as a handful of French girls and many young daughters of those who moved in the glittering cosmopolitan and diplomatic circles. These included the Habisht girls, Polish twins whose parents were friends of Msgr. Wojtyla and with whom he occasionally stayed in Piazza Callisto when he was in Rome. My chaplain and frequent confidant was Father Poupard, who lived at Saint-Do and then worked at the Vatican's Secretariat of State. He afterwards became rector of the Catholic Institute of Paris, then president of the Pontifical Council, and finally minister of culture under John Paul II, a post he retained throughout the papacy. He took a liking to me because of my insatiable curiosity about the mysteries of that seat of power where he carried out his ministry. He was fond of describing the inner workings of the place to me, revealing its secrets, both major and minor, with sparkling eyes and precise words. He had arrived there as a young priest under John XXIII, and knew everything there was to know, just like an influential member of an important ministerial cabinet. Entranced by his captivating tales, I dreamed of becoming a journalist so that I could penetrate even further into this wonderfully enigmatic world, and he encouraged me to pursue my ambitious goals.

The third obstacle to overcome was the almost insurmountable Polish barrier. It is no criticism of Karol Wojtyla to say that he surrounded himself with his compatriots: councilors, private secretaries, and even the humble nuns who served him all came from his country. Since their names were not only unpronounceable but also extravagantly spelled, it was impossible to make the impatient, suspicious nuns on the switchboard understand whom one wished to talk to. The Pope's private secretary, to take one example, was called Dziwisz, a name that, to a French person, resembled something like a sneeze.

And the good nuns were inflexible and rather distrustful, jealously protective of "their" Holy Father.

When, thanks to my friendship with Cardinal Poupard, I was able to attend innumerable audiences, solemn masses and blessings given by John Paul II in order to try and understand how his entourage functioned by closely observing the ceremonies, I was intrigued to see Karol Wojtyla constantly looking at two people who were always close to him: Msgr. Stanislaw Dziwisz and his second secretary, Msgr. Mieczyslaw Mokrzycki, two Poles who were never more than a few meters away from him. And yet the Holy Father was seemingly surrounded by high-ranking prelates of the curia, including a good many Italians. In reality, as one of his Italian colleagues confided to me later, the Pope was only really close to his intimate friends and colleagues, almost all Polish, and a few intellectuals he liked to philosophize with. He shared the surprising characteristic of lacking a court and courtiers with King Juan Carlos, whom I observed minutely when I followed him for a month for *Paris Match*; they both preferred their direct entourage to comprise only those they liked, respected professionally *and* held in deep affection.

Never averting my gaze from the Supreme Pontiff during all of these religious ceremonies, which often lasted hours at a time, I suddenly noticed, from barely perceptible signs, that he must have been a little bored by the protocol, not only because it was tedious in itself, but because it threatened to keep those near and dear to him at a distance. That is when I realized that, to approach His Holiness, I had to play the Polish card, unluckily the hardest card of them all.

One last obstacle remained, possibly to my eyes the most

troublesome: the Vatican was, and still is, a male universe. Even the Virgin Mary would feel ill at ease in this overwhelmingly masculine environment, which only two laywomen in 26 years had miraculously succeeded in invading: Lucienne Sallé, research assistant at the Pontifical Council for the Laity and also a former Dominican pupil, who joined the Council in March 1977 as deputy assistant secretary; and American law professor Mary Ann Glendon, who in March 2004 became president of the Pontifical Academy of Social Sciences.

This shortage of women was not evidently the result of misogyny, per se; these holy men simply have very little contact with the feminine world, apart from the nuns assigned to such secondary tasks as domestic services, cooking, housework, sewing and staffing the switchboard. The ultimate promotion for a nun might be to work as a secretary or, even better, a restorer of old tapestries, a translator or an archivist, like Sister Mary Epiphany, or even—an extraordinary privilege—to be put in charge of running the pontifical sacristy, like Sisters Rita, Adelaida and Elivra, who ironed John Paul II's liturgical vestments to the sounds of Radio Vatican. These humble, self-effacing women moved quietly through the long marble corridors of the Vatican like mice, without ever making their voices heard. They were all, of course, clad in nuns' habits, veiled, carrying large moleskin bags and shod in sensible nun's shoes.

At the time, there were almost no female journalists accredited to the Holy See. The cardinals and *monsignori* had nothing against me: they simply could not understand what I was doing in their closed universe. They took me for a kind of pious laywoman, a deadly-dull diehard, or a possible affiliate of the

Association of Consecrated Virgins or of the Society of Christ the King, members of which are not nuns but laywomen who have taken vows of chastity and poverty, something like a parallel sisterhood of nuns. They were also disconcerted that I was addressing them: in the Vatican, a nun modestly lowers her gaze, does not speak and is not spoken to—though she may perhaps be smiled at. They were likewise intrigued because, so as not to attract attention to myself, I always wore a black, shapeless, cowl-like garment with a little white collar, opaque tights and flat shoes, but no silver wedding ring—after all, I was not wedded to God, which is why I also wore make-up. I did not want to be put in the same category as the women who were part of the Vatican's religious personnel. The curious thing is that any woman who finds herself before the prelates of the Roman curia is generally in an extreme situation. She is either ignored, as though she were part of the furniture, or she arouses the liveliest curiosity, like some rare breed, and finds herself drawn into incredibly long conversations. In any event, the churchmen's attitude toward women remains irrational. Simple conversations in a friendly and detached tone—what we would call small talk—are out of the question. It must be said that these gentlemen are so astute, so cultivated, their minds so keen, that even the most minor conversations with them can never be banal or superficial. In truth, this did not strike me, as it may well have done others, as an insurmountable obstacle—for which I had my past to thank, a past where, lulled by the sound of hymns plus interminable years of Latin, I learned to talk to God and his servants with the simplicity of a young girl familiar with the psalms, her rosary and Gregorian chants. I was also perfectly capable of crossing myself with holy water and genuflecting at the right moment. I had learned how to address a mother superior, an abbot or a confessor, and that one should never take a cardinal's hand but rather kiss his Episcopal ring respectfully, and that you should call him Eminence and on no account Excellence like a bishop.

In the Vatican, I was neither awkward nor intimidated, and people knew it. And it is possible that my modest attitude did not frighten those dignified figures decked out in mauve and purple, usually so quick to slip away with a quick blessing.

When the *Paris Match* news editor, Patrick Jarnoux, suggested in December 1995 that I write a feature on the Vatican because I spoke Italian, I accepted immediately, brimming with enthusiasm, taking the offer as a gift from the heavens. And what a privilege to actually be sent there on Christmas Day! I had long been on the lookout for just such an opportunity as this. Before joining *Paris Match*, I had spent 13 years working at a major magazine staffed by devout writers and a boss who had just rediscovered God, and where John Paul II was the private property of André Frossard. Reporters dreamed of approaching John Paul II and had absolutely no intention of granting this (rare) privilege to a less experienced journalist than themselves, and a woman at that!

In Rome that morning, the heavens were on my side as I called up someone that destiny had already put in my path: Paul Poupard. It was just after the Pope had been struck down by an attack of dizziness during the traditional *urbi et orbi* blessing, which was broadcast worldwide. Cardinal Poupard was concise on the telephone: in fact, everyone in the Vatican distrusted the telephone, thanks to the days when some nuns on the Holy See switchboard under Pius XII used to listen to conversations on behalf of their governor, Cardinal Canali. Cardinal Poupard's words were brief but his tone reassuring: "Come and see me at home at six this evening."

The cardinal lived in the working class area of Trastevere, above the Tiber, in the San Callisto palace, an extra-mural Vatican enclave. Behind this ancient palace, overlooking the Piazza Santa Maria di Trastevere, a number of large, modern, ochre-colored buildings surrounded a courtyard. On the third floor, from where one can admire the cupola of Saint Peter's, live several eminent members of the Holy See. When I left the elevator, I found myself facing a long corridor open to the sky and lined on both left and right with high, varnished doors, all identical. Nobody was in sight to tell me where to go, and not a sound could be heard other than the occasional muffled toll of a neighboring church's bells. No Swiss Guard appeared to guide me around this solemn, soothing, almost monastic place. Finding Cardinal Poupard's apartment was the first test. I was on the point of losing heart when I noticed a gleaming copper plaque, to the left of a heavy oak door, engraved with the name Cardinal Etchegaray. It was not him I was looking for, even if I had read his book (whose title—*J'avance comme un âne [I go forward like a donkey]*—had struck me), but the sight encouraged me to venture farther. I took a few more steps, and finally saw "Cardinal Poupard" on an identical plaque. Feeling anxious, I pressed the copper bell nervously.

As my former chaplain received me at his door with a broad smile, his neighbor, Msgr. De Nicolò, was watering his many plants on the landing. Having congratulated him on his green fingers, the cardinal introduced me; always happy to bestow a compliment, and no doubt wishing to avoid any misunderstanding on the subject of our meeting, he therefore told him, "This is one of my brilliant former students at Saint-Do. She has come to visit me and give me a book." Even if prelates can be suspicious of each other, there was nothing unusual at this time of the year in my sparing a kindly thought for a respected former teacher. Msgr. De Nicolò immediately proved remarkably affable, and his trust in me later on was extremely precious, since he was the regent of the Papal Household and thus one of the organizers of pontifical ceremonies. How could I not believe that the heavens were with me and I was guided by God that day, or at least by one of his angels? Thanks to a chain of unanticipated circumstances, I had finally gotten a toe in the door of the Vatican fortress.

After prayers in Cardinal Poupard's small private chapel, where we were joined by Sister Marie Béatrice and Sister Claire Marie, two French nuns who looked after him, I noticed to the left of the oratory, in a corridor, above a door, the cardinal's coat of arms: a red hat from which hung, on either side of the shield, two cords and 30 tassels in the same color, 15 on each side, with a small yellow boat at sail on an azure sea in the middle, and the Augustinian motto inscribed below: "For you I am a bishop, with you I am a Christian." "My coat of arms, presented to me by the Franciscans of Naples," explained the cardinal, giving me a tiny glimpse into his universe. This was the first confidence he entrusted me with. My former chaplain then led me to his huge library, where some 15,000 works were meticulously archived. Once there, he did not beat around the bush, and told me, with the same frankness he had always used in the past: "There is no way for me to pick up the telephone and ask Msgr. Dziwisz for an interview with His Holiness for you and your photographer. It has never been done before. However, what I can do is work diplomatically toward you being able to approach the Holy Father's entourage; it would then be up to you to seize any opportunity that came along." What this meant in reality was that he was giving me an unexpected chance to break through the great barrier that the Polish circle represented. It would then be up to me to succeed in obtaining a certificate of good conduct—the prelude, as it were, to the precious pass that would grant me entry to the most secret, closed-off place on earth.

It was a highly perilous enterprise, since, if my plan failed, there would never be another way in. I could certainly never hope to gain the favor of Joaquin Navarro-Valls, who would always bear me a grudge for having casually gone over his head. Pinning me with his bright and determined gaze behind unadorned glasses, the cardinal concluded: "I will have you invited to all John Paul II's New Year's ceremonies. I will also arrange for you to be placed close to the front row, discreetly, on the right. After that, you will have to manage on your own."

I quickly understood his message. My past and my experience as a political journalist helped me, and maybe my feminine intuition as well. Surmounting the high walls of the Vatican was proving to be something of a detective game. Who was the most important policeman, the least distrustful papal gendarme? Who did I need to have on my side—the master of ceremonies in charge of all the others? The kindly Swiss Guard? The Pope's close companion, whose attention I would have to catch? The trick would be to succeed in getting on the good side of some people without annoying others, and to be aware that, surreptitiously, people would be observing me coolly. I therefore could not make any mistakes in the liturgical actions or protocol that had to be respected.

At the end of six days of masses, offices, blessings and other celebrations, all those unsympathetic eyes were on me. Was she, like other journalists, going to start by getting annoyed, then become discouraged, and then trip up? My steadiness and silence saved me. Even when John Paul II visited a little suburban church to bless a delegation of road workers, I was there. On the seventh day, Msgr. Dziwisz finally noticed me. On that memorable Sunday, he approached and spoke very politely to me: "I believe that you have come to write an article on the Holy Father? In six days you have surely been able to observe everything you needed to see . . . now you can go back to Paris in peace. You surely have enough information to write your article!"

The trap was sprung! I immediately retorted, politely but very firmly: "I am missing lots of things, the most essential element, in fact! What I would like is to follow His Holiness at close quarters in his daily and private life." I knew from a Vatican gendarme that at six that very evening, the Pope was meant to be receiving some 40 Polish pilgrims in a private audience. I asked Msgr. Dziwisz, "Could I not attend the audience?" He paused for a minute, torn between astonishment that I knew about the invitation, and his inner feeling that, if I knew about it, I must be a well-informed journalist indeed. He then replied, joining his hands in a gesture of piety: "But you would understand nothing of their conversation!" I in turn replied, lowering my eyes: "I wouldn't need a translation. I could read their words on their faces." Then, gently, he took my hand, looked upon me benevolently and murmured: "Come back this evening."

At the appointed hour, I presented myself with beating heart at the bronze door. Behind his light-colored wooden lectern, a vice-corporal in the Swiss Guard stopped me, asking me my name and that of whom I wished to see. I answered in the most natural possible fashion: "The Pope." Looking suspicious, as I had no invitation, he checked by telephoning the second floor to see if I was really expected by the Supreme Pontiff. He then handed me over to a second guard, who led me up the monumental staircase. There a haughty usher escorted me to the stately Consistory Hall, a flamboyant room of intimidating proportions, harmonious frescos, magnificent tapestries and rare marble statues. Agitated, I waited alone for a few minutes until the arrival of the euphoric Poles dressed in black and white. We had to remain standing and to surround Karol Wojtyla at a distance. A little while later, he entered by one of the two doors at the back of the hall, blessed us all together, and then sat on his throne, as straight as it was simple. On his right was a cardinal, to his left a bishop and, a few meters away, a large bouquet of white lilies and yellow roses.

I then discovered a very different Supreme Pontiff from the one I had been seeing on television over the years. With his compatriots, he left his official persona behind, so transported with joy did he seem. He joked and laughed with them. That evening, I even heard him sing airs from his native land in their company. Msgr. Dziwisz had placed me at the end of the line of Poles. Everyone had to be presented to the Holy Father. When he approached me, Msgr. Dziwisz whispered in his ear: "This is a former pupil of Father Poupard's at the Dominican convent in

Via Cassia," before adding kindly, "Mme. de Gaulle was also a pupil of the Dominicans." This detail was the little extra piece of comfort I needed before such an intimidating moment in my life. John Paul II then took my hands in his and asked me: "Are you pleased with Rome?" I replied: "Very much so, Holy Father, I am dazzled by this décor and impressed by Your Holiness' celebrations, but I would be even happier here if I could follow Your Holiness at close quarters to write a splendid article on His Holiness!" The Pope smiled at me, blessed me and walked away. Msgr. Dziwisz, who then took me to one side, murmured in a reassuring tone, "You will be called." "But when?" "You will see. It is in God's hands. In the meantime, may heaven bless you."

I did not dare leave my hotel all the next day—although I was very tempted by the sales at the luxury boutiques on the Via Conditto, on the corner near where I was staying. The day after, at 10:45 A.M. precisely, the telephone rang. "Hello? This is Msgr. Dziwisz. His Holiness will receive you at midday in his private apartments on the third floor." I was so astounded that I made the caller repeat his words—I found it almost impossible to believe them.

An hour and a half later, along with Jean-Claude Deutsch, one of the top photographers at our paper, I joined John Paul II at the heart of his apartments. The Holy Father welcomed us in his private office. He gave us a piercing look, and those moments when we were, for the first time, alone with him seemed to me an eternity. I was immediately struck by the serenity that emanated from his radiant face. We bowed low before him, full of emotion. I kissed his gold ring without really daring to look at his hand. The Holy Father smiled at me. I had tears in my eyes. Msgr. Dziwisz motioned to the photographer to begin his work. He hesitated a few minutes. The Pope then asked him in perfect French, "Is there perhaps a lighting problem? Would you like me to move closer to the window, or maybe further away from it? Would you like me to move back a little?" He was well aware that his white chasuble and capelet were hard to see against the light. This spontaneity and simplicity from the most famous man on the planet, who appeared to have all the time in the world for us, came as something of a surprise.

After the photo session, which lasted a good 20 minutes, the Holy Father blessed us. We then bowed low once more and thanked him profusely before he moved away. At that exact moment Jean-Claude noticed that there was no photo of the Pope at his desk. "Get him back immediately!" he cried out to me. "That's impossible, he blessed us and he's gone," I said. It did indeed seem to me unthinkable to run after the Supreme Pontiff of the Catholic Church down the corridor of his own apartment. I still ask myself today how Msgr. Dziwisz, who overheard snatches of our conversation, managed to catch up with the Pope and talk to him. Nevertheless, here was John Paul II, returning to our side and agreeing to pose again in a session that lasted for quite a while. He was infinitely accommodating in his behavior toward us, complying with all our demands, always governed by simplicity.

And that was how my second meeting with John Paul II turned out. When he smiled at me that day, I instinctively understood that I was beginning to win his respect, which, over the years, evolved into trust, a privilege that allows me today to share with you the private existence of this extraordinary Pope, a unique experience as recounted in the pages of this book.

Chapter Two

JOHN PAUL II: NEVER FAR FROM KAROL WOJTYLA

As ecumenical as he could be, the Holy Father could not prevent the spirit of his native land from subtly permeating his Roman palace. I had noticed this tendency on my very first contact with the Vatican. After all, what could be more natural? The French Popes gave the Holy See a distinctly Gallic, not to mention Provencal, flavor when it was installed at Avignon.

But the ties that linked John Paul II to his mother country were more than cultural: they were visceral and political. To properly grasp this close-knit relationship, we need to recall the history of Poland, particularly its recent history.

Throughout its history, this unhappy country has constantly swung between glory and disaster. In the 15th century, Poland was unified with Lithuania and Livonia—a former Baltic province of Russia that corresponds to present-day Latvia and Estonia—and a significant portion of the Ukraine, comprising the greatest power in Eastern Europe and the forefront of resistance to the Turks. In 1611 during the fight against the Russians, Polish troops even entered Moscow! But the Russians and Prussians soon joined forces to carve up Poland, which was divided in the 18th century. The history of Poland was then marked by a desperate struggle to restore its unity, which was finally accomplished via the Treaty of Versailles.

The Second World War began with Poland being divided up once again, this time between Hitler and Stalin. According to the German-Soviet non-aggression pact, everything to the west of the three rivers that formed the border—the Narew, Vistula and San—was occupied by the Nazis, and millions of citizens perished, both ordinary Poles and Polish Jews. In the Eastern area, occupied by the Soviets, the elite were slaughtered: 15,000 officers of the Polish army were executed and buried in mass graves at Katyn before the Soviets' victory over the Germans, which saw the total destruction of Warsaw. The Yalta agreement then provided for Polish reunification, at the price of the country's "Sovietization," as happened to all Eastern European countries. The Polish people's resistance to this new tyranny could only be expressed via religion, as was once the case in France's Vendée region: were not the Jacobins of that era the equivalent of the Communists to some extent?

This resistance was initially personified by Cardinal Wyszynski, primate of Poland and part of a generation still haunted by the terrible events of the 1940s. Long persecuted by the totalitarian government, he later sent the Black Virgin of Czestochowa on a journey through 10,000 villages as a gesture of protest. Wyszynski was in perfect communion with all the people who, full of faith and ardor, gathered in the churches, their only outlet for freedom. Karol Wojtyla also participated actively in this Resistance movement as the leader of the Polish Church's spiritual resistance and Archbishop of Krakow, a see he occupied for three and a half years from January 13, 1964, until June 26, 1967. When he was then elevated to cardinal by Paul VI, the public authorities in his country were delighted with this flattering promotion, since the main figures of the regime thought that Wojtyla would without doubt oppose Primate Wyszynski and thus divide the Polish Church; but the new cardinal was far too shrewd to fall into such a primitive trap, and therefore remained close to his older colleague. That is why his election as the 264th Successor of the Prince of the Apostles in 1978 was viewed by all his fellow citizens as a first and encouraging victory in their fight against Soviet tyranny.

During his first papal trip to Poland in June 1979, a visit the Communist regime was obliged to accept, John Paul II exclaimed, "Do not be afraid of welcoming Christ and accepting his power! Do not be afraid! Open, open wide the doors for Christ! To his saving power, open up the boundaries of states, economic and political systems, the vast fields of culture, civilization and development! Do not be afraid! Christ knows what is in man. And he alone knows it!" These words uttered by Karol Wojtyla thundered like a battering ram against the walls of the Soviet fortress.

"Do not be afraid!"—of totalitarianism, that is—are words that have now became famous, words he had already proclaimed in his vigorous and inimitable voice from the balcony of Saint Peter's on November 16, 1978. The call was soon taken up by workers at the shipyards of Gdansk, who founded

Solidarity, the free trade union inspired by Christianity that spread across the entire country to become, under the leadership of Lech Walesa, the spearhead of Polish liberation.

This memorable visit immediately made it very clear to party leaders that they had an adversary to deal with, and from now on the regime would have to reckon with this "man in white," far more spiritually potent than if he had the power to set armored divisions on the march. Subsequent events confirmed their fears, since the striking workers of Gdansk and their inspired leader, Walesa, positioned themselves very visibly under his far-off authority, choosing prayers rather than tirades and hymns rather than subversive songs. Walesa and his followers sported just one emblem: the Black Virgin of Czestochowa.

As it turned out, in June 1989 Solidarity transformed itself into a political force and won almost all the elections the Communist authorities had resigned themselves to. Walesa was elected president of Poland in November 1989 and stayed in power until 1995.

Throughout this grueling struggle for freedom, the Church fully supported Solidarity. In the wake of the Prague Spring, Poland's emancipation from Communist repression was the second portent of the eventual fall of the Berlin Wall.

Solidarity and the profound desire of an entire people to reclaim their freedom certainly contributed to the end of Soviet occupation in Poland, but we can now see how many more years such a resurrection would have taken without the spiritual and political support of John Paul II. Present-day Poland owes him almost everything.

It was therefore impossible for this Polish Pope to hide his roots and his attachment to the land of his youth, which he had helped to save. Karol Wojtyla publicly proclaimed this passionate attachment to the land of his childhood in 1982. John Paul II, who had gone to Livorno in Tuscany to visit a Solvay factory, a firm that had employed him as a stonebreaker during the war at the quarries in Krakow, declared, "Poland is my homeland, even though, since I have become Pope, the whole world has become my homeland; but what I do owe to Poland is this: it is a country that has suffered greatly and has given me an understanding of all those who suffer, both from a lack of goods and a lack of freedom. A feeling of solidarity with all peoples who suffer therefore comes to me naturally."

It is indisputable that love for his nation held a special place in the Holy Father's heart. Indeed, his close friend Cardinal Deskur recounts how he would always have been capable of leaving the Vatican within the hour to bring succor to his people, who felt the same way about him. Wherever he set foot in his native land, the Polish people put up a statue to him, always in bronze and including a telling detail: when he is represented on monuments, the Holy Father's cassock is always symbolically turned up on the right, as if by a wind blowing from west to east!

Everything relating to Poland affected him—absolutely everything, even sports. One day Luigi Accattolu, the brilliant Vatican correspondent for the *Corriere della Sera*, asked John Paul II, "Very Holy Father, will you be watching the Poland-Italy football match live on television tomorrow?" "I do hope that I won't miss the broadcast!" exclaimed the Pope. "I am praying that my compatriots win." This conversation took place on June 14, 1982, in the Aerolinas Argentinas plane that was taking John Paul II and his retinue back to Rome from Buenos Aires. The Holy Father and his Polish private secretary later watched the ill-fated game, which ended in a scoreless draw, in his office-cum-library.

In a complete break with traditions upheld by the Italian Popes, as soon as he arrived at the Vatican Karol Wojtyla created an intimate, almost exclusively Polish inner circle around him—his "Little Poland," as the irritated Italian prelates called it. In his private apartment on the third floor of the apostolic palace, he chose to live surrounded by only six compatriots: the ever-faithful Msgr. Dziwisz, whose name no one had yet succeeded in pronouncing or writing correctly after 25 years at the Vatican, and five nuns from the congregation of the Servants of the Sacred Heart of Jesus, who lived at the back of the apartment where, in Paul VI's era, the Maria Bambina sisters from Milan had lived, having followed the Pope from the archbishopric of that city.

These six people formed a little Polish bastion around the Pope, falling somewhere between a personal bodyguard and a religious community. Karol Wojtyla was happy to be able to speak Polish with them and not to have to spend too much time alone after his exhausting days. Differing from his Italian predecessors, John Paul II refused to live in splendid isolation, taking his meals alone in a religious silence and only meeting people as part of his official audiences. For this Pope from the East, the first non-Italian Pontiff since the Flemish Adrian VI in 1522, it was important to come back to a familiar environment in the evening, a moment of comforting relaxation after the long, arduous days this polyglot spent speaking Italian as well as English, German and French. He also thought in

Italian, German and French. When he knew a language, his knowledge was not, as he explained to me once, merely phonetic, but also grammatical; he was familiar with its nuances. He was also familiar with the literature of other languages, since he liked to read in the original. In English, however, he had a pronounced Slavic accent and was less at ease, sometimes forced to grope for the right word when he was tired. The Pope could also write perfectly in these languages, as well as in Latin. Cardinal Deskur explains that, though he didn't speak them faultlessly, he was also at home speaking all the Slavic languages and had as musical an ear as the Beatles! I observed this for myself in Slovakia in September 2003 during one of his last trips abroad, when, despite being worn out, despite stumbling over his words because of breathing problems, he still managed to speak in Slovakian and Russian.

But let us return to the deep-seated reasons behind the former Krakow archbishop's creation of his little Polish circle. He did not want to lose his "Polishness" and mocked the wagging tongues of the curia, feeling exasperated rather than moved. And some cardinals even today are malicious enough to assert that the new Pope's main task will be to take the Polishness out of the Vatican!

The loss of his family over the years had left Karol Wojtyla with a gaping hole in his life: when he was just nine, his mother, Emilia, died of kidney disease; three years later, his brother, Edmund, a doctor, died of scarlet fever he caught while caring for the sick; and then, when he was 20, he found his father and last close family link, retired staff officer Lieutenant Wojtyla, lying lifeless in his bed one night. The Pope's friends helped fill this emotional and familial gap, and immersing himself in a Polish atmosphere was his way of keeping a slight distance between his personal life and the Roman curia and its various cliques. The exceedingly Italian cardinals, who found it hard to resist witticisms, were not terribly indulgent toward this robust Slav, whose solid girth, laughing eyes and high cheekbones made him so physically different from themselves.

Thanks to the circle he created, Karol Wojtyla was surrounded by people who understood him without a word being spoken, and over time they became his real family. If he had not gathered these close colleagues and friends around him, the Holy Father would have risked living in great solitude. In these secular places, the previous Supreme Pontiffs were for the most part very pampered, surrounded as they were by brothers, sisters, cousins and nephews, as numerous as they were intrusive.

John Paul II, who only had one cousin, Natalia Mrzycxod (once a resident of France), had therefore created his own emotional universe. This was naturally not to the liking of high-ranking Italian prelates at the curia, who, aside from the fact that they did not understand Polish, found it difficult to accept having access to the Pope only through these foreign intermediaries who spent their time whispering together. "Karol Wojtyla is a half-time Pope and full-time Pole—he has become the Emperor of the Polish Holy Roman Empire," the Italian cardinals often complained. Even if they admired him, some of them were not impressed by his modest origins. He was the grandson of a tailor on his father's side and a tanner on his mother's side, whereas many of his noble predecessors were princes born in splendid palaces like the Barberini, Pallavicini, Aldobrandini, Chigi, Rospigliosi, Orsini, Pignatelli and Odescalchi, to name but a few. These Supreme Pontiffs, princes of the Renaissance, tended to have large courts and families, and therefore many heirs, along with, above all, beautiful palaces. They were the exalted descendents of highly noble dynasties that often gave the papacy and Holy See precedence over the Church. Even today, despite Pope Paul VI's efforts to abolish the Palatine Guard, tone down the pomp, remove regalia and do away with many functions linked down the centuries to these great Roman families, their descendents still often possess spectacular palaces with gorgeous chapels where mass is regularly held and where the baptisms, marriages and funerals of the princely proprietors take place. Their sumptuous entrances are usually embellished with a high purple canopy bearing the papal arms, and when they receive a cardinal to dinner—as does the Princess Pallavicini, for example—he is always preceded by two *flabelli*, elegantly dressed porters bearing flaming torches.

These witnesses to the luxurious 16th-century past have left their mark: Alessandro Farnese, who became Paul III, bequeathed the Farnese palace, now the French embassy; Ugo Buoncompagni, later Gregory XIII, left his son the Villa Aurora, the largest private property in the center of Rome (two steps from the Via Veneto), which is now in the hands of his direct descendent (he fathered a child before being elected Pope); Ippolito Aldobrandini, who went on to become Clement VIII, left behind the Villa Frascati and the famous vineyard bearing the same name; Camillo Borghese, Paul V, built two huge palaces in the city center; Matteo Barberini, later Urban VIII, also built a palace in the heart of Rome; Giambattista Pamphili, later Innocent X, bequeathed a palace with a mirrored gallery as impressive as that of Versailles and a fantastic art collection, including the famous portrait of Pope Innocent X by Velasquez, plus a block of houses containing over 150 apartments; Fabio Chigi, later Alexander VII, bequeathed a palace that now houses the Chamber of Deputies; Benedetto Odescalchi, later Innocent XI, chose the heart of the Eternal City to build a palace five times larger than Paris' Elysée; Lorenzo Corsini, later Clement XII, built the Corsini Palace in Florence, which still belongs to his family and where Italian haute couture's most magnificent fashion shows are now held; and Ippolito Aldobrandini (ancestor of Olimpia Aldobrandini, another former pupil of the Roman Dominicans and wife of banker David de Rothschild), who became Clement VIII, added the Clementine Hall to the Vatican during his reign (1592–1605), as well as the Consistory Hall, which boasts a gilded, sculptural wooden ceiling. These last two rooms are the largest in the palace, and John Paul II used them for audiences with various groups of people.

There are still some 50 or so palaces that remain in the hands of the princes of the apostles. This illustrious, prestigious papal aristocracy, known as the Black Nobility, cultivates a sense of discrimination; its members are known to look down on other aristocrats, even those of England's Royal Family, since they consider themselves the embodiment of, and the continuity between, the glorious Rome of Caesar and the universal Rome of the papacy. These luxury-loving Popes sometimes erected their imposing properties on top of vestiges of ancient Rome or propped their palaces against ancient walls and broken columns. The Massimo alle Colonne palace, for example, which remains the property of the Massimo princes (Rome's most ancient family), was built on the ruins of the Emperor Domitian's Odeon. These dazzling palaces, their interiors bedecked with sacred frescos and works by Velásquez, Giotto, Carrache, Poussin, Caravaggio and other major artists, are the relics of an era when only a very thin line, as thin as the Host, divided the nobility from the highest-ranking clergy. They are also the fruit of what has been called nepotism, a word whose roots lie in *nipote*, or "nephew" in Italian. As underlined by Prince Jonathan Doria Pamphili, heir to Innocent X: "In earlier times, the Supreme Pontiffs appointed their nephews as cardinals, and allowed them to buy land and build churches and extraordinary palaces where one ecclesiastic after another tried to outdo everyone else in terms of luxury and refinement." As Prince Buoncompagni Ludovisi, heir to Gregory XIII and his palace, points out, "We received so much at birth that our duty is to preserve this heritage down through the generations and to ensure that it lasts. It belongs to the history of the papacy as much as to our family."

During John Paul II's papacy, the head of the curia's aristocratic clan was the noble, conservative, Piedmontese archbishop Andrea Cordero Lanza di Montezemolo, nuncio to Nicaragua in 1983 under the Sandinista government and uncle of Luca di Montezemolo, (President of Fiat, Ferrari and an Italian employers' federation), who was received along with Jean Todt at the Vatican in January 2005. Influenced by the Marquis Sacchetti, general administrative councilor for the Vatican City, he did not hide his feeling that the Holy Father, with his humble rather than aristocratic origins, was lacking in noble ancestry, even if Countess Isabelle Potocka d'Ornano, a relative of Prince Cardinal Sapieha who had met

John Paul II in Poland and Rome, believed that "The Holy Father, in unconscious imitation, adopted certain attitudes similar to our illustrious uncle."

The little Polish community that surrounded the Holy Father had nothing prestigious about it. The closest man to the Pope, Msgr. Dziwisz, was smaller than John Paul II, slightly plump, with a high forehead and sparkling eyes; he never left the Pope's side and was present at all his meals. He lived on the fourth floor of the papal palace, in a modest apartment just above the Pope's that comprised an office, a bedroom with a bathroom and a small kitchen. He therefore only had to take a short trip down a spiral staircase to join the Pope as soon as the latter rose in the morning. He was also at his side when the Pope went to pray and meditate in his private chapel. The relationship that developed between Karol Wojtyla and Dziwisz was not very different from that of father and son. "You have shared in my troubles, worries and hopes. Today let you be filled with joy at my side," proclaimed John Paul II on February 7, 1998, when he appointed him Bishop of San Leone in Calabria, an honorary office since the bishopric was essentially symbolic. Later on, in October 2003, he made him a titular archbishop (again, without an archbishopric) and deputy prefect to the Papal Household. He had also ordained Dziwisz into the priesthood in 1966. With a doctorate in liturgical theology from Jagiellonian University, where Karol Wojtyla had also studied, Dziwisz had been his closest, longest-standing and most faithful aide since the Krakow days. Early on, when Karol Wojtyla was looking for a young assistant, Dziwisz had been pointed out to him as a person of superior qualities. Their shared taste for sports, especially skiing, immediately created a strong link and a feeling of affinity between them, as Dziwisz was also the university skiing champion. He was born 64 years ago in the little ski resort of Raba Wyzna (known as Poland's Chamonix), near Zakopane in southern Poland's Tatras Mountains. The two of them regularly skied at Zakopane, and they continued skiing even after Karol Wojtyla ascended to the papal throne. It incited the less-than-charitable *monsignori* to joke that Msgr. Dziwisz "was just as good at slaloming through the Vatican!" These activities lasted until John Paul II fractured a femur in 1994 when he slipped in the bathroom. Not long before, when the Pope fell while skiing in Abruzzo, Msgr. Dziwisz took a tumble while trying to break the Pope's fall and broke his own arm.

The Episcopal promotion of the Pope's private secretary came as a big surprise at the Holy See, as it was an unusual gesture in the history of the modern papacy. Msgr. Dziwisz now wore the purple sash. These successive, significant appointments were a well-deserved reward for some 40 years of being unfailingly available to the Holy Father, as well as the best way of protecting his vulnerable confidant for the future—in other words, preventing the Roman curia from palming him off with an obscure, unrewarding post. A great many private secretaries attached to John Paul II's predecessors had fallen victim to just such a sad fate. Until the end of Pius XIII's reign, private secretaries only looked after the mail and a few minor administrative tasks; there was certainly no question of them sharing a meal with the Pope. And the hierarchy-conscious Supreme Pontiffs never brought up this taboo subject: at the very most, they would do their private secretaries the honor of drinking a thimbleful of *grappa* in their company on New Year's Day and then generously offer them the opened bottle.

However, John XXIII made a telling confession to General de Gaulle during the latter's state visit to the Vatican on June 27, 1959: "I do not like to dine alone. I get bored on my own," he told the general, his voice husky and sad.

Paul VI took the unusual step of inviting theologian Henri de Lubac, the Council auditor, writer Jean Guitton, and protestant Oscar Cullman, the craftsman of ecumenical dialogue, to eat with him on the last Sunday of Vatican II.

Pius XII's housekeeper, Sister Pasqualina Lehnert, was a legendary figure. She was a formidable, inflexible Bavarian nun he had discovered in a Swiss clinic where he was being treated before ascending to the throne of Saint Peter. When he died, she inherited the modest gift of her master's famous canary, which always sat opposite him at the table in its golden cage, symbolizing his own imprisonment! After she spent some time in purgatory under John XXIII, Paul VI allowed her to open the Pastor Angelicus retirement home in Rome, where she herself retired and consoled herself with the view of Saint Peter's dome from her room.

At age 88, Msgr. Loris Capovilla, secretary and executor of John XXIII's will, took away the private papers of the Pope he venerated and dedicated himself to preserving his memory. Paul VI named him prelate emeritus of the Territorial Prelature of Loreto, a modest gift. He is still alive, and is now the bishop emeritus at Loreto.

Paul VI had two close collaborators: Abbot Bruno Bossi, who disappeared one day not long after the Pope's death (a mystery that has never been cleared up), and Msgr. Pasquale

Macchi, now 80, who was seen as the most influential figure of Paul VI's papacy but who had to wait for the advent of John Paul II for his appointment as archbishop. Abbot Diego Lorenzi, briefly secretary to John Paul I (whose tragically short reign lasted a mere 33 days), rapidly returned to his parish in a Venetian village. His name is not even included in the heavy tome—bound in red and gold cloth and stamped with the papal arms—of the papal directory, which serves as the bible-cum-Who's Who of the clergy. During his short term, poor Luciani was only able to secure a place for his niece, Lina Petri Tormenta, who serves as the invaluable archivist of the Holy See's pressroom in Viadella Conciliazione.

During John Paul II's very long reign, Msgr. Dziwisz was, in contrast, the most influential figure at the Vatican. He played an essential role there and enjoyed a level of power that had no official representation within the Holy See's organization. Yet everyone at the Roman curia knew perfectly well that he was the power behind the papal throne, the person who spoke in the Pontiff's name. He had more real power than the cardinal who served as secretary of state, 76-year-old Angelo Sodano, the Pope's prime minister, or than his substitute, in this case his head of cabinet, 60-year-old Argentinean Msgr. Leonardo Sandri, or even Msgr. Jean-Louis Tauran, a son of Bordeaux and his former foreign affairs minister, who was appointed archivist and librarian of the Holy Roman Church, responsible for the extraordinary Vatican library as well as a member of the four dicasteries (ministries): the Secretariat of State, Doctrine of the Faith, Western Churches and Bishops. John Paul II appointed him cardinal in October 2003, after he had practiced 13 years' worth of subtle diplomacy at his side. His former post was filled by Msgr. Giovanni Lajolo, an Italian-Argentinean and former nonce to Berlin. All three were from the prestigious Pontifical Academy, the Holy See's college for senior members of the Vatican (formerly the Academy of Pontifical Nobles). Even though they handled highly important, sensitive matters, they were nevertheless obliged to go through the filter of Msgr. Dziwisz, who, if only to protect the Pope's health, set the times and dates for their meetings. He was with the Pope before and after their visits, and so had the last word. He was the vital cog in the Polish machine that made the Vatican work and, inevitably, the guardian of all Karol Wojtyla's secrets.

However, the curia members proved to be fairly indulgent toward this character, who came from a world so alien to them. He won just about all of them over with his serenity and subtlety. Endowed with pleasant features and a sense of resolution tempered by level-headedness, his skill in understanding people immediately won him the respect and liking of his colleagues—and the cleverest of them quickly grasped the prelate's increasingly important role in John Paul II's existence and daily activities.

He was also skilled in handling the Roman Catholic Church's unwieldy, bureaucratic official system of government, and everything got back to him, officially or unofficially. He closely followed everything related to the major questions handled by the Synod of Bishops, the Secretariat of State and the College of Cardinals, as well as nine Congregations, 11 Pontifical Councils, three Offices and three Tribunals. All of this ensured that he was never caught without an answer to even the most minor of the Pope's questions. In addition, he was in charge of John Paul II's precious purple leather diary, and intercepted all calls on the Pope's private line from his own telephone in the neighboring room. Together with the Holy Father, he decided, according to criteria that escaped ordinary mortals, whom to invite to morning mass in the private chapel located to the left at the end of a long corridor opposite the papal office. Such invitations often gave the Pope the chance to meet some of the ordinary people who would never have caught the attention of the highly formal heads of the Secretariat of State and Papal Household, the people theoretically responsible for selecting from amongst all the audience requests.

Msgr. Dziwisz, whose only ambition was to serve the Pope, was the person who dined most often with John Paul II and his second secretary, Mieczyslaw Mokrzycki. Karol Wojtyla also occasionally liked to have guests at his meals, except toward the end of his life. But it was most often with Msgr. Dziwisz that he watched television after dinner. Since he found it hard to master the art of channel-hopping, the Pope often managed to detune the television, so Msgr. Dziwisz would then have to ask his friend Father Tucci, head of Radio Vatican at the time, to send his technicians over to repair it. He was indisputably the man who shared the most sacred moments—and the most difficult—of the Pope's existence.

For the rest of his life, Dziwisz's worst memory will always be the horror of Black Wednesday, May 13, 1981, in Saint Peter's Square. He was positioned, as always, just behind the Pope in the back of the white Toyota. At 5:21 P.M. the Pope, hit by four bullets from Ali Agca's gun, literally collapsed in his arms. Dziwisz kept his head and had the presence of mind to guide the ambulance driver, whose vehicle had a broken, never-tested siren and flashing light, through the streets of Rome, ignoring one-way signs in an effort to save those few precious minutes that no doubt saved the Supreme Pontiff's life. Even though Dziwisz never took credit for it, preferring to humbly point to the providential hand of the Virgin of Fatima, John Paul II knew what he had done and never forgot it. The Holy Father always felt comforted and protected by his attentive and calming presence, especially during his last years when he could only move around, depending on the circumstances, with the help of a platform, walking frame, elevator or wheelchair. An extraordinary bond had built up between them, sometimes of a mischievous nature. Endowed with an excellent sense of humor, on occasion Msgr. Dziwisz gave John Paul II a running commentary on the artificial attitudes and self-satisfied tone taken by certain visitors. On several occasions I saw the Pope laughing heartily at the pertinent and funny remarks of his treasured aide after listening to the obviously preplanned words of people who could not stop themselves from talking to him about Christianity; without being able to speak Polish, I of course could only guess what they were saying from the expression on their faces.

Dziwisz, who accompanied John Paul II on all of his trips, including those in the Popemobile, saw everything. One Wednesday at the end of the general audience in Saint Peter's Square, he spotted me far away among the pilgrims with his eagle eye (especially vigilant since the assassination attempt), and immediately gestured for me and my photographer to join the members of the Vatican gendarmerie just behind the Popemobile, an astonishing four-wheel-drive vehicle that could go up and down stairs. He wanted me to enjoy a unique experience for a journalist: being able to recount the Pope's departure from Saint Peter's Square in the famous white vehicle, with its personalized license plate SCV 1 (*Stato della città del Vaticano 1*), at a distance of less than two meters. Unfortunately, the zealous members of his bodyguard did not allow me to get close to John Paul II that day since I did not have a special badge.

In the early morning, under the luminous stained-glass window of his private chapel (created by the Hungarian artist Hajnal, who had also been designing the Vatican's stamps for the previous 30 years), John Paul II gathered his thoughts and meditated at length at the foot of the altar, while Msgr. Dziwisz placed a small black leather case on his prie-dieu (and in later years, on the narrow armrest of his wheelchair) containing the names of those who had written to the Holy Father to ask him to pray for them. A new list was drawn up twice per week. Msgr. Dziwisz supported him and watched over him, as he always did, to make sure that he did not stumble. When, in early 2003, John Paul II decided that he would appear without hiding his state of health—much weakened by Parkinson's disease, he was therefore wheelchair-bound—Dziwisz seemed almost reassured, given that once he was comfortably wedged into his seat, the Supreme Pontiff no longer risked falling backward, forward or sideways when celebrating mass. He stayed silently by the Pope's side, his ever-faithful shadow, sharing those first, long moments of prayer from which the Pope drew his strength for the day ahead. ("Prayer is what gives him life, and before making important decisions he meditates and prays for hours at a time, because he knows that—in contrast with heads of state, be they governments or kings—he is unique of his kind and that his function isolates him. That is why it is so important for him to spend many hours praying," his friend, Archbishop of Krakow Cardinal Macharski, explained to me.) Then Dziwisz assisted him in his round of official and unofficial meetings and morning duties. He was always careful to pass the Supreme Pontiff the speeches he had to read, pointing out as he did so, with a quick coded sign, one of the faithful to be greeted, a pause to be taken or a person to be blessed.

Such reminders are important at the Holy See, as the following anecdote shows: the day after his election on October 17, 1978, when he was going to see his friend Msgr. Deskur at the Gemelli Polyclinic, the new Pope forgot, in his enthusiasm, to bless the hospital staff. He was quickly reminded by the head of protocol. "They are teaching me how to be Pope!" said John Paul II with a smile.

Msgr. Dziwisz was a past master in the art of never being intrusive in front of the cameras or around the Supreme Pontiff, in whose vicinity a number of obsequious high-ranking prelates sometimes jostled for space. He knew better than anyone else at the Vatican that there was only one star: the Pope. It was not important to the private secretary to be in the limelight since, outside of the institutional structures, he controlled the workings of John Paul II's daily life. He did not have the keys to Saint Peter's but knew how to enter its gates. He also had the gift of improving the atmosphere by defusing tensions that arose when the Pope was receiving the century's most notable players. Ronald Reagan, Mikhail Gorbachev, Fidel Castro, Boris Yeltsin, George W. Bush and Jacques Chirac were all a little stunned by the solemnity and majesty of the place as well as the fixed secular protocols of this ostentatious institution. Msgr. Dziwisz always knew how to provide the necessary social glue, yet it was easy for him to invoke the Holy Father's tiredness to avoid a meeting or put off a visit until an indeterminate date, and he could always sense if someone was being a nuisance or risked wearing the Pope out.

The central Polish colony of the Eternal City was organized around Msgr. Dziwisz. A handful of close associates held strategic posts: Father Adam Boniecki, former director of the Polish edition of *L'Osservatore Romano,* the Vatican's official mouthpiece (this Polish edition, which appeared following Karol Wojtyla's election, came out just once per week, unlike the Italian daily; it was a profitable publication, as it sold very well in Poland); Msgr. Mieczyslaw Mokrzycki, second private secretary to the Pope; Msgr. Henryk Nowacki, head of the Polish section of the Secretariat of State; Msgr. Pawel Ptasznik; Father Konrad Hejmo, Dominican, organizer of Polish pilgrims' visits to the Holy See; Msgr. Antoni Stankiewicz, senior member of the Tribunal of the Roman Rota; and other compatriots with less specific functions but who also communicated directly with Msgr. Dziwisz, bypassing the inflexible bureaucrats and slow-moving official channels. They operated as a closed circuit, sustained and protected by their shared language. The same was true of the five Polish nuns cloistered in the private apartments, who could sometimes be seen in the Annona (the Vatican's tax-free supermarket), where the cheese was Polish, the butter Danish, the alcohol French and the poultry, said to be the best in the capital, came straight from the papal farm at Castel Gandolfo. The Annona also has a very handy delicatessen counter. This supermarket is where the nuns did their shopping, buying the basic products needed for the Pope's private household, and it was almost the only opportunity they had to leave the third floor. It was very rare for all five of them to get away from the apartment at once: one such occasion was in August 2000 during the World Youth Day gathering, when they all went to see their "boss" venerated in Saint Peter's Square by hundreds of thousands of young people from all over the world, and another was on October 19, 2003, for the beatification of Mother Teresa. On these exceptional occasions, they made themselves as inconspicuous as possible so as not to be caught out by the photographers. And during the Wednesday general audiences, at least one of them always watched their "God" from the third-floor apartment. Their faces were known to neither public nor press, and they remained one of the best-guarded secrets of the Holy See. I myself, however, had a lucky encounter one day when I was lost in the interminable corridors of the Holy Father's private apartments. I was meant to be joining His Holiness and Msgr. Dziwisz on the terrace of the hanging gardens that crown the papal apartments for a series of photographs. Instead of finding my way, I came face to face with Sister Germana, the Pope's cook. Even though I was very concerned that she might imagine I had slipped into the apartments with malicious intent, I was far from unhappy with the circumstances. Our encounter quickly turned sour, however. Panicking and refusing to listen to my explanations or even look at my badge (the much-envied laminated card bearing the papal arms and my name), she immediately called a Swiss Guard and asked him—in a voice so firm and severe I felt I was being sent directly to the gates of hell—to conduct me back to the bronze door. This left me, however, with enough time to observe her, allowing me, as if by magic, to approach one of the Pope's mysterious servants and satisfy the curiosity of a great many of my colleagues, who were always avid for details.

Members of the order of the Servants of the Sacred Heart of Jesus (founded in 1894) can be distinguished by the burning red heart embroidered on the breast of their habits. In winter they are dressed in black, in summer they wear white. They wear an ebony cross bearing a silver Christ, a silver wedding ring, a large, dark wooden rosary on the left side, a white cord belt knotted on the right, a veil and headdress, a little white collar and black sandals. There are 600 sisters, with a presence in Poland, Italy, France, Bolivia, Libya and the US, and the mission of their order is to come to the aid of the most disadvantaged members of society as well as young girls in difficulty. When he was archbishop of Krakow, the "Little Rome" of a hundred churches as the Poles call it, Karol Wojtyla was already in close contact with these nuns. It was therefore important to him that they join him at the Vatican.

Sister Tobiana, his nurse-cum-doctor, always dressed in clothes as white as a communion wafer, was the superior of their little closeted community on the third floor, seconded by Sister Germana, Sister Fernanda, Sister Matylda and Sister Eufrosyna. They looked after the secretarial work, shopping, linens, cooking and the infirmary.

They aimed to protect the Holy Father as much as possible from the outside world. As Cardinal Poupard explained, "To them, a stranger they could not understand was a suspect character whom they found it difficult to get on with." I tested the truth of this observation myself when, at 8:30 one morning, invited by Msgr. Dziwisz to give the Supreme Pontiff his own personal copy of the *Paris Match* whose cover he graced, I could sense the sisters' nervousness as soon as they spotted me. They stared at me anxiously. They were visibly asking themselves: "Who is this 40-year-old woman? A devout laywoman? A nun without her habit? Or maybe she has nothing at all to do with the institutions of the Catholic Church? Whatever the case, what is she doing here?" They consulted each other, murmuring, perplexed and suspicious—they were having such trouble placing me! According to their criteria, I was young and perfectly respectful of their dress customs and protocol, especially since I was wearing my usual "Roman" uniform, which was not so different from the outfits worn by the few nuns you came across outside the papal buildings. However, as I have already mentioned, I wore a modest amount of makeup—mascara, a little powder and some lipstick—to make it clear that I was not in fact a nun. The holy sisters could not believe that John Paul II would stoop to joking with me. Wanting to reassure me, Msgr. Dziwisz whispered in my ear that I made him laugh. This was my great strength, he revealed to me one day. It is true that the Holy Father was always relaxed when he received me in his private apartments.

Sister Tobiana, known as a nurse in Rome since her Polish doctorate in medicine did not authorize her to practice medicine in Italy outside the Vatican State, kept a watchful eye on the Holy Father's health at all times and, since the visit to Cuba in 1998, accompanied him on almost all of his trips. Cardinal Tucci, then in charge of papal travel, revealed that she traveled almost secretly, boarding before or after everyone else so as never to be seen. She was also in charge of stocking the dispensary.

Sister Fernanda was the housekeeper, managing the daily running of the household, doing the housework and making sure that all domestic matters ran smoothly.

Sister Germana looked after meals. Each day she received a box of fresh fruit and vegetables from Julio, the gardener who cultivated the Holy Father's kitchen garden, behind the gallery fountain, with care and pride. The kitchen was simple and rustic in style, with a large pine table covered with a flower-patterned oilcloth. There were few modern machines: no ice cream machine, no sophisticated blender, just a new espresso coffee machine, offered by some jubilee pilgrims in 2000 and used mainly for passing guests, as the Polish prefer plain coffee. On the beige-colored, slightly faded walls hung a framed photo of the Pope walking in the Vatican gardens and others in the same style. The nun in charge of cooking wore a large apron, a veil tied at the nape and a little collar.

As for Sister Eufrosyna, a converted Polish Jew like Cardinal Jean-Marie Lustiger, she spoke almost as many languages as the Holy Father: Polish, English, German, Italian and French. She looked after his private correspondence and, using an antiquated typewriter and small laptop computer, replied to mail and prepared letters on thick off-white vellum paper embossed with John Paul II's coat of arms and the apostolic stamp. The Pope then corrected and initialed them with his navy blue pen, or directly appended his signature in Latin: Joannes Paulus II.

Sister Matylda was responsible for the papal wardrobe. This may raise a smile, but it was no easy task. John Paul II had some 30 cassocks made by Annibale Gammarelli of 34 Via Santa Chiara near the Pantheon, tailor to the Popes since 1798. Before each conclave, the firm prepared three papal cassocks in different sizes so that few alterations would be needed for the new Pope's first public appearance on Saint Peter's central balcony. Handing down the business from father to son, the Gammarelli family tailor-made the Supreme Pontiffs' clothes in the best quality material. They have a file with all the papal measurements going back centuries, information that is preciously guarded in a safe. The walls of the soberly decorated boutique feature the signed portraits of six Popes for all to admire. The portrait of John Paul I is not signed, as Albino Luciani did not have time to add his Latin signature during his short papacy.

As a general rule, a Gammarelli tailor would go to the Pope's apartment once per year, as his ancestors did before him, armed with his tape measure, pins, scissors and chalk. John Paul II's winter cassocks, always in white, were made of very warm pure wool lined with white silk, while his summer cassocks were of cotton and silk. Outside of the Roman bishopric the nuns of Asia, Africa and Latin America often wear white habits in their countries, but in the Eternal City, only the Pope wears a white cassock. For an extra touch of elegance, the papal cassocks' buttons are embroidered in white thread to create white-on-white crosses, and the cassocks themselves have an almost invisible white-on-white border. Shorter and narrower than the old versions, they are worn over a white shirt with a clerical collar and French cuffs. John Paul II was very fond of cufflinks, and he often received them from friends who knew he was partial to them.

Cassocks, moiré sashes, detachable capelets, shirts, *mozettas* (short, cape-like, open-fronted garments with small buttons and an ornamental hood), and white or scarlet floor-length coats featuring double rows of buttons: Sister Matylda had to immaculately iron all these garments so that they hung with no creases whatsoever. She also had to look after thick white sashes, long cream-colored coats and a series of elegant purple capes trimmed with braid plaited in red and gold thread, with a cape-shaped upper part. The latter were reserved for use on solemn occasions only. The sister always remembered to give the Pope the stole embroidered with his arms, the sign of his spiritual power, for such important, solemn Vatican occasions as receiving heads of state or being presented with the credentials of Catholic ambassadors.

According to 12th-century ritual, white clothes symbolize innocence and charity, whereas red clothes, which the Pope only wore outdoors, recall the blood of the martyrs, authority and compassion. It was naturally unthinkable for the Holy Father to have the slightest mark on his various white habits, despite the numerous activities that made up his day. As one of his former colleagues confided to me, "At working lunches or official meals, he never ate salad, spaghetti or tagliatelli so as to avert the risk of a fatal drop of vinaigrette or sauce falling on his immaculate capelet. In private, however, he did not hesitate to tie a large napkin around his neck."

Sister Matylda was not the only one in charge of the Pope's liturgical garments. Under the careful eye of the master of papal liturgical celebrations, Msgr. Piero Marini, two other sisters, Rita and Adelaide, helped her look after the many miters and ceremonial chasubles: green for ordinary days, white for

Christmas, Easter and All Saints, violet for Lent and masses for the dead, red for Pentecost, Martyrs' Feast Day and Good Friday, and the highly unusual violet, red and gold version that the Pope wore for the opening of the Holy Door. There was also Sister Trinidad Ruiz, whose task was to hand out the mass books in the same venue. Once clothed in his vestments, John Paul II descended from the papal sacristy via an imposing elevator of varnished mahogany directly to Saint Peter's Basilica.

His pockets were always empty. Since he was the best-known man in the world, he had no identity papers on his person and, naturally enough, he never carried any money. Just like the Queen of England, if something needed to be paid for, his retinue took care of it. Popes do not receive a salary, unlike cardinals, who receive about 2,800 euros per month. Instead, like the presidents of the French Republic, all their expenses are paid for. However, once a year on June 29, the day of offerings for the feast of Saint Peter and Saint Paul, the faithful can bring gifts for the Supreme Pontiff, and the Pope has a personal account he uses to make charitable donations as he sees fit.

Sister Matylda had to make sure that the Holy Father had innumerable skullcaps available, since the wind often sent them flying away, and she also shined his shoes, usually burgundy slip-ons made by a Turin shoemaker (size 43 at first, and later size 44 because, as he gained weight, his feet became more fragile and had a tendency to swell up). The Holy Father also had a shoemaker in Krakow who sent him sturdy shoes. The chasubles and stoles embroidered in gold thread were subject to the meticulous care of nun-embroiderers, a delicate task since gold thread tarnishes and frays so easily.

On his right ring finger, John Paul II always wore the papal ring given to him by Paul VI on June 28, 1967, when the latter appointed him cardinal. A large gold ring carved by the sculptor Monfrini, it showed an image of the Crucifixion with Paul VI's arms on the inside. Attached to his cassock was his gold pectoral cross, an imposing object that was nevertheless nowhere near as flamboyant as the one decorated with deep-green emeralds worn by Pius X at the dawn of the 20th century. John Paul II also possessed several papal rings, since they numbered among the rare personal gifts, along with cufflinks and watches, that he could be offered. However, this Pope did not attach much importance to the value of the gifts he received. Imagine my surprise when, during a visit to Rome, I gave him an amusing little metal watch stamped with my paper's logo and with a camera as the second hand, and the Holy Father immediately put it on his wrist right next to a heavy, gold Rolex President Oyster Perpetual model with a ridged wrist strap, given to him by the Polish community of Paris! This visibly annoyed some members of his entourage, but not Msgr. Dziwisz, who found the watch so novel that later on I also gave him one. Most of the time, John Paul II wore an ordinary round Seiko watch on a leather strap with no date indicator, which had its battery regularly changed by Francesco Rocchi, the Borgo Pio watchmaker. One day, when the Pope gave him the joyous honor of being received at the Vatican with his wife and son, he exclaimed to Rocchi, "You are the one who makes me late for my meetings because I'm always short on time!"

One of his nuns, often Sister Matylda, regularly gave him a manicure, and every month the Holy Father's barber Antonio, whose salon was behind the Vatican, came to cut his hair.

On Sunday, the Holy See's Polish community swelled in number. The Pope liked to surround himself with familiar faces on the Lord's Day. Firstly came Cardinal Andrzej Maria Deskur, 79, his closest friend since his seminary days. A member of Poland's upper-middle class and born into a formerly very wealthy family (one of his brothers was a renowned horse breeder), he was raised by English and French nannies at the family mansion in Kielce (long since confiscated by the Communists). He also spoke many languages without the hint of an accent, including, naturally, French and English. A high-ranking theologian, very at ease in society, and an excellent bridge player with a lively, caustic wit, he was for many years president emeritus of the Pontifical Council for Social Communications and is now its honorary president. Despite his advanced age, and thanks to his gourmet hospitality, he remains one of the best-informed members of the Roman curia. The only misfortune suffered by Deskur, surely the closest cardinal to the Pope, was being paralyzed at age 50 following a heart attack during the 1978 conclave. However, although he has been confined to a wheelchair for a quarter of a century, his brain still functions very well! This influential intellectual with a scathing sense of humor campaigned zealously for the election of Karol Wojtyla, who, before occupying Saint Peter's See, regularly stayed with him when he visited Rome. Almost every Sunday, Cardinal Deskur used to come to lunch with the Pope at about 1:00 P.M., and always celebrated their respective birthdays together as well as November 4, the Saint Charles feast day of the Supreme Pontiff.

"I rack my brains all week to find new jokes to tell His

Holiness!" he confided to me one day when he had invited me to his home to taste the best smoked tea to be found in the Holy See accompanied by the most delicious shortbread cookies. "Jokes on what subject, Eminence?" "On Saint Peter. On Cardinal Tisserant and his famous beard, which the less tolerant *monsignori* of the era claimed he would certainly set afire one day! And on other characters, particularly certain Italians at the curia. I do not lack for subjects." "Do you mean to suggest that the Italians annoy him?" "No, not exactly. He does not always understand what they are trying to explain to him. He sometimes finds them convoluted and confusing. As he is not at all inclined toward conflict, he often tends to settle discussions with them using a concise, well-directed argument." During these Sunday meals, the Pope allowed Cardinal Deskur a freedom of expression that always astounded the other guests.

These convivial repasts always began with grace, after which Sister Germana served a number of Polish dishes: a slightly acidic barley soup, Wadowice-style tripe with basil and wild onions, and pork cutlets cooked with mushrooms and white wine accompanied by cabbage, a spinach tart and strong cheeses. This "dining pastorale," to use John Paul II's own expression, was often the moment when the Polish figures of the Holy See, that "parallel curia" living in *palazzi* belonging to the Vatican, gathered together outside the bounds of protocol along with Polish intellectuals, a group that included Msgr. Tadeusz Pieronek, rector of the Krakow Papal Academy, Father Mieczyslaw Malinski, writer and childhood friend of the Pope, visiting bishops, friends from the Polish college of Aventin and, of course, whenever he was in Rome,

Jerzy Kluger, Karol Wojtyla's oldest friend from his days at Marcin-Wadowita college. A Polish Jew living between London and Italy, Kluger trained as an engineer and went on to become a businessman, and was the only person with whom the Pope could still share far-off memories of their childhood in Wadowice, the little town in southern Poland where he was born on May 18, 1920. The war separated them, but in the 1970s Jerzy was reunited with his brilliant classmate before he became Pope. It was Kluger who inspired Gianfranco Svidercovski, former deputy editor of *L'Osservatore Romano,* to film a made-for-TV movie for TAO II—the production arm of Media 7, Berlusconi's channel—based on the beautiful friendship between a young Jew and a little Catholic boy. He now hopes to sell the film to television channels the world over.

The Slavs thus gathered together for a relaxed meal accompanied by much joking and, sometimes, singing. Contrary to legend, the Holy Father did not drink Polish vodka, just his usual glass of white wine diluted with water or the occasional beer. His Polish guests, on the other hand, paid full tribute to their national drink, claiming that Polish vodka is less harmful than its Russian counterpart. In their company, John Paul II was relaxed as he could never be during more official meals and was happy to re-create an intimate, affectionate world that had been so lacking in his life.

It is doubtless thanks to this almost family-like atmosphere, and supported by his great faith, that John Paul II succeeded in remaining balanced and in getting through the trials that arose throughout his very long papacy.

One Sunday, while he was in one of the large audience halls receiving a number of fervently excited Polish pilgrims, some of whom even danced and spun around under the gaze of the apostolic palace's marble statues, he said to them laughingly, with the familiarity he always showed toward his compatriots that so annoyed the Vatican's Italian personnel: "We are all cousins! You just need to say that you have a relative in Rome and it will be easier for you to get a visa." A simple joke, but one that perfectly illustrates the visceral attachment he felt for his people. When receiving his Polish visitors, the Holy Father paid particular attention to the priests who had been seminarians at Krakow when he was archbishop of the city (from January 13, 1964, to June 27, 1967, when Paul VI appointed him cardinal with the title Saint Cesare of Palatine). He was in the habit of seeing them individually and making himself available to listen to their problems, and had seen at least 1,000 of these priests come and go. As one of them, Father Pawel Sukiennik, once explained to me in Krakow, "This created profound links between Karol Wojtyla and us, links that still existed 30 years later." Father Sukiennik is now the parish priest of Niegowic, where John Paul II served as vicar, 1948–1949.

The Successor to the Prince of the Apostles—who, since the start of his papacy, was invested at all times in his pastoral commitment, his mysticism and his liking for theology—had placed his daily existence under the protection of the Black Virgin of Czestochowa, so named because of her dark-colored face. As a Pole, he worshipped her more than any other representation of Mary; he even had a reproduction of the icon hung in the chapel of his private apartments. The Black Virgin of Czestochowa carrying the infant Jesus is the patron saint of Poland. Her followers credit her with miraculous gifts, and are convinced that during the darkest hours of their history she rekindled the country's faith and saved it from the Russian threat. Karol Wojtyla thus entrusted her with his life and his ministry when he was ordained in 1946, a gesture he renewed in 1999 on his knees at the foot of the Czestochowa shrine on Jasna Gora Hill in Poland. He had also sent the wide, white, bloodstained sash he was wearing the day of the assassination attempt on May 13, 1981, to the shrine, for, as he declared a few weeks later to the faithful who had gathered in Saint Peter's Square, "The Virgin deflected the fatal bullets with her own hand." When he went to Poland, the Holy Father met with his former fellow seminary student, Cardinal Franciszek Macharski, his successor as archbishop of Krakow and another close friend. He always stayed with him at the archbishop's palace, his home between 1964 and 1978, and when Macharski visited Rome, he always ate at least one meal with John Paul II.

Cardinal Macharski received me in July 2000 at the Krakow archbishop's palace, which boasts highly Italianate baroque decoration and an atmosphere to match. The floor was covered with elegant slabs of black and white marble. Magnificent apartments in pastel tones were embellished with 17th- and 18th-century frescos and paintings representing saints supported by angels, the Virgin with child, the evangelists, Christ in majesty and other religious allegories, not to mention a gallery of Popes reaching back to the Renaissance. The cardinal told me, "Right from his youth, John Paul II knew what the focus of his life would be. Of course, he did not imagine he would one day become Pope, but he was already the person who, on the day of his election in Saint Peter's Square, was capable of saying: 'Do not be afraid.' He was very mystical, and prayed a great deal even at a young age. He had a lot of control over himself and did not really like imposing decisions. What he really wanted was for people to be responsible for themselves. What always struck me was the attention he paid to other people, that benevolent way he had of listening to each person who spoke to him, listening to everything they said. His profound piety did not prevent him from also being a man of action: as a priest, bishop and cardinal, he had the gift of encouraging the faithful, especially the young, who he knew how to address: 'I cannot create the world without you. I need you. You are the lifeblood of the Church,' he liked to remind them. Poland was always present in his prayers."

Another relevant Polish characteristic of ecclesiastics of his generation, as was explained to me by Cardinal Poupard and others, was John Paul II's innate penchant for secrets. Once a victim of the totalitarian regimes of the east, the Pope was as distrustful as he was careful and had been so ever since his youthful experiences, which left him with a dread of being observed and spied upon. "I never saw him take any written notes during or after a conversation," emphasized the cardinal. "Although he always questioned me on a variety of subjects in great detail, he wrote nothing down; he did not want any written trace left behind and, almost to the end of his life, he relied solely on his exceptional memory, reporting on meetings only verbally to a close aide. At the very most, he would ask the person he was receiving to give him an information sheet, which he never signed." These were the naturally cautious reflexes of a Pole whose roots lay in the Church of Silence, a Church that, throughout all the years of the totalitarian regime, was the only venue for Polish freedom of expression, the only place the secret police did not enter. When Karol Wojtyla was ordained on November 1,

1946, in Krakow—long after the Nazi invasion and his years at the clandestine seminary—it was done in secret at the private chapel of Cardinal Prince Adam Stefan Sapieha. An imposing, emblematic figure of the Polish Church, this eminent aristocrat, known as the Prince Cardinal and referred to by Karol Wojtyla in his correspondence as "the Prince," was related to Radziwill, Sanguszko, Lubomirski and Czartoryski, the exceedingly noble Polish families who gave Poland her kings.

At the end of his reign, the Holy Father's prudence, nourished by the experience of half a century, was amply justified: during those last years, when the huge papal palaces buzzed with rumors about his succession, it was always conceivable that malevolent ears were listening in, which is why the Vatican's electronics specialists were always looking for hidden microphones (they found several). This form of espionage, ever more sophisticated, is worrying. A number of precautions were incorporated into the Apostolic Constitution in 1995 and then reinforced in late 1999 in anticipation of John Paul II's succession; he had always considered it a personal duty to plan for and organize his successor's election transparently. These texts specified that, during the conclave, no recording or transmission apparatus that could connect the outside world to the cardinals (such as laptop computers) were allowed in the Sistine Chapel, where the members of the Sacred College assembled to elect the new Pope, or in the Domus Santæ Marthæ, the hotel run by the Sisters of Charity where College members were lodged within the Vatican. This task was made especially difficult by the fact that it was easy for outsiders to use the nearest antennae to intercept transmissions carrying all the Vatican's communications, and it was not really feasible to install scramblers because the Holy See's means of communication were not terribly modern, and installing such mechanisms would risk interfering with all the Vatican's other links to the outside world.

John Paul II nurtured such a powerful love for his native soil that he went there nine times during his papacy, the last of these visits in 2002, though only eight trips are actually counted because, when he went to Poland July 1–9 and August 1–13, 2001, he made it clear that it was a single trip taken in two stages in order to avoid going through the official greeting and leave-taking ceremonies twice. Be that as it may, he was always welcomed with huge enthusiasm in Poland. Nearly 10 years after the fall of the Communist regime, every Sunday at midday the leading Polish national television channel and national radio channel sent out a live broadcast of the Pope's blessing from the window of the Vatican apartments. And not only was the Krakow airfield baptized John Paul II Airport (de Gaulle and Kennedy only achieved this honor posthumously), but the advertising campaign run by the national airline LOT urged people to "Come and visit the Pope's country!"

On the 25th anniversary of his papacy, the inhabitants of Wadowice, his native town, fêted Karol Wojtyla all day and into the night with a variety of religious ceremonies and sporting events that culminated in an evening fireworks display. At 5:45 P.M. local time throughout all the parishes in Poland, the church bells began to ring, a magnificent chorus of chimes that pealed out as a reminder that, a quarter-century ago at that moment, the man who had once been their archbishop became the first Polish Supreme Pontiff in history, suddenly and providentially transforming Poland into the center of gravity for all Catholics the world over.

Chapter Three

HIS DAY BEGAN AT 5:30 EACH MORNING

WHEN DAWN BROKE, THE ADMIRABLY ROBUST John Paul II was already up and about. I remember a day in January 1996 when I wanted to check for myself if he really got up at daybreak while the rest of the Vatican was still piously asleep.

It is so dark and cold in the early days of the year that you can hardly make out the basilica pediment. Giovanni, at the wheel of the motorized cleaning machine the Roman municipality lends to the Vatican, is spraying the Saint Peter's Square esplanade copiously, careful to avoid wetting the life-sized Christmas nativity scene that will soon be taken down. He turns off his nozzles so as not to splash me. It is 5:30 A.M. and still dark, and I am alone with Giovanni on the famous square. He leans out of the door of his machine and gestures to the two corner windows that are lit up on the third floor of the papal palace, the windows of the Pope's bedroom and antechamber:

"*Il papa lavora già!*" ("*The Pope is already working!*"). As moved as Giovanni, I contemplate the little lights that glow above. So it was true: John Paul II, despite his age, infirmities and exhaustion, rose every morning with the sun like a monk to start praying and working, while the Vatican was still slumbering.

When I was told, "The Pope gets up at dawn," I naturally found it hard to believe. The communications directors for our various ministries are always letting slip to journalists, as though confiding a state secret to them alone, that the important politicians they work for wake up with the cock's crow to pen history-making texts. François Bayrou, Dominique de Villepin, Jacques Attali and other political figures even claim to sleep no more than five or six hours per night. And yet, on planes and trains, I regularly observe both senior and freshman ministers and various members of parliament obliviously dozing off and snoring over their newspapers. So how was I to imagine that the poor Pope, afflicted with so many physical problems, could keep the monk-like hours his entourage claimed he did with such admiration and zeal?

Keen to separate truth from legend, I arrived at Saint Peter's Square at 5 A.M., and at 5:30 precisely the two most famous windows in Rome lit up. I was surprised, no doubt about it, but also secretly satisfied: I had not let myself be hoaxed by the Holy Father's hagiographers. I was not sorry to have got up so early. Many years later on October 18, 2003, the eve of Mother Teresa's beatification, when John Paul II asked the Catholic Church's highest-ranking dignitaries to "Include me in your prayers so that I may continue my mission as the Lord would wish," I imagined that, even sustained by the grace of such a declaration, his declining health would not allow him to keep up with such early-morning hours, which is why, on the Tuesday following the festivities, I returned to Saint Peter's Square at 5:30 A.M.—and was amazed to see the same windows lighting up a quarter of an hour later! With the passing of time, the Pope had only allowed himself an extra quarter-hour of sleep.

I was enlightened about the Supreme Pontiff's waking habits, but aside from knowing that he was an early riser, I knew almost nothing about the Pope's daily life. So I asked Cardinal Deskur, his "soul brother," a few other cardinals who were his friends and several people close to him (who asked me to respect their need for discretion and keep their names anonymous) how exactly each hour of John Paul II's day was spent.

Thanks to these eminent figures, I had the pleasure and honor of hearing a great many episodes and anecdotes—always, of course, out of Joaquin Navarro-Valls' earshot! At the Vatican, I discovered, time is king: once my protectors had proof via my writing that I recounted the things they told me without ever mentioning their names, I acquired their precious trust and they then introduced me to the Holy Father's world. This meant that over the years I could see for myself that the information they gave me was not merely a kindly indulgence but was in fact true.

The walls of the Pope's remarkably monastic bedroom were decorated with nothing more than a cross of Jerusalem embellished with a few Easter olive branches and a wooden reproduction of the Black Virgin of Czestochowa. When the Pope opened his eyes at 5:30 without the need for an alarm clock—a habit he had cultivated since his youth—he reached toward his functional wooden bedside table with a long frail hand that bore his pastoral ring (the one worn by all bishops), which he never took off. (The Pope owned two others: the fisherman's ring and a more elaborate papal ring, worn during major celebrations.) He spent a moment skimming his hand over his breviary, the photo of his parents and the heavy pastoral cross laid there, before pressing the gilded metal switch that lit his bedside lamp with the gray lampshade. The Pope put on his dressing gown and went to the bathroom, where the floor was covered with non-slip material and the bathtub equipped with metal handles since the time he slipped and broke his femur on April 29, 1994. The Pope would then shave and take a shower or perhaps a bath.

Sister Matylda had prepared the Holy Father's clothes the night before. His secretary often came to help him get dressed. In his later years, the Polish second secretary often assisted the latter, and together they dressed him completely. Meanwhile, a third nun lit the candles in the chapel. Before his private mass, the Pope went to the worktable near his bedroom, an English-style coffered desk with a bright red leather top lit by a basic lamp in white metal with clips and an adjustable arm. On the left, toward the window, was a large bronze crucifix, and in front of it a beaker set with a silver-gilt bow (designed by Gucci) full of different brands of pens, all of them gold-nibbed. On the right was a mass book along with his own works, the latter waiting to be signed. He worked alone until after 6 A.M. He then made his way to the Carrara-marble-lined private chapel, where he sat in a bronze chair inscribed with the *Our Father* in Latin (in his later years, he remained in his wheelchair). The room was of medium size, decorated under Paul VI with a stained-glass roof representing Christ reborn and, above the altar, an imposing crucifix. This was the most important moment of the Pope's day. Alone in the presence of God, seeming to neither hear nor see anything around him, he knelt on the ground, and then lay down entirely (while he remained fit enough). This is the mystical form of prayer adopted by Polish priests. I witnessed it myself when he invited me to his private mass. Many details of the private chapel must have escaped my notice since I was so intent on observing this Pope, suddenly transformed into a living instrument of prayer. I was very impressed, since it reminded me of ceremonies when novices took the veil at my Dominican school; wearing white veils, they would lie down on the flagstones in a posture of total adoration. The same rite is observed during the ordination of priests and even bishops.

The Holy Father remained thus in prayer for many long minutes. Then he got up and knelt on his bronze prie-dieu, a solid piece of furniture equipped with a flap he could use if he wished to write down thoughts inspired by his latest period of meditation. His secretaries, Msgrs. Dziwisz and Mokrzycki, then helped him put on his thick, white silk chasuble with a red cross and border; depending on the liturgy, this vestment could also be in bright green, or white with blue bands, or embroidered with gold thread. The Holy Father owned countless chasubles, gifts from the faithful the world over. He regularly offered them to bishops and priests he received. What an honor for them to be able to say mass wearing a chasuble once owned by the Pope!

Some 20 guests then arrived to attend private mass at 7:30 A.M. precisely. They took their places behind the Pope's chair on benches arranged in four rows on each side of the chapel.

They hailed from a great variety of places and walks of life: overseas bishops on their visit *ad limina apostolorum [to the tombs of the apostles Saint Peter and Saint Paul]* (each diocesan bishop had to come to Rome every five years to worship at the tombs of the two apostles, meet the Pope, make contact with the Roman curia dicasteries and present the Vatican with a report on the current situation of their diocese); the superiors of religious orders with general chapters in Rome; community groups; and visiting notables like King Baudouin, Raymond Barre, Jean Guitton and Diego Maradona.

Jacques and Bernadette Chirac visited on December 13, 1985, the feast day of Saint Lucia, patron saint of light, a date that was, most significantly, the first anniversary of Poland coming under martial law. The Holy Father wanted to thank Chirac for sending two cargo planes with supplies, medicine and money to Poland in 1981, a generous gesture by the then-mayor of Paris. When mass was over, the Chiracs were granted a private audience, where they were blessed for the third time by John Paul II, having been blessed once before at the Vatican and then on Notre Dame's forecourt in 1980. On the latter occasion, Chirac gave the Holy Father the complete bound works of Molière.

A great many people were thus received over the long years of John Paul II's papacy, even though, in his last three years, invitations to mass were increasingly rare. Guests included known figures, but also anonymous believers from modest walks of life who had written to the Pope asking him to grant them this rare favor. This illustrates how different the selection criteria were from those used at the Elysée palace or the royal courts of England and Morocco. The guests themselves did not really understand why they had been given this extraordinary opportunity and were amazed at being in such diverse company. Those who lived abroad often traveled a great distance solely to attend the religious service. They were informed two weeks beforehand via a letter from Sister Eufrosyna, while those who lived in Rome were told one or two days beforehand via a short telephone call from Msgr. Dziwisz, who would graciously announce, *"Il Santo Padre vi invita a la sua messa dopo domain" ("The Holy Father is inviting you to attend his mass the day after tomorrow")*. The guests were introduced to each other neither before nor after the ceremony; kings could thus be seen gazing curiously at writers, priests, politicians and ordinary men and women. As for myself, the day that I was invited everyone asked themselves who I could possibly be since, aside from nuns and wives, women were rarely in attendance. When it was time to take communion, I was concerned about not having been to confession for a long time and leaned over to my neighbor, a Mexican nun from Notre-Dame-de-Guadalupe, to ask her in hushed tones if I could still take communion. When she answered me in Spanish, and with great assurance, *"Autoconfesión!,"* the entire assembly turned to look at us in the back row. I don't think I have ever been so embarrassed in my life.

The Holy Father celebrated mass in Latin and Italian, but as a gesture of courtesy to the foreigners present, he interspersed passages in their languages. It was his first opportunity of the day to speak in foreign tongues. One of the guests, usually a priest, served mass. Over the years, mass went from 50 minutes to 40 and then 30 as the Pope's mobility became limited with age. The Holy Father gave the Eucharist himself. His secular entourage, namely his majordomo, doctor and photographer, always took communion, along with most of the guests.

In his later years, this mass continued to give him a feeling of serenity, but it also tired him out, which is why one day Msgr. Dziwisz decided to replace the sumptuous and very heavy ciboria, chalices and monstrances of solid 22 carat gold, all wonderful works of art, with lighter gold-plated, silver-gilt or silver articles, along with the other liturgical objects. There was no homily, but mass was followed by a thanksgiving. The faces of the sisters who always attended the service were radiant. Piety certainly accounted in part for their pleasure, but it was also an opportunity for them to leave their humble tasks behind and mix with other people. When a well-known personality was in attendance, they tended to frequently cast furtive glances at him or her.

When the Pope turned toward the congregation and proclaimed *Ite missa est*, the chosen few all suddenly felt a bit anxious; the fact was that no one knew what was going to happen or what the Supreme Pontiff was going to do. They had received no information beforehand. Who would be chosen to stay for breakfast? As it turned out, although there were rarely more than two or three people invited to breakfast, everyone was nevertheless received after mass in the huge, private salon, decorated in beige and featuring religious paintings and an imposing, solid mahogany bookcase. The Pope granted his guests an audience lasting a few minutes, their proud moment immortalized for them by his personal photographer Arturo Mari, an elegant 60-year-old in black blazer and trousers whom I took to be a Jesuit for the longest time.

Then the various guests gave the Pope their carefully prepared gifts, which ranged from a check made out to the IOR (Opere di Religione, the Vatican bank) to a valuable gold watch. The less well-off guests came with more modest offerings, such as tapestry portraits, bouquets of flowers, chocolates, cheese and panettone bread. The day I was there, a couple of Italian farmers gave him the moving gift of a portrait crafted from spaghetti, and the Mexican nuns who were my neighbors during mass had lovingly concocted pots of guava jam for him! Everyone spontaneously held out their gifts to the Holy Father, but it was his worthy gentleman of the chamber, Angelo Gugel (whose title is the only pompous relic of the posts held by the ancient secular families), who moved with assurance to take them and lay them out on a large table, trying to arrange them harmoniously. The atmosphere was not at all solemn, but full of joy. The Pope then gave out medals, key rings bearing his image and mother-of-pearl or perhaps coral rosaries. Pearl rosaries were theoretically reserved for Catholic queens; however, Madame Chirac and I both received one. According to the guest's rank, but also depending on the Holy Father's personal feelings, the consecrated objects he gave people could be in bronze, silver or even gold!

The Swiss Guards struck a more serious note in the midst of this convivial atmosphere, never smiling when they were on duty and always presenting a haughty front. They guided most of the guests to the exit, i.e., the elevator on the landing (and not the staff elevator, which went directly to the Pope's apartment, operated by an elevator-attendant sister), but not the chosen few who—honor of honors—were having breakfast with the Supreme Pontiff.

Breakfast was served at about 8:15 A.M. in the dining room

near the salon, and sometimes lasted until 9:30, especially when it provided the occasion for discreet meetings that, thanks to the strictly private character of mass, were not included in the official register. The Pope met people like Giulio Andreotti and Romano Prodi, to name just two, in this way. The brown walls were decorated with primitive religious paintings and a stunning triptych representing the Virgin with child. Around the rectangular table—covered with a white tablecloth and brightened up with round bouquets of yellow and white roses, the Vatican colors—were placed burgundy velvet chairs with armrests and high backs. The Pope sat alone on one of the long sides of the table, a rare vestige of ancient protocol he had retained that required princes of the Church, just like kings, to have no neighbors at the table in their own homes. The breakfast menu consisted of coffee or tea, milk, orange juice from Saint Peter's orchard, concentrated red fruit or plum jam just like in Poland, scrambled eggs with wild onions or herbs and shavings of ham, cheese and sausage, and, of course, the typically Italian round, rose-shaped bread rolls that the Holy Father adored, served warm—their delicious aroma was the first thing you noticed on entering his private apartments in the morning. "I came to Rome on purpose to eat those bread rolls!" the Holy Father would sometimes joke. John Paul II drank Earl Grey, an English tea flavored with bergamot. He rarely drank coffee except, at times, American-style coffee. He was not a big eater, so this very substantial breakfast *(sniadanie* in Polish) constituted his main meal of the day. He used to say that it gave him the energy he needed to get through his long working days, which is why he insisted on such an abundant breakfast. "When you eat well in the morning, you work better," he declared in September 1996 to the Saint-Sixte Dominicans in Tours, where he was lodging and where, during his visit to France, he received all the bishops of France at lunch.

It was typical of Karol Wojtyla to invite a wide variety of people, from Mother Teresa to former President Pertini, to share his table, morning and night, despite the fact that he was neither a gourmet nor a big eater—which was a good thing, since his personal doctor had asked him to avoid putting on weight following the 1981 assassination attempt. However, this did not prevent him from tasting local specialties when he traveled. Cold pork products with morels, saveloy with pistachios and Bresse poultry: the top chefs of Lyons felt very honored that the Pope ate heartily of all these dishes when he visited Lyons in October 1985.

The ivory breakfast china, featuring a fine gold rim and the papal arms, was the work of the famous Italian china manufacturer Richard Ginori. The glasses were either the Harcourt model from Baccarat, with the papal arms engraved in crystal, or blown-glass tumblers from Murano (the island opposite Venice) in 18th-century Bohemian style, with medallions engraved in the glass. The silverware was in a very classic style, made of either silver-gilt or sterling silver. In contrast with the Queen of England, whose suppliers are allowed to feature the prestigious royal warrant, "Supplier of . . . by Appointment to Her Majesty," the Holy See does not provide "Supplier by Appointment to His Holiness" certification, and if any supplier mentions the papal connection for the purposes of advertising, they receive no more orders from the Vatican.

Usually guests seemed so overawed that they hardly dared touch anything. They were afraid of spilling jam or honey on themselves (John Paul II never got stains on his clothes) or of having a full mouth when the Pope spoke to them. This deprivation was made even more cruel by the irresistible aromas wafting from the sweet loaves, buns and scrambled eggs, not to mention the presence of majordomo Angelo Gugel, who might lean in to whisper benevolently, *"È molto buono!" ("It's very tasty!").* The Vatican's cuisine has always had the reputation of being simple, carefully prepared and, until John Paul II, not very spicy, since the high-ranking prelates who eat there are often getting on in years. (One example was Corrado Bafile, cardinal emeritus of the Congregation for the Causes of the Saints and senior member of the Sacred College, who celebrated his 100th birthday last July.) Unlike the Pope, many of the cardinals are gourmets: spiritual nourishment alone does not satisfy them. They appreciate the fine wines that generous, affluent believers sometimes give them, and when they go traveling or on holiday, they exchange addresses of the convents and monasteries where the best food can be had. If by chance their wanderings take them to Cuba, they are happy to accept famous San Cristobal cigars for themselves or their colleagues from Cardinal Jaime Lucas Ortega y Alamino, archbishop of San Cristobal de la Habana. (This had become something of a tradition since the days of Cardinal Villot, former secretary of state under John XXIII and then Paul VI, who received them from Luis Amado Blanco, Cuban ambassador to the Holy See in the 1970s; he always gave large boxes of Romeo and Juliette cigars to Villot, who kept them in the salad tray of his fridge so that he could graciously offer them to his guests.) These precious addresses served as their *Michelin Guide* to ecclesiastical fine dining, since life in Rome on 2,800 euros a month with no chauffeur, cook or housekeeper and usually just one or two "au pair" nuns was much less gilded an existence than is imagined. For example, the French cardinals in Rome, Poupard and Etchegaray, as well as cardinals of many other nationalities, drive modest cars like Peugeot 406s, and they are lucky if their traveling expenses are paid for—if you take into account the function they fulfill in representing the Church, their salary is less than sufficient. Some countries are an exception to this rule, such as Germany, where the Episcopal conference grants German cardinals monthly compensation. One day in October 2004, after the beatification of Emperor Charles of Austria, I found myself in a taxi queue on Saint Peter's Square behind two eminent cardinals. I asked them, "What has happened to your chauffeur? Why are you waiting for a taxi in the rain?" "What can you do? There is a priest who acts as my chauffeur and secretary, but it's his day off, so we're going to share a taxi," replied one of them, lifting his arms to the sky while looking at his colleague.

Toward 9 A.M., the Vicar of Christ went to another office in his private apartments, where he received his colleagues. The mahogany desk had an extension so that one of them could sit at the end of the table and put his notepad there. Mobile phones had trouble picking up a signal here and, in any case, the powerful Radio Vatican transmitter sometimes interfered with the lines. In addition to an ivory-colored telephone that served the private apartments and secretary's office, there was a gray telephone the Pope could use to call the Holy See's departments, and a black one with an outside line. Up until the era of Paul VI, the idea of making a direct telephone call to the Supreme Pontiff was inconceivable. John Paul II, however, sometimes took calls, but only after a three-way filter comprising the general switchboard, Sister Eufrosyna and Msgr. Dziwisz. Poor John Paul I, who to begin with had no idea how the filter worked, always answered everyone who called in the early days. One morning, journalist Bruno Bartóloni from the AFP *(Agence France-Presse),* who also contributed to *Gazette de Venise*, wanted to contact his secretary, but got the Pope himself on the line! He was so stupefied that he started off apologizing profusely and offering all sorts of good wishes before taking advantage of the opportunity to conduct a short interview, which naturally enough was a great scoop.

At the side of the desk, within John Paul II's reach, lay the current purple and gold papal directory featuring all Church notables. This bulky, 2,600-page tome, which he leafed through nervously when he was annoyed by what was being said to him, was the work of an editor and some 10 contributors, including the head of the Church's Central Office of Statistics, under the direction of Secretary of State Cardinal Sodano. Each year in early February, the Pope received the first copy of the latest edition as well as the telephone directory for all the religious communities, bound in white calfskin. In front of the Holy Father's brown leather writing case lay a bronze and crystal clock and a crucifix on a black pedestal.

The Pope stopped every day on the way to his office to pick up a selection of daily papers from the console table, including *La Stampa, La Repubblica, Il Corriere della Sera, The International Herald Tribune, Die Welt* and *Le Figaro*. He was also handed a white leather folder stamped with his coat of arms containing the day's first copy of *L'Osservatore Romano*, the official Vatican mouthpiece with a daily print run of 5,000 copies.

The Holy Father, with seven languages at his command, read the main headlines of all these papers, skimming articles that interested him via a rapid reading technique like the one used by John F. Kennedy. He paid special attention to the press review drawn up by the Secretariat of State, and perused the Polish newspapers in more depth, including *Tygodvik Poweszechny*, the Krakow daily paper for which one of his close friends, Father Adam Boniecki, regularly wrote, *Gazeta Krakowska*, *Gazeta Wyborcza* and *Snak*, a monthly publication for the Catholic intelligentsia. He remained in his private office until 11 A.M., dictating his letters to Sister Eufrosyna.

It was in this study, sequestered from the noise of the outside world, that John Paul II wrote his encyclicals and, in 1995, *Evangelium Vitae*, a bestseller that sold over 4 million copies in 52 countries. As with all his writings, his royalties were donated to charitable works via his personal bank account, 16-IRW. In a corner of his study beneath a window, there was a small anti-slip platform, which the Holy Father would mount every Sunday in order to bless the faithful gathered in Saint Peter's Square below.

In keeping with his own character, after his election as Pope and once he moved into the majestic papal palace, John Paul II asked for a simpler décor in his private apartments, despite the wonderful Italian Renaissance architecture's generous dimensions, coffered ceilings, frescoes, trompe-l'œils, porphyry, alabaster, marble, and large, high-ceilinged rooms with delicate gold-leafed plaster walls, which lent an atmosphere that was more religious than flamboyant. There was nothing museum-like about the apartment, even though the Carrara marble floors at the entrance were inset with the enormous coat of arms of some aristocratic 16th-century Pope fashioned in multicolored precious stones, and the arms of John Paul II hung above the heavy front door. His coat of arms, designed for him by a heraldry expert during his time as Archbishop of Krakow, featured an offset Latin cross and a gold letter *M* against a deep blue background, symbolizing Karol Wojtyla's devotion to the Virgin Mary; once he was elected Pope, a pontifical tiara and the keys to Saint Peter's, in gold and silver, were added to his arms.

The third-floor apartments contained some 20 rooms (with a small screening room on the left as you entered), which felt not at all pompous or cold thanks to the multitude of commonplace objects and slightly kitschy souvenirs on display. In the midst of allegorical works from the 16th, 17th and 18th centuries representing the Adoration of the Magi, the Annunciation, the Crucifixion, the Judgment of Solomon, Saint Peter's Square and other, similar themes, John Paul II chose to display several works by modern artists: two mosaics—one by Russian Alexander Rüskov, the other by Slovenian Marko Rupnik—and a hyperrealist painting, *Exodus*, painted in 1988 by Jerzy Duda Gracz, Poland's most renowned living painter. During the course of his pontificate, these majestic surroundings were slowly transformed into a convivial place where the ushers, dressed in long, eggplant-colored jackets with white wing collars and gold and silver chains, and the strapping Swiss Guards, standing motionless in front of the door in their two-tone uniforms, seemed almost anachronistic and out of keeping with John Paul II's personal style, which was warm and unique to him. The Pope placed discreet photographs of his family around the place, as well as modern Madonnas, reproductions of Virgin icons, brass and wooden crucifixes, a portrait of Cardinal Wyszinski, a bronze sculpture of a Pope on horseback, a work by contemporary modern Italian artist Ludovico Graziani, and another modern painting by Filocamo. Throughout the apartments could be seen unpretentious, eclectic souvenirs of pilgrimages.

Reassured by the modesty and diversity of some of the gifts on display, I had no qualms during one of my visits in presenting the Holy Father with a matching black lacquer and enamel pen and magnifying glass made by a craftsman in Paris. The Pope was particularly relaxed that day, and the moment he took the magnifying glass in his right hand he amused himself by staring at me through the magnifying lens, to the astonishment of two young bishops from overseas.

These objects of no great value, to which he was nonetheless attached, were at odds with the solemnity of the palace, itself the luxurious heritage of 18th-century Popes with a propensity for building, such as Pius VI (1775–1799), to whom the Vatican is much indebted for its present grandeur. Karol Wojtyla set out to break with a classical Italian tradition, one that valued precious metals and objects from the late medieval and Renaissance periods above all else: console tables in gold leaf, medieval stone statues, 15th-century cabinets inlaid with precious stones, and many other priceless pieces of furniture bearing the coats of arms of his predecessors. Almost every visitor—including myself, though I was relatively familiar with the formality of the Elysée palace's government ministries and haughty functionaries—was astonished to realize that, within these grandiose apartments charged with the weight of history, there reigned a taste for simplicity and disdain for pompousness. With his unpretentious knick-knacks and a few potted plants, John Paul II succeeded in lightening the mood amidst these imposing, time-worn surroundings, in a place where, unlike our own national palaces, the marvels bequeathed by the past had never been spoiled by the poor taste of a minister's wife.

John Paul II would commence the public part of his day at 11 A.M., when he moved from his "house" (as he used to call it) to his official apartments immediately below on the second floor of the east wing, which mirrored the private apartments in that they also comprised some 20 principal rooms laid out according to the same floor plan. Since 1870, these official apartments have served as the stage for all the main papal activities, such as private and semi-private audiences and *ad limina apostolorum* ecclesiastical visits by bishops from around the world, recently including those from Clermont, Moulin, Saint-Flour and Valence, France, accompanied by a group of nuns who work with the destitute. There were also farewell visits from departing ambassadors and the presentation of credentials by new ones, meetings with members of various pontifical councils, directives to staff concerning future speeches, discussions about the status of an upcoming voyage and much more. All in all, the Pope's schedule was every bit as full as that of any other head of state.

John Paul II always received cardinals, other eminent Church leaders and important pilgrims in the magnificent Consistory Hall, while heads of state, monarchs and other powerful figures were received in the main pontifical library.

But while his health still permitted, John Paul II had an astonishing ability to attract gatherings of important guests in each of the 10 imposing second-floor reception rooms. He would then solemnly pass from room to room, doubtless without anyone in the Small Throne Room realizing that he had come via various other halls—the Clementine, Consistory, Saint Ambroise, Corner and Popes Rooms—as well as the Urban VIII Chapel, the Throne Room and the Ambassadors Room! The large library on the second floor is so similar to the one on the floor above in the residence that the notable guests received by John Paul II could imagine themselves at a private audience in his own apartments. This happened to the president of Honduras, the grand duchess of Luxembourg, the queen of England, Prince Rainier of Monaco, Victor-Emmanuel of Savoy and many others, who are perhaps reading of their misunderstanding here for the first time!

In reality, receptions for heads of state (there are three categories of visits to the Holy Father: private, official and state) were always held in the official apartments. This is where the three most recent former French presidents, Giscard d'Estaing, Mitterrand and Chirac, were welcomed. Valéry Giscard d'Estaing was received on October 28, 1978, barely 12 days after the papal election; in order to avoid meeting a foreigner for his first official reception, the Holy Father was forced to accord a last-minute reception to Italian President Alessandro Pertini on October 24. François Mitterrand was received on Saturday February 27, 1982, and Jacques Chirac made a state visit on January 20, 1996.

In 2001, I was writing a book about Chirac, and after much effort I managed to ask him what he thought of John Paul II.

The president was hesitant in responding, for he preferred to keep his feelings secret, but as the subject was a figure of such high standing, and one whom Chirac held in the highest regard, he eventually answered, "It is an honor to be received on a state visit by John Paul II. I hold him in great esteem and have much admiration for him. We have had a few private meetings, and I was impressed every time, to the extent of not feeling completely free, which is quite rare for me. I would say that this is a feeling I have never experienced elsewhere. His force of character prevailed to the extent that I felt there were certain matters that I would never have raised with him myself."

The long-time head of travel arrangements, Cardinal Tucci, recently confided to me: "From his very first visit to France, the Holy Father was always very appreciative of the attitude shown to him by President Chirac. I would say that their relationship was very cordial, indeed affectionate; their understanding was implicit and their liking mutual. If Chirac was able to visit the Vatican so soon after his election, it was because he had always demonstrated humanity and understanding toward the Supreme Pontiff. Although he was disappointed that in 2003 Jacques Chirac did not fight for the inclusion of a reference to Christian origins in the text of the European Constitution, to be honest it was Valéry Giscard d'Estaing who disappointed him most in that regard. But there were so many issues at stake that all he could do was forgive them!"

According to inflexible protocol, a herald—the *decano di sala* and his assistant—would await the VIP guests at the door to the apartments and would accompany them to the library entrance, where the Holy Father would be waiting to greet them. They would then bow low to him, take his hand and kiss the papal ring.

During larger audiences in the second floor apartments, the Holy Father would receive high-ranking international officials and ambassadors to the Holy See. (There are currently 174 accredited ambassadors, plus representatives from the Russian Federation and the Palestinian Liberation Organization—who are not classed as diplomatic representatives—and representatives from the Order of Malta and the European Union. The Holy See is a member of 33 intergovernmental and international bodies, including the UN and the UN Food and Agriculture Organization.) Each and every one of them would try to have a private conversation with him, but he would always make his excuses and leave if he felt an audience was at risk of becoming monotonous and predictable. He had developed an infallible two-tier tactic for dealing with such situations. First, as soon as the conversation started to drag, the Supreme Pontiff would adopt the look of a tired old man, which would discourage the person in front of him (who often already felt quite uncomfortable if they were divorced, for example, or cohabiting and knew that the Pope knew). The other trick was to direct the person toward his Prime Minister Cardinal Sodano while sternly intoning, "Welcome to Rome!" The imposing surroundings also helped to inhibit unwanted conversation.

Although meetings with the Pope were very brief, those that met him were fascinated by his charisma and impressed by his knowledge of history and world politics. As denizens of a milieu where people tried to be as guarded as possible, they were strangely disconcerted by his frank and uninhibited way of speaking, as was explained to me by former French Prime Minister Édouard Balladur, who visited John Paul II in December 1993: "I was struck by his conciseness, his intelligence, the way he spoke very clearly in excellent French, and by the amount he knew, not just about Eastern Europe but about everything. He had a vision of things that was both planetary and historically long-term. He placed events in their context, and he had a very global approach to situations and a very personal scale of the importance of events and values; he was not interested in petty maneuvering. In person, he had great physical presence and a very firm speaking voice. But what impressed me most was John Paul II's aura and natural authority."

In any event, the Pontiff was singularly unmoved by flamboyant personalities from the world outside. When he was given a 2 million franc armored Fiat in 2000 by Giovanni Agnelli, the man known as "the King of Italy," he responded with no more than a smile and gave the photographers a few seconds. That same evening, however, he spent a long time with some Slavonic nuns who had been imprisoned and forced to perform manual labor during years of persecution by their then-Communist governments; he even sang with them. Some of his powerful guests, generally politicians, sought to embarrass him by asking awkward questions. He would always respond calmly, answering in telling, precise phrases. Valéry Giscard d'Estaing has said that he never approached a controversy, and would always stifle debate with a well-turned phrase. Cardinal Poupard emphasizes the fact that "his prodigious memory, broad cultural background and innate gift for the turn of a phrase would always come to his rescue."

At the end of these audiences, the Pope would take gifts

from a silver platter held by the *decano di sala*—including medallions, paperweights and pictures or mosaic reproductions of artworks from the Vatican museum—to present to his most notable visitors. The gold and silver medallions were presented in white, dark green or burgundy moiré silk boxes bearing the papal coat of arms. He usually received similar types of presents from his illustrious visitors.

To mark John Paul II's 80th birthday, president of the Italian senate Nicola Mancino presented him with a copy of the Italian constitution bearing the memorable inscription, "The Pope is also the father of our country." There is no denying that, in Italy, politics and religion go hand in hand; indeed, deputy Marco Pannella presented the Pope with a religious manuscript dating from the 16th century. During celebrations marking the 25th year of his papacy on October 16, 2003, he was showered with gifts from the various heads of state, members of royalty and other delegations in attendance.

His butler, Angelo Gugel, would gather up the gifts in a dignified manner and arrange them on a walnut table. This very rigid ceremony was reminiscent more of the Three Kings than anything at Versailles or a Byzantine palace. The gifts were then catalogued and stored in the *Floreria apostolica*, which served both as the private papal museum and as a collection of objects used to decorate offices in the various dicasteries (ministries) and pontifical councils. Some of the gifts presented to the Holy Father, especially perishable food, were redistributed to Rome's Bambino Gesù children's hospital, to residents of Mother Teresa's house inside the Vatican walls and to other charitable bodies.

The Holy See announced that as of January 5, 2005, John

Paul II had received 38 state visits and held 737 audiences and meetings with heads of state and 245 with prime ministers during his pontificate. This was in addition to all the audiences—the figures for which have never been made public—with cardinals in charge of ministries, visiting bishops (to whom he would generally announce, "You are responsible for preaching the Gospel forcefully and clearly to all mankind"), leading politicians, Church leaders, diplomats presenting their credentials, and distinguished writers and scientists. It was during private audiences such as these that the Pope, who never accepted any decorations or awards himself, would bestow the ribbon of the Order of Pius or some other decoration on those he wished to favor, on condition that they were not divorced (Jacques Chirac was one such recipient).

He took his lunch between 1:30 and 2 P.M. He was not attached to dining at any set time, something that exasperated the Italian prelates who took their *colazione* very seriously! Poles as a rule are not too concerned about the exact time that they eat, preferring to sit down at table once they have finished doing whatever needed to be done. The Holy Father would usually invite those attending his last morning appointment to have lunch with him, perhaps bishops from countries he would be visiting. Menus were Sister Germana's domain, but the Pope was very attentive to his guests' nationalities. For example, when inviting a French cardinal—Cardinal Poupard's visit to Castel Gandolfo just after a trip to Russia—he would ensure that a tasty dessert tart or gateau was on the menu, because he had once been told by Polish nuns that the French were great lovers of desserts. Cardinal Tucci describes how "he would begin meals with serious talk about the matters at hand, and it was only once the dessert arrived that he would relax and begin to make jokes." Once when he was receiving a group of Chinese people, he asked advice from Cardinal Deskur, a man who loved fine dining and, as an expert on Polish and international cuisines, was renowned for keeping one of the finest tables in Rome. Indeed, as soon as Wojtyla became Pope, Cardinal Deskur sent his own cook, Sister Germana, to work for the Supreme Pontiff, which must have been a real sacrifice for him.

One of the Holy Father's Sunday guests would often be a priest from one of the parishes in Rome or its environs that the Pope would be visiting to celebrate mass the following week. This was a habit that became less frequent and eventually ceased completely during the final years of his reign. Over the course of his 25-year pontificate, John Paul II did, however, visit 241 of Rome's 300 Catholic places of worship.

The Holy Father would eat Italian-Polish food at lunch, dishes that were in general fairly rich. Toward the end, however, he ate little; at times, he barely touched the food in front of him. The extra weight and puffiness around the face that he showed during the last years were a result of the great number of drugs, including cortisone, that he was required to take. Menus varied, but might include pasta, steamed potatoes, vegetable pies, roast meat, fish, *pirojki* (puff pastry filled with meat or cabbage), jellied fish terrines (on Fridays), fruit salad and pastries (including the famous *kremowka*: Polish layer cakes made with cream, fromage blanc, and poached cream—a type of Polish molded custard). Dessert courses were often expanded to include delicacies brought by Polish pilgrims. The wine served was white, from the Holy See's own vineyards. Some wines were lightly sparkling and sealed with the type of stopper generally used for sparkling lemonade. The Holy Father would dilute his wine with water, generally San Paolo, which was still and had a low mineral content. Sometimes in summer he would drink beer, but always in very small quantities; as a youth, Karol Wojtyla had been a member of a temperance movement. Aside from vegetables grown in his Roman kitchen garden, most of the fresh products—eggs, chicken and mozzarella—were delivered in a refrigerated truck direct from the farm at the papal villa in Castel Gandolfo, the Pope's summer residence, some 60 kilometers from Rome. Although over time John Paul II's menus became blander, he never lost his love for seasoning. Once, during a grand meal attended by cardinals and eminent Italians, the guests, seeing him liberally sprinkling his salad with what looked like parmesan, asked whether this was his way of Italianizing his food; in fact, he was adding a typically Slav condiment: horseradish!

Meals at the Vatican were always made with great care, regardless of who the guests were. On June 15, 2000, when John Paul II hosted 200 poor homeless people in the atrium of the Nervi Hall to celebrate his jubilee, the menu comprised ravioli, roast veal, sautéed potatoes, cheese and fruit salad, accompanied by Italian still wines and finished off with a glass of sparkling wine. The meal was served by students from Rome's seminary.

John Paul II was relaxed from the outset, and was a lively host, with the ability to encourage his guests to join the conversation. As he sat down to eat, he exclaimed, "So, which languages are we speaking today?" The Holy Father ate little and quickly, which allowed him to spend more time concentrating on his guests. He tended to begin by asking them relatively complex questions, which would then offer him the chance to eat a few mouthfuls as he listened to their replies before asking a follow-up. In the words of the cardinal archbishop of Vienna, Msgr. Schönborn, who was invited to share a meal with John Paul II on many occasions, "When I was there, I never spoke very often, as I was fascinated and inspired by the Pope's discussions with his guests!"

There was a pause for prayer, conducted in the chapel before and after the meal, and then, on doctors' orders, the Pope would have a siesta of about an hour—nearer two hours in later years—in his room, installing himself comfortably in one of his two red damask armchairs. He rose a little later in the afternoon, sometimes pulling on a black cap and throwing his old black cape, which dated from his time as a bishop in Poland, over his shoulders before slowly making his way to the terrace just above his apartment overlooking Rome and the Courtyard of Saint Damasus, which had been recently renovated by Paul VI. It was on this famous terrace that I was scheduled to meet my colleague from *Paris Match* in order to photograph the Pope as he walked in prayer. The terrace is in fact a hanging garden complete with trees in large pots, a fountain and a pond stocked with goldfish. Every morning, a gardener waters the plants and feeds the fish. John Paul II liked to read or recite his breviary as he walked a short way. This represented both his daily physical exercise and a spiritual exercise, a moment when he could pray and meditate in absolute silence.

Some time around 6:30 P.M., the Supreme Pontiff would return to the study in his private apartments and summon his closest colleagues, his Prime Minister Cardinal Angelo Sodano (who was summoned back from Chile in 1988, where he was the papal nuncio, and who served as his first minister for foreign affairs), Msgr. Sandri, the substitute, and, until 2003, Msgr. Jean-Louis Tauran, his minister for foreign affairs and one of the few French prelates to have come through the Pontifical Ecclesiastical Academy at the Gregorian University (and, as the son of a wine merchant, he was also a redoubtable connoisseur of Bordeaux wines). In October of 2003, Msgr. Tauran was replaced by Msgr. Lajolò. Also present on an informal basis and without particular hierarchical order were the devoted Polish priests who assisted John Paul II at all times: Msgr. Stanislas Rylko, Msgr. Henrik Nowacki and Father Stanislaw Szlowieniec.

When he had guests, after dinner John Paul II would descend once again to his official apartments. There might be delegations from abroad or pilgrims, often from Central and Eastern Europe, in groups of never more than 40 people. In his later years, as his Parkinson's disease and the legacy of the 1981 attack left him increasingly weakened, the Pope consented to hold audiences such as these only for those whom he felt were closest to his heart. Naturally, he no longer made the warm and brilliant speeches for which he was so famous; instead, the cardinal secretary of state would solemnly hand out a photocopied speech in person.

The days were long, and sometime around 8 P.M., the Holy Father would show clear signs of fatigue. He would go up to his apartment accompanied by Msgr. Dziwisz, who would take the opportunity to slip a note into his cassock pocket listing the schedule for the following day. John Paul II was happy to return to the intimacy of the private papal apartments. (He was the seventh Pope since Pius X to occupy them.)

He would first visit his chapel for a moment's prayer, kneeling on his prie-dieu. Then he would return to his study to watch the news headlines on the main Italian state channel, TG1. He was also fond of popular science programs, saying that when they were well made they served as an antidote to a tendency to forget certain values; he also enjoyed the quality TV movies made by Ettore Barnabei about Mother Teresa and John XXIII. He would occasionally watch Polish channels TF Polonia and Polsat, which he received via a small satellite dish hidden in a corner of the *attico*, his flower-filled top-floor terrace, where he had also installed a small Stations of the Cross that was a favorite place to pray in the afternoons. John Paul II took little interest in the cinema; he did however enjoy *La Porta del Cielo*, a film about Fatima by Vittorio De Sica, *Life Is Beautiful* by Roberto Benigni, *Our God's Brother* by Polish filmmaker Krzysztof Zanussi, *Pan Tadeusz* by Andrzej Wajda, *Mother and Son* by Alexander Sukurov and Roman Polanski's *The Pianist*. Sometimes he was presented with films by filmmakers invited to take part in Spiritual Cinema Week. And even though he did see Mel Gibson's controversial *The Passion of the Christ*, John Paul II saw no more than 15 films in his entire pontificate.

His favorite pastime had always been reading, losing himself in works of philosophy or history taken from his own shelves, not from the famous official library on the second floor where he was always photographed. The latter was run by the state secretariat, which took charge of the countless books that arrived for the Pope every day; the latter books were, for the most part, reviewed by his staff, who would pass on to him all manner of documents that they felt might be helpful to his own output. The Vatican's apostolic library in the Belvedere courtyard housed a collection of manuscripts, illuminations, incunabula, maps, and precious and rare books that was used more by social scientists and academics than the Pope. For this reason, John Paul II built up a personal library in his apartment; run by his two secretaries, his collection was already very large when he brought it with him from Poland to the Vatican.

His evening meal was more frugal than at midday, often comprising a hot, low-fat light soup plus vegetables and fruit. The Polish custom is to take a light meal in the evening, sometimes merely a selection of cold snacks. Karol Wojtyla's guests in the evening were usually his two Polish private secretaries. He was little given to conversation, saying, "In the evening, I am the silent Pope." While Angelo Gugel served the midday meal, Sister Germana served the evening meal, performing her duties wordlessly (whereas Angelo was forever encouraging guests to eat plentifully!).

Shortly before midnight, the Pope would again kneel in prayer in his study or his bedroom, wherever he might be. Before going to sleep, he would lie in his bed and read a few pages from a book or his breviary, a thick bound work that he kept in a black leather slipcase fastened with a zipper. The nun who kept vigil in the adjoining room listened closely for the quiet sound that meant that the Holy Father had replaced the breviary in its case and that "her" Pope's day had drawn to a close. Then John Paul II's delicate, bony hand reached for the light switch on his bedside table, and he fell asleep reciting his rosary. In 2003, once he had resigned himself to being wheelchair-bound, Msgr. Dziwisz, Dr. Buzzonetti and Sister Tobiana altered his late-evening timetable, the period that was most dear to him throughout the course of his long days.

Chapter Four

A YOUNG GIRL, MY OWN CHILD, AMIDST THE PILGRIMS

Many of my memories of John Paul II are very personal. He received me several times at the Vatican and at Castel Gandolfo, and he granted me a number of interviews during his pastoral visits around the world—special treatment, indeed. Perhaps it was because his entourage had been kind enough to commend my concept of journalism to him. I had a reputation for being respectful and conscientious, but also for being very determined and not mincing my words. I feel this was something that pleased the Holy Father, who was on occasions riled when surrounded by an overly deferential entourage. I also believe that he was amused by my daring tenacity and the simplicity that I exhibited when I approached him, a belief that was confirmed for me by a cardinal who was also his friend. Deeply aware of the favor bestowed on me, I instinctively paid more attention than ever to ensuring that I did not overstep the mark. Looking back now, it is with great emotion that I relive these special moments, like a DVD that I return to again and again.

Sometime during the winter of 1995, under the exasperated gaze of certain Italian colleagues who seemingly took offense at the sight of starlets in racy advertisements, I offered the Holy Father several back issues of *Paris Match* that told the stories of his three predecessors, and he read them with care. "I am very touched, for I knew these articles already," he told me. "Did you know that in the old days, under the Communists, this magazine was smuggled into Poland and acted as a true message of hope for us, as we saw images of far-off France and freedom?"

It was clear that he had a soft spot for the magazine I worked for, and I daresay for me as well. For instance, on the day I presented him with the magazines, he handed them to his faithful manservant and quickly turned to look me straight in the eye, saying warmly, "I invite you to return here at your convenience with your daughters so that I may bless them." Almost overcome with emotion, I thanked him fervently for this thrilling suggestion.

On my return to Paris, I wondered whether I should take Marina and Cosima—then aged seven and five, respectively—together or one at a time; the latter would, after all, have the advantage of giving me two chances to visit the Holy Father. Bearing in mind the severity of the very dignified Vatican staff, the idea of taking them both at the same time also worried me somewhat, for I was forced to remember the time they accompanied me to a reception at Paris City Hall, when they got up to much mischief by treating the mayor's highly polished marble floors as their very own Olympic skating rink. In order to avoid unnecessary stress, I therefore decided that for the first visit I would take only my younger daughter, Cosima. The first order of business involved choosing a dress for her to wear that day. Influenced by movies she'd recently seen—*Un Indien dans la Ville* and *Pocahontas*—she was determined to visit the Vatican dressed as a Native American! I managed to convince her that a white cotton dress was far more suitable when you were privileged to receive a papal blessing. She was very taken with the idea of making the journey, even though, despite the halting religious education she was receiving at school, she did not yet really understand who the Pope was. In fact, she asked me, "Mummy, who is the person who always dresses the same and that you always write lots about on little pieces of paper?" She was intrigued by the Pope, for there were many photographs of him in our home and she told me that when she saw him on television he looked much gentler than other TV stars. However, she had a lot of trouble understanding why he always dressed in white, and why the imposing gold pectoral cross he wore was so very much larger than the one her godfather gave her for her baptism. What excited her most was the prospect of spending a few days in Italy with Aunt Sophie and missing a few days' school during the week, plus the chance to eat big bowls of spaghetti with tomato sauce, just like the big-hearted mongrel from the Disney film *Lady and the Tramp,* all to visit an old man who probably looked like the grandfather she'd never known.

It was Tuesday, June 25, 1997, and we were on a plane to

Rome. Although she was scarcely able to comprehend the spiritual significance of this audience with the Pope, Cosima was still enchanted to be able to see the Vatican for herself, as she had already seen it in innumerable photographs. She was also proud to think that when she returned to Sainte-Clotilde school, during playtime she would be able to describe Saint Peter's Basilica to her schoolmates, the very building that, according to Father Tessier in his short catechism classes, was erected to honor the memory of Saint Peter. Doesn't the phrase, "You are Peter, and on this rock I will build my Church" amply show us the true measure of the place? But best of all, she would surely be able to touch the man in white, whose every appearance on TV made me cry out: "Be quiet—I want to hear what he says!" Given that one of the two televisions in our home is permanently tuned to the Vatican channel CTV, this means that there are sometimes long silences, and scarcely controlled bouts of impatience, that stretch for minutes at a time.

I told her that she must start by genuflecting, and that she was to address him as Holy Father; I made her practice this a few times. I then tried to explain to her, without using the Vatican jargon that bore so little relationship to the real world, just what the general Wednesday audiences were about, for at the end of this religious event we were to have a discreet meeting with the Holy Father.

John Paul II's weekly public audiences started at either 10 or 11 A.M.; the most impressive were the ones held in Saint Peter's Square. The Pope used to make his way to the foot of his platform in the famous Popemobile 4x4 vehicle and take his place in a high-backed chair on the dais, facing the crowd assembled in the square in front of the basilica. He then addressed the gathering of pilgrims and pious tourists in at least seven languages, a habit he continued until 2001. He would bless the crowd in the same way that he blessed devotional items such as medallions, rosaries and missals. These audiences lasted more than two hours, or an hour and a half from 1993 on. Depending on the weather, the time of year and the numbers present, the audience was also on occasion held in the basilica (the capacity of which was 5,000 to 6,000) or the Paul VI Hall (capacity of 8,000), which was built by Milanese architect Nervi at the behest of Pope Paul VI. Except in his final years, the Pope often divided his audiences, receiving all the overseas tourists in the immense hall and the Italians in the basilica. However, until his dying day and if the weather permitted, Saint Peter's Square remained the place where he performed masses, beatifications and the innumerable Wednesday audiences.

In any event, the pilgrims always sang and applauded, no matter where the audience was held. Everyone was required to show a ticket, which was obtained the day before by going to the bronze Vatican gate and asking one of the ramrod-straight, uniformed Swiss Guards where to go for tickets, only to receive a response that never varied from a man that never looked at you: "Turn right by the Pius XI staircase, and enter the Saint Damasus courtyard."

Two-thirds of the way up the stairs and already disoriented by the sheer scale of the place, pilgrims would find a magnificent door surmounted by a majestic tiara bearing the words *Prefettura della casa pontificia*. These words indicate the place where pilgrims obtain their long-dreamed-of tickets. The tickets themselves are plain numbered pieces of paper, to be guarded carefully as the office will not issue a duplicate. The ticket is the key to an experience that is very often the main purpose of a visit to Rome: to hear and see John Paul II at last. Newly married couples were always given special treatment; as well as their tickets, printed on symbolic white paper, a prelate also presented them with a medallion and rosary on the Supreme Pontiff's behalf. Brides were requested to wear their white wedding dresses during the audience.

Literally hundreds of thousands of pilgrims passed through the *prefettura* during John Paul II's pontificate, seeking their tickets to an extraordinary, wholly unforgettable Wednesday audience.

When the *prefettura* was required to send tickets to special guests or to people organizing groups of pilgrims who were unable to come in person or whose tickets had become lost in the post, it delivered the "celestial" invitations personally via vehicles from the *autoparco vaticano*'s elegant fleet of dark-blue vehicles. Special guests received tickets for the front row immediately in front of the Pope; there were never more than 30 of these spots, to which were then added places for the handicapped, the sick and newlyweds, who were always placed to the left and right of the first rows. People in these positions were certain to be presented to the Pope by the head of the Papal Household, so that they might kiss the papal ring. Better still, close-up photographs would be taken of them with the Pope by his personal photographer, as if they were in a one-on-one meeting. These were delivered to their hotels the same evening. In return, they were asked to leave an envelope provided for the purpose containing just 2 euros for a 10x15-cm print, 3 euros for a 10x20, 4 euros for a 20x30, and 9 euros for a 24x36. This was a wonderful opportunity for well-known people, whose features would sometimes appear in black and white in *L'Osservatore Romano* and who would then attempt to ensure that the photograph showing them side-by-side with the Pope was first printed by newspapers in their own country before being artfully displayed in their office or living room.

Many such people knew little about the complexities of Vatican protocol, and were thus persuaded that they had received a private audience. In truth, aside from official visitors and high-ranking political and religious leaders, it was very hard to obtain a truly private audience with the Holy Father, although he did meet in private with over 700 heads of state and government. In his final years, the Holy Father limited the number of invitations as much as possible, but even by cutting his private audiences by one-half or two-thirds he still met with some 500 people per year.

Fortunately, the very popular Wednesday audiences, with the chance to kiss the papal ring for those in the *prima fila*, were an opportunity for Karol Wojtyla to greet people who, although often well-known in their own countries, were not sufficiently notable in the eyes of the Holy Father to warrant a private interview with him. It actually mattered little, for the relatively privileged people seated in the *prima fila*—anyone from politicians to Brigitte Bardot—often harbored illusions (subtly reinforced by the diplomacy of their respective ambassadors to the Holy See) that they had been favored with a private audience. As ever, it is a question of nuance, and it also proves that time is a great healer, even at the Vatican: in 1970,

Brigitte Bardot posed for photographs as a scantily clad nun, which caused a great scandal at the time and was censored by the Vatican—but since then, an angel has wiped her slate clean!

The Wednesday audiences, which were fabulously staged and admirably choreographed, remained events suffused with warmth, for John Paul II loved the spontaneity and fervor of the believers who, week after week, came to bear witness of their love for him. The waves of happiness he felt continued to nourish and sustain him until the very end of his pontificate. The audiences were attended by thousands every week: theater companies in costume; Italian generals in full uniform; students from the naval academy; members of the Orfei circus troupe (Italy's national circus), complete with tightrope walkers, clowns and even acrobats who installed their trampoline just a few meters from the papal throne; rangers from the Val Grande national park; members of the Bologna civil protection corps; pilgrims from across Latin America; young girls from Legion of Honor educational establishments; students from European universities; parish choirs; and even Cossacks from the Ukraine, plus members of innumerable associations, priests, nuns and missionaries from far-flung lands. Every Wednesday was different, but the enthusiasm of the reception never varied. According to the most recent Vatican figures issued on October 16, 2004, over the course of his quarter-century papacy a total of 1,150 audiences were attended by 18 million of the faithful from every country of the world.

It was strange indeed to witness the look of happiness etched onto every face as the Bishop of Rome, accompanied by a tidal wave of cheers, applause and cries of joy, made his way slowly across Saint Peter's Square aboard his strange white vehicle. I saw thousands of pairs of eyes glaze over with tears, fascinated by a man who bore not just the weight of his years, but that of the entire Catholic Church as well. It was an unforgettable experience that most of those attending would know only once in their lifetime. Indeed, images of this famous audience were buried in the subconscious memories of all of us thanks to the infamous audience of May 13, 1981, when Turkish gunman Mehmet Ali Agca shot the Pope. The powerful images from that day were shown again and again by television channels around the world every time John Paul II's health was the subject of anxiety.

Prior to that fateful day, it was not unusual to see the Pope sitting in a standard open vehicle as he slowly made his way through the admiring crowds in Saint Peter's Square. In the early days of his papacy, Karol Wojtyla would even descend from his car to mingle with the crowds. Heedless of the astonished looks on the faces of certain cardinals from the Roman curia, the Holy Father at times went one step farther and was occasionally seen to sign a few autographs. It was a regular occurrence for him to return to his quarters at about 1 P.M. with his wrists covered in scratches, almost bleeding, and the sleeves of his robes torn. In a state of great excitement and fervor some nuns, especially from Africa, South America and Asia, had trouble restraining themselves as the Pontiff approached, rushing to touch him and, overcome with passion in scenes reminiscent of appearances by the Beatles, they often attempted to tear off pieces of his cassock. The Pope, in his great indulgence, naturally understood the irresistible compulsion and great devotion of these women, who venerated him to such an extent that some threw themselves at his feet, at which point he would always murmur, "Get up! Get up!"

Following the assassination attempt, his security advisors forbade the Holy Father from exposing himself to the excesses of such filial love. One day, therefore, he announced to the crowd assembled in Saint Peter's Square that he would no longer be able to walk among them. The crowd was in such a pitch of excitement that many applauded his words even before their meaning had sunk in—no matter, for what counted was not so much hearing him but rather seeing him and experiencing a sense of communion with him.

Why were Wednesdays chosen? The idea was that those whose stay in Rome was too short to allow them to attend Sunday's Angelus mass would have another opportunity to see and hear the Supreme Pontiff. This meant that those who were there at the beginning of the week could attend the Wednesday audience, and those who came for the weekend, the Angelus.

Earlier Popes were very much cloistered within the Vatican, and the audiences that they held, albeit far less regularly, represented a unique chance to meet their flock; they rarely left their palace and never traveled, with the exception of Paul VI, who visited other countries on nine occasions between January 1964 and December 1970. At the time, his decision to travel was seen as nothing less than a palace revolution. First, he visited the Holy Land during the Second Vatican Council in 1964, before traveling to Berlin, Mumbai, New York, Fatima, Istanbul, Bogotá, Geneva, Kampala, the Philippines, Samoa, Australia, Hong Kong and Sri Lanka, thereby keeping the promise he made on June 30, 1963, the first day of his pontificate: "I shall travel in order that a great fire of faith and love shall pass over the entire world and engulf all men of goodwill." He was the first Pope in Vatican history to travel on an airliner! The last Pope before him to have crossed the Italian border was Pius VII (1800-1823), who was sent into exile by the French in June of 1812.

Every Supreme Pontiff left his own unique imprint on Christians' moments of grace and fervor. The debonair John XXIII (who was appointed patriarch of Venice at the age of 72 before acceding to the papacy on October 28, 1958, at the age of 77) improvised conversations-cum-sermons with the faithful; at times these were so convoluted that neither the prelates, past masters themselves at exercises of this type, nor the enthusiastic pilgrims were able to follow or understand what was said. John XXIII had a sense of humor: the great Vatican specialist Bruno Bartoloni tells how, during an audience, the Archbishop of Milan and future Pope Giovanni Battista Montini uttered a few respectful words to Pope John, who, answering in a voice heard by all, began to talk with the poetic verve of the crocodiles that lived on the banks of the river Ganges. We later discovered that the Pope, who had just celebrated his birthday, had perhaps consumed a small glass of the Lord's wine, with less sugar and more alcohol than communion wine—something that he was not used to!

In those days, information about the Pope's activities was so slow in coming and so dull that the handful of Vatican and agency correspondents had no compunction about telexing dispatches ahead of time, lovingly relating the Pope's prayers for the world's latest victims of natural disasters and accidents. They were all too aware that a communiqué in just those terms would be not long in coming, so they found it preferable to anticipate things a bit. This led to a situation where, when there was a day marked by a succession of disasters or accidents, the series of official announcements made it appear that the Pope, with astonishing speed, had visited his private chapel some dozen times in an unbelievably short space of time!

This sudden flurry of communiqués expressing the Pope's sadness was in reality the only official activity at the Holy See, which ritually issued the following text: "As soon as he was informed, the Supreme Pontiff went immediately to his private chapel to pray." These days such communiqués, as was the case regarding the terrible tsunami of December 2004, are signed by the cardinal secretary of state, and express "The pain felt by the Holy Father, who through prayer shares in the pain of the people, and who asks the Almighty to welcome the victims into his kingdom and to bring comfort to the injured and their families."

Given the growing success of this new style of direct physical contact with the crowd during the Wednesday audiences, Paul VI commissioned Nervi, one of three architects at UNESCO's Paris HQ, to design the reception hall that bears his name, on the former Radio Vatican site.

All of John Paul II's predecessors, when presiding over one of these increasingly popular audiences, were obliged to use the heavy and ornate *sedia gestatoria*, a ceremonial sedan chair in thick, purple gold-trimmed velvet bearing the papal coat of arms. The Supreme Pontiff of the Roman Catholic Church was borne aloft in this mobile throne on the shoulders of high-ranking secular Vatican officials, escorted by the papal guard. Although this method had the undoubted advantage of making the Pope visible from afar, and pilgrims have always wanted to be able to see and approach the Catholic Church's spiritual and temporal leader, it also tended to leave Popes feeling nauseous, as the unequal height of the bearers made the chair move like a boat in a small swell. Paul VI was a shy man who suffered seasickness in the *sedia gestatoria*, and he tried in vain to finish with a tradition he felt was every bit as outmoded as the heavy diamond-encrusted tiara, which he was more successful in refusing to wear. It was John Paul I, then in poor health, who first refused to use it during his enthronement ceremony, and had it consigned to a museum in August 1978.

This meant that John Paul II was never required to submit to what he saw as the outdated masquerade of the sedan chair. This was the first sign of a new era at the Vatican, an era that as of October 1978 was destined to cause much disruption for the guardians of papal protocol. The Pope had to compromise for the first few months, agreeing to use an inelegant sort of mobile platform. However, he was unhappy with the restrictions that this platform placed on his movements, and so he decided to use it no longer. This was where the Popemobiles, the white open-topped vehicles that replaced the sedan chair, came in.

For a time, the general audiences took place in two stages. The first part was devoted to contact with the assembled faithful. When John Paul II was more active, in order to have a chance of getting near and perhaps touching him, it was necessary to stand in the first row next to the metal barriers in Saint Peter's Square, or the length of the central aisle in the basilica or the Pope Paul VI Hall, where the Pope moved from left to right and from the front to the rear. John Paul II would often take children in his arms, much to the disapproval of the watching Vatican police and pontifical gendarmes, who spent every moment anxiously assessing the risks faced by the Pope as he worked the crowd. Any one of the people present could have injured him, stabbed him or injected him with a deadly poison, but he scarcely gave the matter a thought. Karol Wojtyla greatly enjoyed his weekly communion with the faithful, an occasion where any Mexicans in the crowd inevitably made the most noise. Once he had prayed with them and blessed them he greeted them in Italian, English, French, German, Spanish and at times in Slavic tongues (Slovakian, Lithuanian or Croat), on occasion speaking in a dozen or so languages before ending in Polish, which signified the end of the audience.

These moments of freedom and trust came to an end with the assassination attempt of May 31, 1981. The Holy Father no longer descended to mingle with the crowd, and the people attending the events were strictly monitored by the Italian police, who worked to assist the Vatican force. Ticket holders were required to pass through metal detectors before being shown to their allotted places, strictly in the order indicated on their tickets, before finally sitting on the gray plastic chairs provided. Several police cars and two Order of Malta ambulances stood by at the edge of the square. John Paul II gave his sermon during the second part of the audience. When in the Paul VI Hall, he no longer walked up the central aisle, entering the platform instead via a side door as he moved to the rear of the Hall beneath an immense, stylized bronze Christ who appeared to be emerging from a burning bush. This sculpture was commissioned by Paul VI from Italian sculptor Pericle Fazzini, who was also responsible for Paul VI's cross, which was in fact a staff to solicit Christ's aid. Beneath this monumental work of art sat the Pope, in a high-backed, golden-colored wooden chair upholstered in thick, cream-colored velvet; it looked nothing like a throne. The sermons, to which John Paul II attached considerable importance, were a physical strain on him. When the audiences were held in Saint Peter's Square, John Paul II at first required assistance to climb the steps leading to the podium from which he would give his sermon, before he had definitively opted for a wheelchair. During the summer, the Wednesday audiences were especially wearing, as he found the heavy summer heat difficult to bear. However, seeing the enthusiastic, colorful crowd would miraculously give him sufficient energy to speak in Italian, with brief excursions into French, English, German, Spanish, Portuguese, Polish and more. Much later, his sermons were read for him by various prelates from the Secretariat of State. As the weeks went by, this very strict catechism, begun in 1978, allowed him to address many areas of Christian faith and current affairs, as well as to comment on his journeys. Up until 2001, most of these sermons were still translated into 16 languages! For a very long time, the Pope would walk resolutely toward the *prima fila*, but near the end he remained seated and the invited guests would come to him, bowing with a mixture of great emotion and respect.

But it did not happen like this for Cosima. Intrigued by the experience of the public spectacle, sitting amidst the crowd of the faithful, she went on to have the benefit of two private audiences after the ceremonies, one in the Paul VI Hall and the other in Saint Peter's Square. The first took place on June 26, 1997, when Msgr. Dziwisz—breaking with traditional protocol with his habitual verve, under the disapproving gaze of Dino Monduzzi, the very severe prefect of the Papal Household—discreetly motioned us to quickly leave by a side door that led into a small hall. Once inside, Cosima looked at me, uncertain whether to speak or remain silent. However, as the Holy Father stretched out his hands toward her I saw my daughter, who was usually shy and had found the ceremony a bit too long, suddenly become fascinated by the radiance and goodness of John Paul II's gaze, to the point where she spontaneously and unhesitatingly opened wide her arms, not in any way seeking my approval, almost as if it was she who were welcoming him. Was I anxious or proud? I cannot say which feeling dominated, only that for a moment I understood, through my daughter's reaction, the extraordinary magnetism of John Paul II. Knowing as I did the uncompromising nature of Cosima's character, that day I too felt the reassuring warmth and inexplicable aura that obliged her to act so out of character. I was reminded of the words of the Gospel, "Send the children unto me," that the Dominicans repeated to us so often. From that day forth, I paid more attention than ever to the Holy Father as he greeted children, fascinated by the gentleness with which he bent down toward these innocents, very much the protective grandfather figure. I saw him fuss over them, embrace them, even take out a handkerchief to wipe a child's perspiring brow.

Cosima was received once more at the Vatican when, in February 2001, the Holy Father invited me to personally present him with a copy of my book, *Le Pape en Privé*. "Since your daughter is on the cover, you should bring her, too. The

Pope is very fond of children," Msgr. Dziwisz told me in a telephone conversation. Cosima was now nine years old and had already taken her first communion. She now of course knew exactly who the Pope was, and was so delighted to return to the Vatican that she never questioned what she would wear, picking out a white dress all by herself. When the day came, she was so overawed that she called him "Very Holy Father."

As a rule, on the day before a general audience Msgr. Dziwisz and the cardinal secretary of state would not make any official appointments for the Pope. It was a day devoted to meditation to allow him to concentrate deeply on the topic of the sermon for the next day's audience. The chosen topic was an austere one, and John Paul II spent some time on it. These homilies were highly intellectual and often went over the heads of the assembled faithful, who for the most part paid attention only when they heard their group's name pronounced. A few unkind souls within the curia whispered that they were written by others. It seems that the truth is that Karol Wojtyla almost always wrote some of the sermon in Polish, which was then polished up in the Italian translation, except in later days, when he simply gave guidance on the ideas to be explored, which were then written up by staff members of the Secretariat of State.

The symbolic aspects dominated this astonishing audience. In a country blessed with clear skies from May to October, weather permitting he would take evident delight in making a slow progress around Saint Peter's Square in one of his 4x4 Fiats, Mercedes or Toyotas, which were fitted with a comfortable armchair at the back and two seats at the side. When the weather became too hot, he switched to one of his air-conditioned Popemobiles. Following the 1981 attack, he was far better protected than at the beginning of his papacy. His bodyguards surrounded him and ceaselessly scanned the crowd. There were markedly fewer members of the security detail during the first three years of his pontificate; indeed, the first reaction of the plainclothes Swiss Guards and Vatican gendarmes when the Bishop of Rome went by was often to kneel respectfully instead of keeping an eye on the crowd. The Italian police reacted in the same way.

The Italians had always been responsible for guarding Saint Peter's Square, even though it was extraterritorial and therefore beyond their jurisdiction. The Italian police force was theoretically barred from entering the basilica, but it cared so deeply for the Pope's well-being that, when the Wednesday audience was held in this sanctuary, it continued to provide close surveillance. However, the Italian police did penetrate as far as the Paul VI Hall, which was deep inside the Holy See and not on the border.

When she retuned to Paris after her first visit to the Vatican, Cosima talked to her sister at such length about her morning spent at the Vatican that Marina decided this was something she wanted to experience for herself. Since John Paul II had invited her, the two of us set out for Rome together in September 1997. There were no arguments about the white dress. At the age of seven, Marina remembers every instant of her blessing and, although she was generally a quiet child, she had not counted on the Pope's unique blend of solemnity and simplicity, for as she approached him he asked her in French: "Do you speak Italian as well as your mother?" My daughter, despite being almost overawed, replied in a clear and unwavering voice: "Yes, Very Holy Father, and I also speak English." John Paul II laughed, disarmed by her aplomb, and Msgr. de Nicolò, the regent and master of ceremonies, smiled approvingly at Marina.

I always felt such joy when attending these audiences that, when I had to go to Italy, I always made sure that I would be in Rome on Wednesday. I was always given a shady spot in Saint Peter's Square thanks to the faithful friendship and support of Marjorie Weeke, the longtime press manager for the Pontifical Council for Social Communications. In the words of Dennis Redmont, head of the Associated Press for Southern Europe: "The ceremony at Saint Peter's Square every Wednesday is the last great show on earth. It's a must-see for any visitor to the Italian capital!" He was right. Today, when we miss John Paul II's presence and charisma so much, I cherish the memory of these extraordinary moments.

Chapter Five

AROUND THE WORLD 29 TIMES: INSIDE SECRETS OF THE TRAVELING POPE

I TRAVELED WITH JOHN PAUL II TO CUBA, BERlin, Jerusalem, Bratislava, Lourdes, Kiev, Sainte-Anne-d'Auray and Vienna.

The abiding memory of the Holy Father is as a pilgrim, in the original sense of a religious traveler, and his witnessing of the Christian faith in 129 nations, comprising almost all of the 1 billion Roman Catholics on earth. He spent 540 days of his pontificate on the road: no other Pope traveled the world as he did or took his message of peace to so many new frontiers. John Paul II gave 2,372 speeches around the world. All of this came at no little cost to his fragile health, which was further impaired as a consequence of the attack in Saint Peter's Square. This meant that, toward the end of his pontificate, he could only celebrate mass from a wheelchair, while other prelates read his homilies on his behalf.

I truly believe that few details of his pastoral missions escaped my notice, even if at times I had to be a bit sneaky! I feel that it is permissible to reveal such details here, all the more so as they were motivated by a very wholesome curiosity.

Having already made up my mind to discover the Pope's secrets when in Rome, I decided it was time to see what John Paul II's cabin looked like in the airliner taking us to Cuba. I was fascinated by everything about the Holy Father, and I knew that the readers of *Paris Match* felt the same.

We took off from Rome on January 21, 1998, and landed in Havana 13 hours later. This was the first time a Pope had set foot on Cuban soil. During this memorable pilgrimage, which the Pope described on the flight home as "a milestone of reconciliation and a historical step along the path to a new evangelism," more than 3,000 journalists, predominantly from the Americas, awaited him in Havana. While he headed off with his entourage across the tarmac of José Martí airport, I had taken advantage of the bustle of disembarkation to hide in the toilets at the front of the Alitalia MD-11. My plan was to wait until all the passengers had disembarked and then sneak a peek at the papal cabin, which no journalist had ever seen. I was also keen to confirm the presence onboard of John Paul II's personal nurse and doctor, Sister Tobiana, who in general never left the confines of the Vatican. Back in Rome, I'd been told that, for reasons of discretion, she always left the aircraft long after the other passengers. I opened the toilet door very slightly from time to time to check on the progress of the disembarking passengers, only venturing out once they had all left. I made my way immediately toward the papal cabin with the intention of taking a quick peek. I did find

Sister Tobiana inside, but her back was toward me and she never noticed my presence. I took my time and spent a good 10 minutes taking in all of the details before heading back down the plane with the intention of leaving by the rear door. Looking out the window, I became aware of the large police and army turnout for the Pope's arrival. Fidel Castro and all his ministers were there, as were members of the diplomatic corps and local bishops, preceded by Cardinal Jaime Lucas Ortega y Alamino, the dashing archbishop of San Cristobal, Havana. I was very nervous and feared being spotted leaving the plane alone. I had no means of identifying myself because, for security reasons, when traveling with the Pope our papers were taken from us by Vatican officials as soon as we set off; we were in some ways hostages of the Holy See until we landed again at Rome's Ciampino airport. I anxiously pondered the best way to slip out of the aircraft while the national anthems were played and the interminable speeches of welcome made. It would have been unpardonable to be seized by the police, distracting my colleagues and the thousands of believers who crowded the airport to witness the warm and friendly handshake between the Holy Father and their *leader maximo*. Sister Tobiana unwittingly came to my rescue. When I saw that she was preparing to leave the aircraft, I decided to follow close behind, hoping that my calf-length black dress would be enough for the security forces to think I was a nun. Sister Tobiana never so much as turned to look at me, for she never spoke to strangers. Thanks be to God, the airport official who came to collect her did not ask me any questions and let me leave with her. You might think that I acted with a lack of discretion, but as Karol Wojtyla's diocese was the whole world I think that my insatiable curiosity was amply justified. Anyway, as the Pope himself said, "The plane is like my second home."

For the first time in history, as the Holy See announced on October 16, 2003, on the occasion of the 25th year of his papacy, a Pope had traveled over 1,159,185 kilometers, spending 5.9% of his time abroad and traveling a distance equal to three times the span from the earth to the moon! He also made 145 pastoral visits within Italy, so many Italians, from mountain dwellers at the foot of the Gran Sasso alpine glaciers in Abruzzo to fisher folk on the shores of the Adriatic, were able to welcome their primate where they lived. Almost every Italian who wished to receive the papal blessing had the chance to do so at some stage.

This giant of the faith made his longest journey between November 18 and December 1, 1986, as he traveled from Bangladesh to New Zealand with stops in the Seychelles, Australia, Singapore and Fiji for a total of 48,974 kilometers in 13 days, six hours and 15 minutes. His shortest-ever trip was made on August 29, 1982, when he visited San Marino, the tiny Roman Catholic state—at 60 sq km, it is only slightly bigger than the Vatican's 44 sq km—near Rimini, Italy. The Holy Father, who returned to Rome the same day, spent only 300 minutes there.

The most pain-wracked trip was his third pilgrimage to Slovakia, in September 2003. It was, for four days, his very own way of the cross, from Barska Bystrica to Bratislava, where the 83-year-old Pope was to beatify two martyrs in the presence of Slovakia's entire Roman Catholic population.

In visiting 129 counties, the first of which was Mexico,

January 26–31, 1979, John Paul II went to Muslim-majority countries like Turkey, Morocco, Egypt, Jordan, Azerbaijan, Kazakhstan and the Palestinian territories, as well as to Protestant lands like the Scandinavian countries, Hindu-dominated India, and, of course, Israel.

Karol Wojtyla hoped one day to celebrate mass in China, the world's most populous country, and to stop over in Russia to build bridges with the Patriarch of Moscow. The Lord decided that it was not to be, and this was one of the Pope's deepest sorrows.

So despite the difficulties caused by his age and his many physical frailties, which meant that he could only move around in a wheelchair, why did Karol Wojtyla continue his globetrotting ways? What was it that kept driving this exhausted man who was in constant pain, his head ever more bowed, his speech hesitant and his breathing labored, even past his 83rd birthday? Toward the end he had real difficulty in pronouncing his speeches in the language of the host country, and he tended to slip back into his mother tongue without realizing it.

Was it absolutely necessary for the man whom some described harshly as a "tired, old prophet" to continue to follow the letter of Christ's commandment, "Go ye therefore and teach all the nations"? After two unforgettable decades, during which the US press dubbed him the "Pope Star," did John Paul II have anything left to offer in this regard? Yes, unequivocally, he did, as the miracle of his very presence generated such compassion amongst the crowds who continued to glorify him, for they well understood the redemptive value that he placed on daily suffering. Herein perhaps lies the justification for his ever more exhausting voyages.

I'm sure that in a funny way he was also trapped by his own legend, which had made him the center of world media attention. No Pope before him shared his ability to come up with a shockingly memorable turn of phrase, to the extent that he at times aggravated a good many traditionalists in senior Church and Vatican circles.

Despite his personal commitment, toward the end John Paul II was nonetheless forced to cut back on his official engagements as well as his semi-private and private appointments. During the first days of 2004, he canceled the grand ceremonies due to be held on the 6th and 12th of the month at Saint Peter's for the appointment of new bishops, as well as infant baptisms in the Sistine Chapel and the highly sought-after invitations to his private early-morning mass, even for bishops who came on *ad limina* visits only once every five years. This decision doubtless had the benefit of sparing the faithful and his close entourage the pain of seeing him endure so much suffering. He, however, was ever anxious to spare his intimates, and would tell them, "The Pope continues to speak, but he now speaks the language of the soul." Indeed, in the face of such suffering, he acted "as a direct disciple of Christ," explained German theologian Joseph Ratzinger—then prefect of the Congregation for the Doctrine of the Faith, now Pope Benedict XVI—who was one of the cardinals that John Paul II trusted most. It was Ratzinger who, in September 2003, confirmed that the Pope was ill and that the faithful should pray for him.

His pastoral visits abroad bear no comparison to tourist travel, neither for John Paul II nor for those who traveled with him. Everything was planned with the goal of reaching the largest possible number of people and places in the shortest possible time. During the course of a two-day trip to Paderborn and Berlin June 23–25, 1996—a trip I took part in—he presided over 13 events, from religious services to meetings with the faithful to political and ecumenical receptions. Seven years later in Slovakia, September 11–14, 2003, by which time he only moved with the aid of platforms, hoists and wheelchairs, he nonetheless conducted three masses and led prayers in four towns, driving himself mercilessly onward.

As a young man, Karol Wojtyla was a great lover of the theater, and he retained his belief in the importance of a gesture. To speak of forgiveness was abstract, whereas to be filmed on December 27, 1983, at Rome's Rebibbia prison in private conversation with Mehmet Ali Agca, the man who tried to kill him, was a gesture that stuck in people's minds. Similarly, being photographed in Mexico in January 1979 wearing a sombrero, or in 1986 in Brisbane, Australia, cuddling a koala, served to greatly increase his popularity amongst the young; talking about ecumenicalism didn't really have the same effect. To see John Paul II several times at Assisi in 1986, sitting on a dais alongside representatives of the Orthodox and Protestant Churches and of the Buddhist and Jewish faiths, plus an Amerindian chief in plumed headdress, was a surprising image that gave pause for thought. There was no government leader or head of state, no star of the arts or show business, that could rival his media appeal.

Wherever he went on his travels, he dymanized the faithful, encouraging them to take up the fight under the banner of faith without slipping into demagogy or making the slightest moral or ideological concessions. He spoke to peoples and rulers, his words at times causing anxiety when morality and ideology were allowed to enter the political or diplomatic arena. Every one of his speeches was taken up and relayed by the media to all corners of the globe. For instance, millions of Cuban viewers were able to see the scarcely imaginable image of Fidel Castro, high priest of Marxism, lost in the midst of a crowd at prayer.

On Wednesday, January 21, 1998, his entourage, the *seguito*, was as usual aboard the airliner carrying the Holy Father to Cuba. I was getting to know them well; at the time, there was the Cardinal Secretary of State Angelo Sodano; the substitute secretary of state; two Polish private secretaries; the master of pontifical ceremonial liturgy; the Pope's personal physician, Renato Buzzonetti; Camillo Cibin, the inspector general of the Vatican police; a smattering of cardinals, bishops and monsignors; as well as the man responsible for the Pope's travel, Father Roberto Tucci; an Anglo-Italian theologian; the director of Radio Vatican, Father Pasquale Borgomeo; and the director of *L'Osservatore Romano*, the very severe and distant Professor Mario Agnes; who was nicknamed "the ears of the Vatican"; as well as a few laypeople; a disparate group of distinguished advisors; and Arturo Mari, the Holy Father's personal photographer. The plane also carried a complement of seven Swiss Guards and Vatican gendarmes; the Pope's close protection detail had grown since the 1981 assassination attempt. The entourage was of such a high level that if, by some horrible misfortune, the plane crashed, the catastrophe would have terribly weakened the Church of Rome—imagine the chaos if half the government of any country were wiped out, let alone the fallout from the sudden death of this prestigious group, which represented the heart, soul and driving force behind the entire Roman Catholic Church. But death held no fear for John Paul II.

Invitations to travel on the papal plane were so highly sought after that no one was permitted to join the prestigious group during stopovers.

During his trips, the Pope was very keen to keep close to those he referred to, in private, as his "family." This included, naturally, Msgrs. Dziwisz and Marini, the master of pontifical ceremonial liturgy. The latter was a very good-looking, distinguished Venetian with movie-star looks who was as efficient as he was good-natured. Discreetly omnipresent, he organized the running of all the masses and religious events with panache. For years, he never betrayed the slightest anxiety or shortness of temper, except toward the end, when what he feared the most was that the Pope would stumble sideways or forward, or that, once in his wheelchair, he would somehow fall from it. He attended to even the smallest of liturgical details. He took pains to make certain that the special giant communion wafers, the size of a Neapolitan pizza, were on board; custom-made by a community of nuns in southern Italy, they were big enough to be seen by all who attended the giant masses, no matter how far away they were.

Angelo Gugel was also aboard the plane, sitting close to the Holy Father. He kept him permanently in sight and was in charge of all the practical details: it was Angelo who fetched his stick or his scarlet cape, and he was in charge of the supply of specially blessed rosaries that John Paul II always presented to the flight deck and cabin crew, most of whom would kneel to receive them. Gugel, whose cat-like gait matched his perfect physical presence for his job, had previously served John Paul I. His love for Karol Wojtyla was such that he had learned a little Polish, and he became so adept at using a computer that he was in charge of the Holy Father's personal computer, on which coded details of his schedule were kept.

This little world, which was far less hierarchical and remote than the rest of the Vatican, lived solely and above all else to protect the Pope at all times, everywhere. For example, on one occasion aboard the papal plane, I was amazed to see one of them leap up to intercept a hostess who had just placed a glass of Coca-Cola on the Pope's seat-back table! Lost in study of his breviary, John Paul II was heedlessly about to sip a beverage that he had been forbidden to drink ever since the damage to his intestines caused by the assassination attempt. The hostess swiftly exchanged it for a glass of freshly squeezed orange juice.

Aside from Msgr. Dziwisz, Gugel and first minister Cardinal Casaroli, succeeded in 1991 by Cardinal Sodano, other members of the papal entourage traveled business class.

Unusually, 75 journalists from around the world (traveling in economy class) were also aboard the trans-Atlantic flight to Cuba; there were owners and editors from major international newspapers, radio and television stations, as well as sound recordists, still photographers, camera operators and various ordained correspondents from the assorted organs of the Holy See. Although this may seem a large press corps, it is in fact a modest number once divided by the total number of my journalist colleagues seeking to cover the event. Every one of my lucky colleagues had managed to pass a selection process as strict as it was mysterious, for there were always many, many requests for accreditation made by all the most important media organizations on the planet.

The Pope himself always sat in the first-class section of the cabin. In theory, we were all kept apart from him and his entourage by the usual arrangement of curtains; however, during short-haul flights, John Paul II's democratic wish was that they remain open most of the time. The cabin crews were visibly impressed to be welcoming aboard the direct successor to Saint Peter. As regulations required that a hostess be seated facing the first-class passengers during takeoff, the airline always took pains to ensure that she was attractive and had shapely legs. The hostess on the plane taking us to Cuba served the Pope with a gourmet meal: Parma ham with melon, beef steak with broccoli, a cheese platter, baked apples and pears, fruit salad and olive-oil soaked, pizza-like *fugazza*. When traveling with Air France on another papal trip, the cheeses served all had names with religious connotations: Saint-Nectaire, Saint-Marcellin and Caprice des Dieux! At John Paul II's specific request, we always enjoyed the same menu as he did. Alitalia often liked to serve the Pope a Châteauneuf-du-Pape to drink, which he always diluted with water as was his custom. He then drank a large glass of *canarino*, a lemon-peel infusion that was once the tea drunk by the poor of southern Italy. I'm sure it was his herbal tea that gave him the energy to hold a memorable press conference on the plane as it cruised toward Cuba at a height of 10,000 meters above the Atlantic.

The Holy Father, who had slowly made his way up the aisle, sat ahead of the bulkhead separating economy and business classes and began by blessing us. A keen sense of euphoria reigned that day as, for once, the Holy See's terse and generally uncooperative spokesperson, Joaquin Navarro-Valls, was not able to keep us in check as he had been obliged to leave for Havana earlier, hoping to persuade the managers of Cuban state television to provide live coverage of the Pope's arrival and open-air mass. Better still, we were also spared the presence of his very severe and disagreeable colleague, the Belgian Vic Van Brantegem, who had a broken foot. What a stroke of luck! We were happy and excited in equal measure, for it was the Pope who had approached, and for once he could not escape. The Patriarch of the West was no more than two meters from us. His left arm trembled, for his Parkinson's disease was clear in his every movement, yet his face was radiant. In an instant, the cabin was transformed into the world's most extraordinary press conference venue. For once, we were not trapped inside some media bubble; instead, a group of top journalists came face-to-face with the successor to the apostles. Some of the big-name journalists who were traveling with the Pope for the first time appeared to be terribly impressed, although reluctant to show it. These leading journalists, who had never previously found themselves so close to the Bishop of Rome, only then became aware of the powerful aura he radiated. The thought of asking him a challenging or awkward question of the type often put to politicians never crossed anyone's mind—not the old hands, not even the Americans, who were in the habit of being direct, critical and even rude when addressing leading figures. The Pope answered our respectfully phrased questions with dignity and humor, speaking successively in Spanish, English, Italian and, for me, French.

As no one had yet asked a question in French, I took it upon myself. I was one of only three female journalists present (the others were from a Latin American TV station and the *New York Times*) and our chivalrous colleagues had allowed us space in the front row. Taking my courage in my hands, I rose a little self-consciously from my seat to ask the question that none of my colleagues had yet put. "How are you feeling, Holy Father?" "I get all my news from the newspapers," he replied with a smile that made his eyes wrinkle, his tone midway between joking and serious.

Having spent a good hour with us, John Paul II blessed us all once again and returned to his cabin at the front of the MD 11. He spent such a long time with us that from time to time one of the red-capped cardinals would anxiously poke his head around the curtain and sigh disconsolately, all too aware that the more time we spent with the Pope, the less we would write about them in any future articles. Yet the cardinals only ever divulged the scantest of information, seemingly despite themselves. The Holy Father then slowly made his way into the cockpit to bless the flight crew. Laying his long, frail hands on the shoulders of the captain of flight AZ 4668 (it was always Alitalia's senior pilot who had the honor of commanding the Holy Father's plane), he asked him: "What is the weather like in Cuba?" The pilot later recounted how he felt as though an angel had descended when the white-clad Pope's silhouette was suddenly reflected in the cockpit windows.

Contrary to what one might imagine, the Holy See does not operate its own fleet of aircraft, despite the fact that every president of a small country or head of state of an emerging nation often has a fleet available. For every trip originating in Italy, the Holy See would charter a plane from the Italian national carrier, Alitalia. The plane would be fitted out to suit the needs of its illustrious client. Depending on the length of the flight, Alitalia would provide a DC 10, a DC 11, a 747 or an Airbus. Alitalia would invoice the Holy See only for the seats occupied by members of the papal entourage, whereas journalists were required to pay for their tickets directly. However, at the end of each year the airline would make donations to papal charities equal to the amount received from the Vatican, to a certain extent a gesture in recognition of the unparalleled prestige that the Pope's journeys brought the airline. Millions of TV viewers would see the man in white descend the steps of one of its planes—invaluable advertising at a time when Europe's traditional airline monopolies were collapsing. This was something that did not escape the notice of start-up airline Sky Europe, which offered the Supreme Pontiff one of its jets for his September 2003 trip between Bratislava, Banska Bystrica and Kosice, Slovakia.

There was nothing about the planes provided for use by the Holy Father that could be compared to Air Force One, the mighty 747 used by American presidents. As was apparent in the aftermath of the 9/11 attacks, when President Bush spent the day aloft, Air Force One is a flying White House complete with bedroom, bathroom, dressing room, a situation room equipped with 84 telephones, and no less than six toilets. "John Paul II traveled far more simply," said Father Tucci, someone I considered one of the most fascinating and discreet Vatican insiders. He organized 79 of the Pope's pastoral journeys, until he was replaced in 2001 by Msgr. Renato Boccardo, a fine-looking, 53-year-old Italian with a touch of Alain Delon about him, who has since also been appointed bishop acquapendente and secretary of the Pontifical Council for Social Communications. Father Tucci added, "If it had been up to John Paul II alone, he would have traveled more modestly still, for he viewed airliners primarily as places for talking and working."

The Pope's cabin was always installed by the same group of carefully selected Alitalia staff members. They would completely remove the existing first-class accommodations in the relevant aircraft in order to install the Holy Father's small study and sleeping quarters. The white blankets, under-sheets and sheets were of the utmost smoothness and, although a standard size, were woven specially for the Pope from the finest linens and wools. They bore his coat of arms, embroidered in a close-stitch red and blue thread with gold and silver topstitches. The headboard of the papal bed was covered in cream-colored leather and was placed close to the windows. To the right of the bed, a large ivory and light-colored wooden crucifix hung upon a dark blue drape. There was a heavy curtain in brilliant scarlet separating his sleeping quarters from his office area, which was fitted with an upright armchair upholstered in a light beige and sky blue fabric. Facing it was a large table covered with a white tablecloth, upon which a bouquet of yellow and white flowers and a selection of international newspapers and magazines were placed, including, of course, papers from Poland.

His entourage had no qualms about leaving around magazines sporting critical headlines, things like "John Paul II Must Go!" or "Battle for Succession Underway at the Vatican." Although he rarely read such articles, the Supreme Pontiff nonetheless skimmed through a lot of them. There was a four-seat upholstered bench facing his table.

Clearly visible on the outside of the fuselage, the Pope's coat of arms was always visible to the right of the gangway when ascending, and at the front flew the white and yellow pennants of the Vatican State. These had become unalterable traditions since 1978, and they were respected even on May 2, 1989, when the Supreme Pontiff traveled via the Concorde to Lusaka from the Indian Ocean island of Reunion. During his last years, the fact that he could only move around in a wheelchair had some impact on his onboard habits; henceforth, he entered and left the plane via an elevating platform. His weakness also meant that he no longer came back to talk to members of the press, saving his strength for his meetings with the faithful, gospel in hand.

Will the Holy See one day operate its own aircraft? This is an issue that, prior to the election of Karol Wojtyla and owing to the infrequency of travel by his predecessors, had never arisen. Previous Popes hardly ever traveled to preach the gospel around the world, and the first Bishop of Rome in the history of the papacy to set foot on an airliner was Paul VI in January 1964.

At the age of 67, heedless of the image of a Pope as static as a marble statue, Paul VI took his pilgrim's staff and quit the 48 hectares of the Vatican to at last go out to meet his flock, at the same time ushering in a new era in the papacy. The line had been crossed at last. Better still, in the symbolic choice of Jerusalem as the destination for his debut trip in January 1964, Paul VI was laying ground for the future. At the time, the event was felt to be of such importance that the press proclaimed, "Paul VI Writes the 5th Gospel." *Paris Match*, which devoted two special issues to his trip, went so far as to dispatch

60 journalists, including 25 photographers, who made the Paris–Jerusalem–Paris journey aboard a specially chartered Caravelle airliner converted to a newsroom that was in constant radio contact with the magazine's management team, themselves installed at Paris' Orly airport. People at *Paris Match* talk about the event to this day!

This return of the Prince of the Apostles to the Holy Land proved to be a seed that was to germinate, 36 years later, under John Paul II. Traveling outside Italy was a courageous initiative on the part of this reform-minded Pope, and one that might have ended tragically on a trip to Manila. Shortly after landing at the capital of the Philippines, a man dressed as a priest accosted him, lunging at his chest with a knife. Miraculously, Paul VI escaped with a few scrapes to his right hand and a slight chest wound that bled quite profusely. The public was never really aware of what occurred, for the Pope was wearing a thick flannel vest that absorbed most of the blood, leaving his immaculate cassock unblemished.

Although it started so badly, the truth was that this 10-day, 5,000-kilometer pastoral odyssey was a triumph. That did not, however, prevent the appearance of some signs of discontent with the Catholic Church or the ecumenical movement. However, to actually see a Pope in the flesh rather than on the front page of *L'Osservatore Romano*, sitting in his *sedia gestatoria*, was a truly revolutionary change. These immense audiences (1 million people came to Manila's Rizal Park) were to produce some of the last memorable images of Paul VI, and this was his final overseas voyage. He received his share of criticism, as did John Paul II, for traditionalists found major events such as this distasteful.

For instance, Paul VI was harshly described as a "summer storm, less nourishing than the gentle rains of autumn that penetrate deep into the soil." His speeches were also subject to criticism. They were judged repetitive, and it was rumored that wherever he went the Pope would talk, but not listen. During the final eight years of his papacy, Paul VI was rendered increasingly immobile by arthritis, so his meetings with secular personalities and people of the faith were restricted to the Vatican.

Prior to Paul VI, John XXIII was another Pope who set a historical precedent. On October 4, 1962, he set out from the Vatican for a train to the shrine of Our Lady of Loreto (the patron saint of fliers), whose shrine was near Ancona. This was the only time he ever ventured to the Vatican station, which lies adjacent to the governor's office; it is a modest station that had only ever been used for receiving goods via the Italian rail network. For seven centuries, Loreto had been Italy's most revered place of pilgrimage as well as one of Europe's leading religious tourism destinations, visited by some 4 million people annually. The Santa Casa and portrait of the Virgin Mary are the subjects of intense veneration. The Santa Casa is claimed to be Mary's Nazareth house, transported by crusaders to the *colli del Lauri* and encased during the 15th century within a protective, fortress-like basilica.

This trip by train away from the Vatican was a historical first—an 81-year-old Pope who dared climb aboard a train and travel a full 650 kilometers! What were, by the standards of the day, large crowds lined the entire length of the route, sometimes since before dawn, for a chance to see the Successor to the Prince of the Apostles as he ventured forth from his realm. The faithful, both curious and reverent, waved banners on which could be read, "Long Live the Pope! Long Live Peace! Long Live the Healing Pope!"

Several thousand people awaited the Blessed Angelo Giuseppe Roncalli at Loreto, with the same number again crowding the train station to greet the arrival of the pontifical train. There were nine cars in total, transformed into salons, offices, a dining car and a sleeping car. The train itself had been lent by the Italian president, for evidently the powers that be at the Holy See had never imagined that the day would arrive when the Pope would set off across Italy and leave the Vatican by train.

Upon his arrival, John XXIII was formally welcomed by Italian President Antonio Segni, who, having lent his train, had made the trip by air. After making a closely listened-to speech, the Pope placed a gold crown upon the head of the Black Madonna of Loreto. The crown had previously been seized by Napoleon in 1797 and returned in 1801. He then dined alone, taking a simple meal prepared for him by the nuns from a neighboring convent. In an adjacent dining hall, Italian Prime Minister Amintore Fanfani, who had also made the journey, was the guest of honor of several cardinals and leading Church figures, and they enjoyed a vast menu. After the meal, the Pontiff, who had left the Vatican 12 hours earlier, headed to Assisi. Once there, he walked a short distance along the narrow streets to reach the basilica, where he prayed at the tomb of Saint Francis.

As night fell, thousands of oil lamps lit the way for a tired John XXIII as he went back to the train that would return him to the Vatican at the end of a memorable day. At Rome's

Trastevere station, the Pope was again formally welcomed by the prime minister before finally returning to his apartments.

Roncalli had traveled previously, having been named papal nuncio to Paris on January 15, 1945. France's General de Gaulle, head of the provisional government of the day, had noted that, as of December 23, 1944, the day of the departure of the previous nuncio Msgr. Valerio Valeri, and in the absence of a representative from the Holy See, "the traditional and constitutional doyen of the diplomatic corps," the man he would have to salute on January 1, 1945, would be Alexander Boglomov, the ambassador from the Soviet Union—a Marxist and atheist to boot! De Gaulle lobbied Cardinal Tissaernat, a Frenchman close to Pius XII, to send a new nuncio to Paris as quickly as possible. So it came to pass that Angelo Roncalli, the future John XXIII, landed in Paris on January 1, 1945, aboard de Gaulle's personal plane, a DC 4 Skymaster maintained by the air force at Villacoublay, presented to him by US President Roosevelt after the French had resumed control of their capital. After a difficult flight through storm and wind, Roncalli finally landed at the airfield, just in time to make it to Paris by 11 o'clock, when he presented the first official goodwill message to de Gaulle on behalf of the diplomatic corps. He stayed at his Paris posting from 1945 until 1953, his demanding yet friendly character endearing him to the leader of the Free French.

John XXIII had left his pontifical palace on two previous occasions: first aboard a black Mercedes 300—with his coat of arms (two fleur-de-lis surrounding a silver tower and a lion of Saint Mark) depicted in bronze affixed to the two rear doors—to visit a convent and orphanage at San Vito Romano, a small village at Monte-Calvo some 30 kilometers from his summer residence at Castel Gandolfo (he then continued on to pray at the shrine to Mary at Genazzano); and later a 70-kilometer journey from Rome to the summer house of the Roccantica seminary. Hesitant as they may appear, at the time these journeys seemed nonetheless revolutionary. Under the terms of the Lateran agreements between the Vatican and the Italian government, Pius XI and XII only left the Vatican to travel within Rome or to Castel Gandolfo. Only 50 years later, it is hard to imagine how things were in those days, without all-seeing TV cameras and zoom lenses!

How were John Paul II's voyages paid for? Who exactly picked up the considerable tab? Raising questions of money with the Vatican was always difficult and frowned upon. It certainly appeared that, although their ceremony and pomp were faultless, they were organized on far simpler lines than those of former President Mitterrand and his ministers, who often brought a planeload of friends and leading personalities with them. In the spring of 1989, John Paul II arrived at the island of La Reunion to celebrate the beatification of Brother Scubilion, a missionary originally from France's Morvan region. French Prime Minister Rocard flew by Concorde from France to greet him, accompanied by an impressive retinue of ministers and functionaries, who had taken advantage of the jaunt to make a quick, low-profile side trip: a safari in Kenya. John Paul II's escort seemed modest indeed in the face of all these higher-ups. After the ceremonies were complete, the prime minister charitably lent his Concorde to the Holy Father so that he could complete the 3,000-kilometer flight to Zambia more quickly. Despite the fact that it had received the papal blessing, 11 years later this same aircraft, *Sierra Charlie,* crashed at Paris' Roissy airport; god-fearing Alitalia crews maintain that the papal blessing offers protection only when the Pope himself is onboard.

The Pope's 1987 trip to the US cost in excess of 20 million dollars, but it was paid for by American dioceses and a consortium of manufacturers, including a computer firm from Silicon Valley.

Subsequent to his first visit to New York in October 1979—one that, according to press reports, cost the US government and the well-off American Church (a most generous group that donated 23.5 million euros in 2002) some 3 million dollars—a journalist referred in the Pope's presence to his travel expenses. This was one of the very rare occasions when John Paul II lost his cool in public, and he answered with real anger: "I do not consider it something to account for when you remember that we humans were bought for a price beyond measure. There is no way to calculate that. It is stupid. People talk about cost as a way of trying to stop the Pope. People say that he costs more than the queen of England. That is just as well, for the message he carries is of transcendental value."

Karol Wojtyla could not abide the thought of money-changers in the temple. He refused to allow the issue of the cost of his travels to become the subject of controversy. As a man born in a poor country, someone who had never had any interest in money, he was gravely troubled by comparisons to the queen of England; at Christmas in 2003, for example, he had trouble comprehending how the death of one of her pet corgi dogs could be headline news for a British tabloid! As a grand propagator of the faith, he took no interest at all in the financial, practical and material problems faced by his entourage. In this regard he was very similar to France's General de Gaulle, who throughout his life would affirm in confident martial tones, "What's needed will follow." For John Paul II, his trips were simply an extension of his missionary and ecumenical zeal. He was driven to develop religious and inter-religious dialogue, culture and a new evangelization of the character of Jesus himself. In his view, nothing else was of any importance.

As for the Popemobile, Father Tucci explained to me after he had invited me to join him in business class for a while during the flight back from Havana, "It is absolutely not about a desire for walkabouts, as some would have you believe. It is about seeking a way to meet the popular desire for a sense of almost physical contact with the Pope. The Popemobile, which is a little like a modern version of the *sedia gestatoria*, is not something invented by the Vatican; it is an armored vehicle that the local authorities have required us to use since the events of 1981." Indeed, leaving aside their futuristic looks, there was nothing pompous or triumphal about these various 4x4s fitted with bulletproof glass boxes. They looked more like white-painted fire trucks than the poetic flower-decked carts pulled by innocent mules when the Popes lived in Avignon, or the fancy carriages of previous centuries. Anyway, what could be more natural than moving around in an armored vehicle for the planet's most famous and most photographed personality? This was someone who held the absolute record for the largest-ever crowd, the 4 million who gathered to see him at Manila's Rizal Park in January 1995. As for jet travel, it is no more than common practice for heads of state and prime ministers, as well as leading business figures on both sides of the Atlantic. And in the Internet era, how terrible it would have been for John Paul II's image if he had traveled around Samoa in an old pickup covered in ribbons and hastily repainted white, as Paul VI did in November 1970.

Local leaders were always disappointed not to be invited to join the Holy Father in his Popemobile on his overseas tours; instead, it was always local bishops and archbishops who were invited to be at his side. In this way, they too could benefit from the Pope's popularity. It was, on occasion, a privilege that was also extended to various patriarchs from the Orthodox, Romanian, Syrian and Georgian Churches.

The practice was to bring several drivers from the host countries to Rome beforehand so they could get a handle on these vehicles, which were very heavy and cumbersome. For example, in Paris in August 1997 it proved necessary to carry out a series of difficult nighttime tests using a Popemobile air-freighted in from Rome on a Transall military freighter. The tests in the courtyard of the Elysée palace showed that the test subject, President Chirac, felt queasy owing to the uneven gravel surface. The Holy Father always preferred to be driven by one of his two personal chauffeurs: Piero Cicchetti, who was in charge of standard vehicles, and Orlando Santinelli, who was in charge of the three Popemobiles. In later years, he was invariably driven by one of these two men, for they knew their vehicles so well that they were able to drive far more smoothly than anyone new to the task.

The Poles could have saved some money by not scrapping the Popemobile they had built for him when he made his first visit in 1979. Little did they realize that Karol Wojtyla would return to his motherland no less than eight times. They had to build another, which cost them another 80,000 dollars.

Insiders maintained that, in the final analysis, the cost to the Holy See of John Paul II's peregrinations was far from excessive. As I explained earlier, the amounts charged by Alitalia were symbolic, and no non-Italian airline ever dared ask to be paid the cost of his ticket, which was always issued in his name. His close collaborators too often benefited from airlines' generosity, as they were all well aware of the incomparable prestige afforded them by papal travel. Standard practice was for the Pope to fly out on Alitalia and return to Rome on a carrier representing the last country visited. However, during the voyage to Cuba, the Holy Father preferred to return to Italy aboard the Alitalia MD 11, which was felt to be a safer option than the Cubana Antonov 24 or Ilyushin 62 that Fidel Castro had provided for his return trip. These matters exercised Father Tucci's diplomatic skills to the fullest, as he was required to explain to Castro's people that Alitalia did not want their long-haul plane tied up in Cuba for six days (January 20–26, 1998), so they would be sending another over from the US. The Cubans were so affronted that when Tucci explained to them that their plane was too small to carry everyone, they offered to provide two! Tucci replied that everyone with the Pope always traveled in the Holy Father's aircraft. In the end he got his way, for he was a man whose combination of tact and reasoning always prevailed.

When traveling overseas, the Holy Father and his closest associates always stayed at the Nunciature, or the apostolic delegation in countries that had no Vatican embassy. The remainder of the papal entourage slept in bishops' palaces, in accommodations belonging to the local church, in convents or in hotels. When John Paul II visited Tours in 1996, he stayed with the Dominican Sisters of Charity, a fact they were most proud of.

Travel expenses for the papal bodyguards, doctors and ecclesiastical and lay-staff, as well as for the journalists from Radio Vatican and *L'Osservatore Romano,* were not ruinous, as together they rarely comprised more than 30 people. In truth, journalists were the only ones who actually paid for their travel, and even then prices were set low to allow access by under-resourced media organizations. In any event, the prices were more than reasonable set against the 20,000 dollars minimum that the White House charges journalists who want to travel abroad with President Bush.

The Pope was often formally welcomed as a head of state, and in these cases the considerable expenses involved were covered by the host nations, providing of course that the invitation actually came from the government of the country concerned. In certain very Catholic countries, such as Poland, Slovakia and Brazil (a recent survey found that Brazilians were happiest at mass or on holiday), there was often a special public holiday granted the day he arrived, and often also on the day of the main open-air mass. The local Catholic Church would take responsibility for staging religious events and ceremonies, but relying strictly on donations and volunteers. Many months prior to John Paul II's arrival, the faithful would be encouraged to come forward by priests during mass as well as via media announcements, mail shots and e-mail. In almost every country, successful Catholic businesspeople and ardent admirers of Karol Wojtyla would send very large checks to help bridge the gap or would come forward offering to pay for particular stages of the voyage. Take the example of the August 1997 World Youth Day in Paris, where no less than 60 businesses stepped in to play Good Samaritan. The amounts provided ran to several million French francs. Heading the lists of sponsors was Axa, via its aptly named subsidiary Mutuelle Saint-Christophe, which provided 45,000 euros' worth of insurance and subsequently made good on a 150,000 euro shortfall needed to pay for two major claims and various small incidents. The list of sponsors also included Publicis, Nestlé, Auchan, Coca-Cola, Air France, Apple and many others. France Galop made its racetrack at Longchamps available, a donation whose origins lay in the fortuitous fact that Cardinal Lustiger and Jean-Luc Lagardère (president of France Galop and of a leading French industrial conglomerate that bore his name) were neighbors at 32 Rue Barbet-de-Jouy. Renault, despite being headed by Protestant Louis Schweitzer, provided a fleet of chauffeured Safrane cars for use by prelates. For once, the Holy See received very little assistance from public funds for this trip, as it was John Paul II's second French visit within 12 months. During a time when France's right-wing president was working with a left-wing government, President Jacques Chirac (who knew the Holy Father well, having met him many times previously: in June 1980 in Lyon, in 1986 in Rome, in Tours in 1996 and at other times in his role as Paris mayor, French prime minister and president) could do no more than greet him as a head of state on arrival at the Elysée palace.

It was in poor countries, rather than in the West, that donations to the Pope were proportionally the greatest: from local jewelry to simple offerings of local produce. Everyone shared the same pride in contributing to the Supreme Pontiff's journeys.

However, Europeans also showed themselves on occasion capable of generosity. For example, the Holy Father received expensive cars as gifts for use on his travels: in 2002, he was presented with a new Popemobile by Mercedes, and in March 2003, with a deep blue armored Lancia Thesis complete with a single comfortable seat in the back, a gift from Umberto Agnelli worth some 2 million euros but which was of inestimable value to Lancia, because until that time most of the papal vehicles were by Mercedes.

On his trips abroad, John Paul II was assailed by innumerable gifts of every possible type. I well remember how cramped we were on a trip from Rheims back to Rome in the papal Air France Airbus. The ground crew had to remove a number of seats to make enough space for all the crates of champagne the Pope had been given. It appeared that the competing manufacturers were all vying to outdo each other, with the result that the Pope was offered literally thousands of bottles. The prelates on the flight certainly seemed happy, accustomed as they were to Italian sparking spumante rather than these fine wines. As well as the alcohol, there were many other gifts: pictures made from seashells and other handicraft items that had been lavished on the Pope during his four-day stay at Sainte-Anne-d'Auray in Rheims.

From time to time, Popes were presented with very considerable gifts. In the past, these included palaces, fine jewels, tiaras (included one encrusted with emeralds presented by Napoleon I in 1804), the gold and jeweled brooches representing the earth supported by angels presented to Leo XIII by the government of Peru, 22-carat liturgical objects, monstrances, ciboria, chalices encrusted with diamonds, precious stones and pearls, and many other objects besides. Ever since Pope Paul VI abandoned tiaras, which he felt were too heavy and ostentatious, these anachronistic three-tiered headdresses were displayed alongside other rare and extravagant objects in cases in the Sistine Chapel's sacristy. Only the tiara originally presented by the people of Milan to the austere Giovanni Battista Montini is absent; Paul VI auctioned off the tiara, which looked like a finely crafted artillery shell, to raise money for the destitute of India.

As pampered and well looked after as any of his predecessors, John Paul II had in theory no need to dip into his account with the Institute for Religious Works when on any of his pastoral trips. However, whenever he visited a very poor country he would distribute large sums to the destitute, children, elderly and sick, and often to local bishops, too, although details of the sums involved were never divulged. For the remainder, he did not have to call on his personal funds for most of the innumerable gifts he made to local churches and good causes, as most of them came from his more or less inexhaustible personal stores.

Although the actual financing of John Paul II's journeys was relatively straightforward, the same could not be said of the arrangements needed for their organization. First, two Popemobiles had to be carried, except to countries where there was already one available, as one was always needed as backup. There are a dozen or so Popemobiles currently around the world, all built specially for John Paul II's visits and carefully preserved by local bishops as souvenirs. This was the very first item on the checklist. The organizers would then have to check that the 50 or so cases and military-style trunks containing all the gifts, medals, cassocks, religious images and mass books were loaded aboard, as well as the hundreds of copies of the Pope's speeches printed in several languages. Also required on the journey was his extensive wardrobe, which included several white cassocks, broad-brimmed hats, miters, chasubles and even the folding travel chapels, which were trunks containing liturgical items and folding tables to allow the Pope to say his private mass, for, according to Msgr. Marini, "Wherever he was staying, every morning at daybreak we would always find him in the chapel; he was capable of spending long minutes on his knees in front of the holy sacrament." The portable chapels also enabled a journalist priest to say mass in the hotel for the handful of his colleagues who wanted to attend.

A check needed to be made to ensure that all the broadcasting equipment belonging to Radio Vatican was loaded into the hold; this included tape recorders and editing equipment as well as extra items required by Telepace, the Holy See's television broadcaster. Radio Vatican beamed its programs to all four corners of the globe via shortwave and satellite, reporting favorably on the Supreme Pontiff's every move. They also needed to ensure that everything needed by journalists had been loaded: fax machines, detailed schedules, booklets giving practical information, copies of the Pope's homilies and speeches as well as the microphones needed for use by the Holy Father and other members of his team. But the most important cargo, of course, was John Paul II's medical equipment, especially his oxygen supplies.

As the Pope made it a rule never to accept invitations to official lunches or dinners and much preferred to eat surrounded by his colleagues, his supplies always included Earl Grey tea, his favorite and one that helped him to relax and shake off fatigue, and cases of Toscane Uliveto still mineral water (though in Rome, he usually drank San Paulo). But far more precious were the defibrillators and other medical paraphernalia, and the pouches of rare AB-negative blood. In later years, the Pope traveled with something that came to resemble a field hospital. Wherever the Pope was staying abroad, an emergency medical intervention team stayed in permanent contact with the two most technically advanced local hospitals, whose medical teams were provided in advance with a copy of the Pope's secret medical records. His two personal physicians, Drs. Buzzonetti and Polisca, followed him everywhere like a shadow. Whenever he traveled abroad there was always an emergency medical aircraft on standby at a nearby airfield. Wherever he traveled he was always followed by a couple of ambulances, more so toward the end of his life.

Up until 2001, these arrangements were coordinated by travel supremo Father Roberto Tucci, whose place was subsequently filled by Msgr. Renato Boccardo. Whether by accident or design, the onetime student actor turned Holy Father appeared to always have an innate understanding of how to put on a show, and in public he always surrounded himself with colleagues who themselves exuded real presence.

Wherever the Holy Father traveled, Roberto Tucci was never far behind. He was man of such elegance and distinction that he seemed like a grand ecclesiastical figure from the past, and he had a powerful build and physical grace that matched that of Giovanni Agnelli. You couldn't keep your eyes off him. Always dressed plainly as a priest and wearing a clerical collar, he impressed us all with his sculptural, serene looks, all the more so when, during a September 1993 visit to Latvia, for example, he was forced to converse with the local clergy in Latin, as this was the only language they had in common. He was a man who never lost his cool. He would constantly yet unobtrusively keep an eye on his watch, for he had everything planned and timed down to the *n*th degree. He wore an earpiece that kept him in constant contact with members of the security detail, and was able to alter the papal itinerary at any stage in the event that something unplanned occurred. This brilliant intellectual was a former director of *La Civiltà Cattolica*, a prestigious bi-monthly review for Italian Jesuits, and yet he had something of the circus ringmaster about him. Once he retired, having been appointed cardinal by John Paul II in February 2001 (he jokingly remarked that it was a sop as he was not allowed to vote during conclaves), he preferred to work, in his own words, as a replacement assistant priest who exercised his ministry from time to time in a modest parish in Tuscany rather than mingling with the more worldly cardinals in Rome. Nothing fazed him, and he was always able to step back and retain a sense of humor, no matter what occurred. He was a Jesuit who'd converted to Catholicism at the age of 14, the son of a Neapolitan insurance agent father and a well-born English Anglican mother. He joined the Jesuits at the age of 15, taking his first vows at the age of 17, at which point his mother told him, "Look me in the eye: do NOT become a Jesuit!" After studying philosophy and taking a PhD in theology, he occupied many important posts during his career, the last being the 19 years he spent in charge of Karol Wojtyla's travels. Initially he was not too keen, but as a Jesuit he had sworn a special oath of obedience to the Pope, and so he devoted himself selflessly to his task. He never flinched from making a decision. For example, when the Pope's plane was caught in a storm during a flight to Lesotho in 1988, it was he who gave permission for the captain to make an emergency landing in Johannesburg, which was the closest airport, despite the fact that John Paul II had decided not to visit South Africa because of its apartheid system of government. It was Tucci who always made sure that anti-slip coatings were provided where needed, that the Pope's special steps for entering the Popemobile had been packed along with the white and yellow Vatican City state pennants and Karol Wojtyla's giant coats of arms, which had to be placed on either side of the altar platform during giant open-air masses. His final task was to make certain that white and yellow markers were strategically placed along all the Holy Father's routes. As time went by, the details would change but the strategy and organization varied little. He always made sure that, at the exact moment the papal aircraft flew over any particular country, a courtesy message was transmitted, which said something along the lines of, "As I fly through your airspace, I offer my affectionate greetings to your government and people, and I send my special blessing to all, that peace may reign and you may live in serenity and prosperity."

Of course, things did not always run according to plan. For example, a journey might run more slowly than expected or there might be coordination problems between the local and Vatican security services. On several such occasions, I noticed that the mystically minded Pope would start fingering his rosary, remaining wholly unmoved by the agitation that swirled around him.

On his return from a trip abroad, it was easy to sense just how relieved the members of his close staff were, their relief being very much an indicator of their constant worries during his travels regarding his safety and ever-deteriorating health.

Seen from the outside, over the years these trips appeared to be handled so smoothly that they did not appear any more complex than something that might be put together by any luxury travel operator. This was all an illusion, as in reality preparations were put in place long before the previous trip had even ended. A weighty dossier was created for every mission, and it was not unusual for a trip to require 18 months' preparation.

To start with, the only invitations that the Bishop of Rome would even consider, the *sine qua non* for any papal visit, were those issued by governments. John Paul II considered the primary purpose of his trips to encourage governments through his presence and to glorify the people of God rather than to seek dialogue with local churches and listen to their problems; the latter was something he did on other occasions, first of all in Rome during the periodical *ad limina* visits. When the Patriarch of the West traveled abroad, it was in order to share his message, not to run the risk of having foreign governments try to use his visit as a photo op. Wherever he traveled, he always stressed the importance of discipline and obedience to Rome. He wanted to reenergize a Catholic community in profound crisis, especially in parts of the world where fewer and fewer people were attending church or entering the priesthood. He was also determined to rekindle the ecumenical flame of which he was the source around the world. He would often say, “The need for fresh evangelization requires unity, first and above all.” His aims were very clear, and they required much careful discussion in order to avoid raising unwanted political overtones or offending others’ sensibilities.

The Pope would start by holding a working lunch to discuss the program for a forthcoming visit. As ever, the meal was served in the dining room of his private apartment on the third floor of the apostolic palace. Alongside the Holy Father would be his prime minister, the substitute secretary of state and, of course, his private secretary Msgr. Dziwisz assisted by his second private secretary, as well as the head of the language department for the country concerned, the bishops and leading high prelates affected and, finally, the indispensable Father Tucci, without whom nothing concrete could ever happen. Some of those attending the meeting would subsequently travel to the intended destination to take stock of the situation on the ground, meeting with political and religious leaders and setting out the details of the program; this was what was known as the preparatory mission. It was often a challenge to fit everything into the available time, as the Holy Father’s orders had to be followed to the letter, and he would usually draw up his own list of places he would visit and ceremonies he would attend. This list was broken down into an extremely detailed written timetable, with no stage ignored. Scheduling was made even harder by the fact that the Holy Father was in the habit of promising visiting clerics that he would visit their country, and once his word had been given he was determined that it would be respected, even if this took him to the very limits of his physical strength.

During the Pope's last two visits to France, in September 1996 and August 1997, Father Tucci succeeded in obtaining all that could be expected—and more besides—from a nominally secular French Republic. He was helped in this regard by the subtle, behind-the-scenes work of Prefet Landrieu, then head of the French president's private office, as well as by Jacques Chirac himself, who, in his own words, "admired the courtesy and intelligence as much as the peaceful strength of this man, who is so unlike most of the people I come across." The Jesuit Tucci, ever the canny diplomat, would always take pains to thank hosts for allowing the Pope to visit their country. He would also make an earlier, preview visit to the destination selected, ensuring that the conditions he saw were those that the Pope would encounter. The purpose of these visits was to establish watertight timetabling. He would even check the ceremonial arrangements at Rome's Leonardo da Vinci airport. The Pope would almost always board his plane, via gate C6, at the same time—8 A.M. The Pope and his guests were treated to a red carpet, but other than that only a metal barrier separated them from other passengers.

By 2002, when boarding the Pope onto an aircraft had become harder because of the wheelchair, lifts and other paraphernalia used to ease his discomfort, Father Boccardo paid more attention than ever before, making sure than no last-minute technical problem would interrupt the ceremonial aspects, for, despite his iron will, the previously even-tempered Pope had become more impatient: it was not unknown for him to strike his cane on the ground in barely contained anger, making his bad temper known as his strength of character came bursting through. As one of his close staff members relates, "Karol Wojtyla's character always featured a large dose of pride, an overwhelming need for self-affirmation that toward the end of his life he naturally found harder to keep in check, as he could not fight against both his illness and this character trait, which was also part of what made him so strong."

I was told one day by Father Pierre Riches—a onetime chaplain at Fiumicino Airport, originally a Jew from Alexandria who had converted to Catholicism at age 23, who spoke Italian, Arabic, English, French, Greek and Spanish: "In principle, the Pope was at all times very cordial. He would always ask how I was, whereas his entourage was constantly very rigid and wrapped up in the detailed protocol of the ceremony. Once, just before he boarded his plane, John Paul II jokingly remarked to me that 'Of course it would be most inconvenient were this plane to crash, as there would be hardly anyone left at the Vatican to organize my succession!' There was absolute silence from the members of the Sacred College present that day."

The Supreme Pontiff was always greeted by a number of eminent prelates, such as the *camerlengo* (the title of certain papal officials), the senior cardinal of the Sacred College, the vicar of the diocese of Rome, and senior managers from Alitalia and the airport, all of whom stayed on the ground. As John Paul II traveled so frequently, the Italian president, prime minister and other senior establishment figures no longer came to the airport as they used to when he was first elected.

As soon as they returned from the inspection tour, Father

Tucci and later Father Boccardo—both successors of the infamous Father Paul Marcinkus, known in Vatican circles as the man who diverted the knife-wielding man who attacked John Paul II in the Philippines, and then, a little later, as a man involved in the murky affairs of the Vatican Bank—would present the Holy Father with a paper detailing the intricacies of political and religious thought in the countries he was to visit, as well as setting out the opinions held by local priests; these notes were subject to yet further revision prior to the Pope actually visiting the countries in question.

John Paul II also liked to learn a little about the grammar and phonetic system of languages he did not know; he viewed this task as a personal challenge and a way of expressing an individual homage to these nations. As a man who spoke many languages, he did not have much trouble in picking up the rudiments of new ones. Prior to his arrival in Manila, in February 1981, he received a few lessons in Tagalog from a group of Philippine Dominican nuns at the Vatican.

The Holy Father also took pains with the liturgical aspects of the planned ceremonies, and would ask to be kept regularly informed of progress in planning his future trips. He himself set out the main themes of his speeches, especially when he was keen to make his thoughts about an important subject known. This intellectual exercise interested him above all else, and he would spend any free time he had on it.

The Pope would first make an imaginary journey in his mind, examining all the social, religious, cultural and geographical issues, and then, when the actual trip came, he could concentrate on meeting people in all the places he visited. The parts that he found the least interesting, however, were written for him by a member of the secretary of state's staff, often Msgr. Ptasznik. Although there was nothing secret about this, it was the sort of admission that used to infuriate the people who ran *L'Osservatore Romano*, also known, totally inappropriately, as the *amico della verita* (truth's friend), a publication that has been a past-master of disinformation since time immemorial. In his later years, John Paul II's sermons and speeches were almost always drawn up from notes that the Holy Father dictated in Polish, and were then translated into other languages including French, which was in theory still the language of diplomacy.

Despite his trembling hands, John Paul II did not alter his handwriting, which was large, regular, clear and precise, always free of hesitation and revision. This was the same fine and elegant hand that was so clearly shared by previous Popes, evidence of the traditional concern for calligraphy, a subject that was taught in seminaries until John Paul II's generation. Some papers in his handwriting, 20 to 22 lines long, carried the letters AMDG, for the Latin *Ad Majorem Dei Gloriam* (for the greater glory of God). John Paul II always carefully reread texts written for him by others. Whenever he was not sure he followed the writer's reasoning, he would place a question mark in blue ink in the margin, or enquire of his writer, "Are you sure that this phrase is necessary?" John Paul II was never curt, and texts would sometimes be returned for revision or correction several times before the definitive version was accepted and passed along for translation. Paul VI, on the other hand, wrote endless notes and questions along the lines of "What is meant by 'festive liturgy'?" when he was unable to find the adjective in the dictionary.

When the Pope visited Slovenia in May 1996, the text of his speech was sent without corrections direct to the secretariat of the Slovenian episcopate in Ljubljana. Meanwhile, Cardinal Angelo Sodano noticed that the version of the speech in question mentioned a forthcoming convocation of a new European synod, whereas the main protagonists had yet to be informed. But it was too late, and nothing could be done to prevent the incident. This type of misunderstanding was extremely rare in an environment that thrived above all on nuance and what was left unsaid.

The Pope's speeches were generally provided to the press ahead of time, but subject to an embargo until a specified day and time. This allowed us to follow and analyze his speeches as well as to spot sections that he added off the cuff (something that he stopped doing during the final two years of his life). No journalist would ever have dreamed of breaking the embargo, for to do so would mean never traveling with the Pope again.

Several weeks before leaving, journalists traveling with the Pope were required to provide the press manager with a full list of the contents of their bags, clothes included. The Holy See was far stricter with us than any political leader.

John Paul II's travels were fully documented by his personal photographer Arturo Mari. As a staff photographer at *L'Osservatore Romano* since 1955, he had photographed no less than five Popes. He was a member of the Vatican staff just like any other. He was fond of saying, "It is not a question of money. I work because I believe in the Pope and what he does, and I give thanks to God for my work"—and, partly thanks to Mari's work, the photographic department of the weekly edition of *L'Osservatore Romano* was one of the rare money-making arms of the Vatican. Mari took some 3 million photographs of the Holy Father, a body of work that constitutes a gigantic historical photo archive, including coverage of the memorable political moment when Karol Wojtyla met Lech Walesa in the Carpathian mountains in June 1983—photographs that one picture agency offered Mari half a million dollars for! These documents naturally remained secret. Arturo would shoot up to 800 rolls of film per pilgrimage; his photographs were then sold for a few euros by the *L'Osservatore Romano's* photographic department at the Porta di Santa Anna, which also provided images to newspapers and magazines at much higher prices that were nevertheless relatively reasonable. It was a system that cleverly pulled the rug from beneath the feet of the leading global photo agencies, for in this way the Holy See could control its own scoops. This truly was manna from heaven, part of which was used, under the terms of an arrangement made in heaven, to subsidize the travel expenses of pious Poles who wished to make the trip of a lifetime to the Vatican to receive a blessing from Karol Wojtyla.

Poles were passionate about these pilgrimages to Rome. During the Pope's jubilee year, 35,000 of them came to Rome by bus, bicycle and on foot. Saint Peter's Square hosted the presidents of Poland's upper and lower chambers, its prime minister and its president, accompanied by the nation's cardinals and bishops, all gathered to salute John Paul II.

The Pastor of the Universal Church, never one for nostalgically thumbing through old photo albums, nonetheless always bowed to photographers' demands with grace and patience. He had the knack of appearing to create a genuine sense of involvement and personal relationship with all those he met.

"I want to meet them all. I want to meet everyone who prays in the place where they pray—the Bedouin in the desert, the Carmelite or Cistercian monk in their monastery, the ill on their sickbed, the healthy going about their daily lives. I must cross the threshold of every home," stated the former archbishop of Krakow a few days after his election, and this attitude, this missionary spirit and desire to go out and meet people was something that never left him despite his advancing age and failing health. As Cardinal Tucci maintains to this day, John Paul II was a man who would never give up. How would he have been able to accept his freedom of action being taken from him at a time when his physical handicaps were restricting him more and more? To force him to cut back on his mission would be the same as killing him. He would have died of despair, for despite his powerful spirituality, he would have found it disheartening. It would have loosened his grasp on life, for even though he was the Pope he remained a man, and a strong-minded one at that!

Prior to takeoff, and instead of the usual monotone announcement, "Cross-check doors for takeoff," the senior pilot from the host country's national carrier would use the microphone to make an extraordinary, respectful address to the passengers. He would first welcome the Pope and the rest of us, and then, speaking on behalf of himself and the rest of the crew—who had generally applied for the honor months in advance—he would go on to express the joy he felt in having the Supreme Pontiff on board the aircraft. One memory of when I was traveling with the Pope that left a strong impression on me was when I heard, for the one and only time, the captain conclude with the following words: "For the first time ever, I commend this fight into the hands of God, in the person of his highest representative on earth." Everyone applauded enthusiastically, especially the bishops and ambassador to the Holy See from the country concerned, who, for the first time in their lives, were enjoying the privilege of traveling on the papal plane and seeing the Bishop of Rome up close; they cried out "*Viva il papa!*" I myself was both moved and dazzled, and I had eyes only for him. Better still, thus reassured to be flying in the company of the last intermediary between heaven and earth, I almost forget that I was scared of air travel. But how could I possibly have felt even the slightest fear when, as the captain said, I was traveling under the best protection of all: *his* protection.

Chapter Six

ISRAEL: THE GREATEST VOYAGE OF HOPE

IT WAS NOT UNTIL 20 YEARS INTO HIS PONtificate that, shortly before his 80th birthday, John Paul II was able to realize his long-held dream of walking in Christ's footsteps, standing where he preached to his disciples 2,000 years before.

On December 24, 1978, he celebrated midnight mass in Saint Peter's for the first time, standing beneath Bernini's monumental bronze canopy in praise of God. Assembled in front of John Paul II was the entire Roman curia, the ambassadors to the Holy See, all wearing formal dress and grand decorations, and the senior representatives of the Vatican hierarchy. With the eyes of every member of this illustrious gathering fixed on him, the new Supreme Pontiff declared in his powerful voice that he would have preferred to be celebrating this Christmas mass in the Grotto of the Nativity in Bethlehem. This had been a goal of his ever since 1963, when as a young bishop returning to Krakow from Rome after the second session of Vatican II he made a detour to Jerusalem, where he secretly swore to return one day and celebrate mass. He thus spoke of his regrets, and invited the illustrious congregation to join him in celebrating the liturgy of the nativity with "the profundity, ardor and authenticity of immense inner feeling." This was a defining moment, and all the faithful in attendance joined the Pope in evoking the scene of the nativity in Bethlehem.

The Holy Father had to wait until 2000 to see his wish fulfilled. Of all his trips, the memory of John Paul II in Israel must surely be the most beautiful, the most spiritual and the most moving.

At 11 A.M. on March 25, 2000, at Korazim, one of the most sacred places in Christianity, from which Jesus gave his Sermon on the Mount, it had just stopped raining. Like a sailboat gliding across the water, the Popemobile, which had been sent specially from Rome, climbed slowly up a muddy track surrounded by tens of thousands of the faithful, whose singing rose toward the Mount of Beatitudes. Aboard the vehicle, John Paul II stood relatively erect, his broad shoulders scarcely bent. Terribly moved by the size of the crowd, he tried to smile despite the immobility of his face. The closer he came to the immense altar that had been constructed at this evangelical apex, the more his face lit up.

As always, he found fresh energy in the enthusiasm of the crowd. The weather had improved, and the Pope, surrounded by hundreds of priests, beamed. Behind me, I could hear every language under the sun being spoken, for many of the pilgrims present had traveled many days, coming from all over the world to be present. There were bishops and cardinals, including the charismatic Christoph Schönborn, the archbishop of Vienna, and groups of elderly priests who had traveled all the way from deepest Amazonia and were leaping with joy. There were also Lebanese and Palestinians, mostly young people who had camped out in the surrounding olive groves. Some 45,000 young people raised in the Church, including about 900 enthusiastic French youngsters, some of whom were returning to the fold, sang the *Magnificat* in unison, followed by *John Paul II We Love You!*

The site was decked with Israeli flags, the yellow and white flag of the Vatican, and various banners and welcoming slogans from a host of nations. Patently energized by this immense crowd, John Paul II was able to speak during the homily, and his voice, though slow, was clear, echoing impressively all the way down to Lake Tiberius. He had to pause constantly, interrupted by fervent applause and ovations that grew louder and louder all the way through the mass.

I found myself cast back 2,000 years, and the name Tiberius was still prominent in my mind as it had featured strongly during the religious education of my youth. I was in Galilee, in that place where Christ had, long ago, miraculously multiplied the fish and loaves! I was just a few meters from the Vicar of Christ! I found it hard to take any notes, utterly lost as I was in this feverish atmosphere, my eyes misted with tears. This mass at the Mount of Beatitudes was a ceremony more powerful than any other. In order to reach the site I had to leave Jerusalem at midnight the night before so as to escape the security lockdown that was already being put in place.

As he was returning to his car following this awesome religious ceremony, one of the heads of the police security operation,

Nathan Rotenberg, said to me, "Your Pope is an extraordinary person! The ease with which he switches between languages to deliver his message of peace and solidarity is very important to us . . . I have just lived through a unique experience!" Rotenberg exercised an important, high-stakes role in the Holy Land, if the number of security forces, kilometers-long barriers, innumerable checkpoints, and barrages of screening I had passed through were anything to go by.

John Paul II had accomplished something of a miracle himself, in this region already so profoundly marked by the Holy Spirit. Although it was raining in Tel Aviv, on the Golan plateau and Lake Tiberius area the weather suddenly eased over the site at Korazim, which even saw a ray or two of sunlight during the two-and-a-half-hour service. Another sign was the incredible energy that John Paul II conjured up, drawing deep on those mysterious forces that great mystics are able to find within themselves. Rarely had we seen the Pope kneel or prostrate himself so frequently as he did on this trip to Israel, where, heedless of how hard it was for him to stand up again, he was unable to resist kissing the ground within the Grotto of the Annunciation. He had to walk down a ramp in order to reach it, leaning on his cane with his left hand and gripping the handrail with his right. As always, there was no way of knowing how much of this energy came from his own human reserves and how much from the sublimation of his faith.

The Pope's schedule included a visit to the Dheishe refugee camp for Palestinians; a mass at the Holy Sepulcher, where he entered the dome containing Christ's tomb, kissed the stone and sank deep into prayer, alone with the memory of the crucifixion and dreaming of a Jerusalem at peace; and a poignant ceremony at the Yad Vashem Holocaust memorial, where, standing next to the eternal flame, he performed an act of remembrance accompanied by his Jewish childhood friend, Jerzy Kluger, and greeted 10 Jewish survivors of the death camps. Finally came the moment that will indelibly remain in the memory of all who saw it, one that reached far beyond the frontiers of Israel itself: the Pope's symbolic gesture at the Wailing Wall, toward which he moved with unbearable slowness stemming from a mixture of fatigue and emotion before slipping a letter of repentance between the ochre stones of the 2,000-year-old wall. The letter repeated a request for forgiveness that he had pronounced during a ceremony of penitence in Saint Peter's Basilica a few days earlier, seeking pardon for the sufferings inflicted on the Jewish people. The letter was on Vatican-headed paper and was signed in Latin by the Pontiff. Before placing it in the wall and blessing it, he quietly spoke the words again, surrounded by an utter silence broken only by the flashing of Arturo Mari's camera some 10 meters distant. These images, as heart-rending as they were amazing, unfolded in front of my eyes like a private screening of a silent movie.

Thanks to the relationship I had developed with the Israeli police chiefs I met the night before in the King David Hotel, I was fortunate enough to find myself always placed right on the red-lined papal route, amidst his close entourage and only a few meters from him inside the immediate security perimeter. I was thus able to stay with the Pope for the whole visit, which was very unusual in this highly sensitive land where John Paul II was escorted by some 20,000 police and over 1,000 soldiers.

The military pointed their automatic weapons as helicopters circled low overhead and ambulance sirens wailed constantly, while a strange-looking anti-mine vehicle tailed behind, the latter a real curiosity that always made you wonder whether it was about to blow up in your face!

All of this was more than enough to stress out tourists not used to such impressive displays of force as well as to cause considerable annoyance to residents, although by some miracle they put up with the disruption with calm equanimity, even though the visit caused gridlock throughout Jerusalem's narrow streets. However, the moment they succeeded in hooking a passenger, especially a journalist like myself (there were, after all, 3,000 of us in town), taxi drivers would always proffer an impenetrable Hebrew explanation for doubling the amount shown on the meter! For his part, as he sadly admitted just before the open-air mass to Father Tucci in the temporary sacristy erected at Korazim, the Pope regretted that he had a security cordon all around him, as this deprived him of the restorative walkabouts amongst the crowd that he loved so much.

Working in the background of the official ceremonies, which were attended by thousands of pilgrims, many of whom had flown in via specially chartered planes, Father Tucci constantly had to deal with last-minute problems with the Israeli authorities. The latter had by no means an easy task, as they too were extremely anxious about the health of this elderly man whom they had previously seen only in pain-wracked TV pictures, and of whose inner strength they had little understanding. They were therefore anxious for him to spend as little time as possible walking or standing. They were pleased that the Pope was driven by his Italian chauffeur, Orlando Santinelli, who was highly experienced and knew how to pace things. He had traveled to Israel on a reconnaissance trip a few days beforehand, which allowed him to spare the Holy Father as much as possible from being jolted around, especially when traveling down unsealed roads. It was necessary to find the solution to numerous unexpected situations, some of them simple, such as ensuring that he could return to the Holy Sepulcher on the day he left, but others more complex.

The least difficulty with John Paul II rapidly became insurmountable as the Israeli organizers shrank from taking the initiative, paralyzed as they were by their visitor's standing. Despite this, they managed to move the arrival time at the camera-infested east Jerusalem refugee camp forward by an hour. This brilliant idea came from the Israeli secret service, which realized that the visit could turn into a catastrophe for the Supreme Pontiff. Indeed, no sooner had he left than the Palestinian stone-throwing began.

The Pope was accompanied wherever he went by his personal physician, who carried with him those famous bags of AB-negative blood. The cautious Israelis had offered the Pope an extremely lightweight, flexible, bulletproof vest but, motivated by a mixture of pride and fatalism, he steadfastly refused to wear it. The stone-throwing in the refugee camp was heavily reported on by Gulf TV channels, which were always on the lookout for scoops during the period of the pilgrimage to Mecca. The Gulf stations brazenly interrupted their programming to report an attack on the head of the Catholic Church—were they perhaps a bit jubilant? When I heard the faithful being called to prayer from the muezzin of an adjoining mosque at about 10 minutes before midday and toward the end of the pontifical mass in the square outside the Church of the Nativity in Bethlehem, my first thought was that this was a deliberate provocation, but the Holy Father simply interrupted the mass calmly for a few minutes. This was but a small incident amongst others, and one that, happily for the Vatican, had escaped the notice of the camera operators from the pool and was not aired on Telepace, the Holy See's channel.

There were also moments of humor. In Nazareth, a man proudly presented the Holy Father with a brick supposedly taken from Abraham's house; John Paul II jokingly remarked to him, "I thought Abraham lived in a tent!" As the air force was strictly forbidden from flying during the Sabbath, I remember the last-minute panic and agitation when an olive-green air force Black Hawk helicopter had to be hastily repainted in blue police colors.

During every long and stressful day spent in Israel, Karol Wojtyla was never out of the sight of his immediate entourage: Msgr. Dziwisz, Cardinal Sodano, Msgr. Marini, Angelo Gugel, Camillo Cibin, his two physicians and three gendarmes. They held their breath every stage of the way, forever worried that something might happen to him.

In truth, the Pastor of the Universal Church was driving himself relentlessly. During his stay in the Holy Land, March 20–26, 2000, he visited 10 sites, held five large masses, gave 13 speeches in Latin and English with added phrases in Hebrew and Arabic, and held official meetings with King Abdullah II of Jordan, Yasir Arafat, Israeli President Ezer Weizman and Prime Minister Ehud Barak. He was in pain every step of the way, his movements like so many stations of the cross. The difficulty he had in expressing himself clearly and his shuffling, halting gait lent added weight to his message of peace and to this "irrevocable alliance" with the Jewish people. His close colleagues who accompanied him everywhere he went did their utmost to micromanage every detail of his time, more or less without his knowledge, seeking to minimize as far as possible the tensions that surrounded this exhausting marathon. At the end of each day, John Paul II would return to the apostolic delegation building in East Jerusalem, a pleasant, pale-ochre building with lush gardens. In the small salon next to his bedroom was a ceramic mural dating from the reign of Paul VI, a reminder of the now famous embrace between Giovanni Battista Montini and Athenagoras, the Patriarch of Constantinople that occurred on January 5, 1964, a gesture that at the time was seen as a sign that this fraternal enmity was neither irreversible nor eternal. Once back in his quarters, Karol Wojtyla could at last rest and pray, confident that he had never wavered in his desire to emphasize the spiritual ties that united the Jewish and Christian faiths. It was also a chance to enjoy the simple, rustic fare cooked for him by the Sisters of the Misericord.

Sister Germana was a low-profile passenger aboard the papal plane who traveled shielded from the cameras' prying eyes. Because of the heat of the local climate, she dressed all in white as she oversaw, with kindly authority, the Pope's diet. She made sure that he was served no fried or chilled foods and that the dishes prepared for him were less spicy and rich than is traditional in kosher cooking so as to avoid upsetting his stomach, which had been damaged in the assassination attempt. Such arrangements could not always be made when dining out. John Paul II dared not refuse an invitation to an Ashkenazi meal prepared by members of the large local population of Israelis of Polish origin, which featured carp, schav borscht, matzoh, chicken livers fried in onion, stuffed lamb and apple strudel. These centuries-old dishes were symbolically important foods for the Diaspora. As in Rome, Sister Germana also looked after his clothes and kept his supply of thick white sashes and spotless capelets in various thicknesses, which she carefully ironed every day, in constant readiness.

Thus ensconced between a talmudic college and two leading hospitals, the Hadassah and Augusta-Victoria (both on permanent standby), the Pope was finally able to spend some time alone, meditating in silence as he faced the Mount of Olives.

In the space of six days, and by virtue of a few well-chosen acts, this 80-year-old man with the profound religious aura had—despite his pain-wracked face and thanks to his frank, direct gaze—won the admiration of many people who had seemed wholly indifferent to his arrival a short time before. The emotion grew bit by bit as an intense feeling of sympathy and devotion swelled around John Paul II, even in a country that gives the impression of having seen it all before. In the end, this journey—which in his heart of hearts he had wanted to make more than any other—kindled a real passion on the part of Israeli authorities and citizens alike and eventually won over even the skeptics.

I was flabbergasted to see a number of leading Israeli intellectuals, people not noted for their interest in papal comings and goings, suddenly developing a keen interest in his visit.

This was a paradox, the secret of which was known only to John Paul II. Leading writers and influential authors such as David Grossmann, Amoz Oz and others suddenly began writing lengthy, upbeat articles on his visit. The major dailies, *Maariv*, *Haaretz* and *The Jerusalem Post*, which ran a special banner logo during the visit, each devoted five front-page columns to him for six consecutive days, as well as many of the inside pages as well. This blanket coverage was all the more surprising since the Israeli press had been guarded about his visit prior to his arrival; in fact, their main focus of attention had been a sexual-harassment scandal involving the minister for defense. It then became impossible to turn on a television without seeing images of John Paul II on all the local channels, both Israeli and Arab. One of the Israeli channels even went so far as to add a small cross-shaped logo at the bottom left-hand corner of the screen, to the intense irritation of various Orthodox Jews and shawl-draped rabbis. In every single store in Jerusalem's shopping quarter, which was centered on King David and Agron streets, the most basic retailers and the ritziest antique dealers alike all followed the Pope's visit on televisions perched on store counters, watching as avidly as if it were a football match. John Paul II had worked his magic on them all, from the humblest to the mightiest. Even local children could be heard crying out to *"el baba" ("the father"),* and on the day he arrived in Israel he was chosen as the star of the carnival held as part of Purim celebrations! Everyone was under the spell of the grace and charisma exuded by this exhausted man, who symbolized human frailty and, in so doing, came closer to every human being. Once he returned to Rome, the Holy Father confided to Cardinal Deskur that he was "boundlessly grateful that Israeli television translated all my speeches into Hebrew."

Thanks to his fine political antennae, those who imagined that this brilliant mediator would allow himself to become trapped by the intricacies of the peace process were left disappointed. A statesman and renowned diplomat, the Pope repeatedly showed that he had not waited for his 91st trip abroad to demonstrate his deft touch and steadfast determination. His travels were the backbone of his initiatives, and he was determined to live up to his missionary vocation and not remain sequestered within the Vatican. In his own way, Karol Wojtyla was a great politician, displaying enviable skill as he visited various nations, greeted their ministers and met with their leaders, trying to move the latter's thinking forward regarding such areas as human rights and religious freedom. However, when he was traveling to meet the faithful and his brothers in faith, he devoted nearly all of his time to liturgical events, aiming to remotivate the local churches. As was explained to me at the time by Avi Pazner, the former Israeli ambassador to Rome and one of the architects of the Vatican's recognition of the State of Israel, now the world president of Keren-Hayesod (the United Israel Appeal) and an Israeli government spokesperson: "The fact that we were both born in Poland created evident fellow-feeling between us. Neither side gained more than the other from this historic visit. Everyone was clamoring for more, but the Holy Father, who was far too prudent and wise, never allowed himself to be influenced or carried away. In April 1992, when I ventured to remind him that the Vatican was one of the last countries in the world not to have diplomatic relations with Israel, he gave me a conspiratorial smile and then, in a voice both serious and humorous, said, 'Are you insinuating that we are the worst? Are you not aware that, according to our religion, the last shall be first?' In that instant I knew it would be forthcoming.

"Regardless of his advanced age and illness, I never for an instant imagined it was possible to lead John Paul II anywhere he hadn't already decided to go," concluded Pazner, a man fully converted to the Pope's cause.

People at the Vatican were fond of recalling that John Paul II loved to say that Jews and Christians were all sons of Abraham. "He had lived amongst Jewish people and had Jewish friends, and had mingled with Jews from his early childhood. He was taught the value of fraternity by his father and his teachers. He was also marked by the deportation during the Second World War of close neighbors from Wadovice—that is why he understood us," explained the grand rabbi of Jerusalem, Ismael Mesir Lau, who was one of the leading skeptics about John Paul II's visit prior to his arrival.

Karol Wojtyla's father was a retired lieutenant who rented a modest two-room plus kitchen apartment at 2 Ryrek Street in Wadowice to a Jewish trader, Chaim Balamuth, who kept a store on the ground floor.

The Pope wrote in one of his books, *Crossing the Threshold of Hope*, "I remember, above all, the Wadowice elementary school, where at least a quarter of the pupils in my class were Jewish. I am especially eager to recall my friendship with one of them, Jerzy Kluger. This friendship that began in the schoolroom endures to this day. I can vividly remember the Jews who gathered every Saturday at the synagogue behind our school. Both religious groups, Catholics and Jews, were united, I presume, by the awareness that they prayed to the same God. Although we did not use the same language, the prayers in the synagogue and the prayers in the church were in large part based on the same texts." Karol Wojtyla was a life-long believer in the importance of good relations with Judaism.

It was this conviction that undoubtedly proved to be one of the keys to the success of his memorable Israeli visit, during which he managed to duck the main political obstacles as a man who had never in any way mingled with anti-Semitic circles in Poland—a land where not more than 30,000 Jews were left after 1945. At the Holy See, the conservative-minded Cardinal Angelo Sodano and Msgr. Tauran were anxious to follow the traditional Vatican line, more pro-Palestinian than pro-Zionist, closer therefore to Yasir Arafat than Ehud Barak, and right up to the last minute they lobbied tenaciously in favor of Yasir Arafat's stance, but to no avail. Aided by his many years of diplomatic practice, John Paul II stood his ground yet also avoided upsetting the Palestinians. This was a subtle balancing act, for while the Pope stressed the importance of establishing "a proper relationship with Islam, [one that] needs to be conducted prudently, with clear ideas about possibilities and limits" in March 2000, he also visited Jordan and the Palestinian territories, for he felt there were a number of issues at stake, although it was, naturally, the visit to Israel that lingered longest in the memory. In Jordan, he celebrated mass in front of 60,000 people in a stadium in Amman, as well as at Wadiel Karrar, one of the sites claiming to be the spot where Jesus was baptized by John the Baptist, before traveling to Bethlehem for a day to conduct mass in Manger Square in front of the Church of the Nativity and to pray in the Cave of the Nativity. He then visited the nearby Palestinian refugee camp at Deiheisha, and finished with a meeting with the president of the Palestinian Authority, Yasir Arafat. The Pope visited President Arafat as a pilgrim driven by pacifism, intending to show support for efforts aimed at peace and justice for the Palestinians. His visit to the Holy Land honored the ongoing dialogue between the three religions of the Book: Judaism, Christianity and Islam.

Fascinated by this place where God and history coincide, the Pope was keen to hold a mass to celebrate the 2,000 years since the birth of Christ; he sought thereby to strengthen his brother Catholics from the Melchite, Armenian, Syrian, Maronite, Coptic and Chaldean churches. The numbers of Eastern Church members were continually falling in the Middle East; falling victim to the difficulties of co-existing with Islam over the years, they were plagued by emigration. He exhorted them to remain courageous, urging them to "cling to this land."

This 2000 pilgrimage, which served to strengthen Jewish-Christian dialogue, was the fruit of work done by three figures from the Pope's generation: Father Roberto Tucci; Australian Cardinal Edward Cassidy, a good-humored churchman who was president of the Pontifical Council for the Promotion of Christian Unity; and Roger Etchegaray, the cardinal charged with difficult missions who was at the time president of the Committee for the Great Jubilee. It was Etchegaray who assisted the Pope in the delicate task of wording the request for forgiveness from the Jewish people.

Aside from these eminent Church figures, mention should also be made of the discreet influence wielded by engineer

Jerzy Kluger, Karol Wojtyla's Polish-Jewish childhood friend, now living in Rome and mentioned in *Crossing the Threshold of Hope* as the friend with whom, from the age of six, John Paul II used to play table tennis and ski on handmade wooden skis. The two of them attended elementary and secondary school together in Wadowice, a town that once counted 2,000 Jews out of a population of 12,000. Since 1978, Jerzy Kluger has been a tireless campaigner in working toward rapprochement between Catholics and Jews.

In April 1999, Ariel Sharon visited the Holy Father in Rome. At that time the head of the right-wing Israeli party, Likud, Sharon presented him with a 17th-century map of the world, *Nova totius terrarum orbis tabula*, upon which were inscribed in Latin the ancient regions of Judea and Samaria where the Twelve Tribes of Israel once dwelt. I was told by Uri Dan, one of Sharon's closest associates who was present that day, that the Pope accepted the gift with evident pleasure, taking it in his hands and contemplating it with attention, repeating enthusiastically several times, "I shall finally reach the Promised Land!" Sharon and his entourage were intrigued that the Pope spontaneously referred to the Jewish "Promised Land" rather than the Christian "Holy Land." Speaking of his future trip to Israel, John Paul II then explained, "Since the names have not changed for 2,000 years, I shall take the Bible as my guide," and then, to the astonishment of his guests, with eyes half-closed and a voice husky with emotion, he began to recite the Hebrew names for the holy sites.

An ecumenical cabin crew, assembled in his honor, awaited him when he boarded the El Al flight returning him to Italy from Israel. There were four stewardesses assigned to him: a dark-skinned 24-year-old former Miss World Airline, a black African Catholic of Ethiopian origin, an Israeli whose family, like Karol Wojtyla's, came from Wadowice, and a Muslim Arab, as well as an Arab steward who was a Maronite Christian and a former opera singer specializing in Verdi (and who therefore spoke Italian). For once, the Pope was unable to avoid eating kosher, for El Al was intransigent in this regard. The Holy Father must have savored the memory, for he had little occasion to eat kosher in Rome, where the Jewish community numbered some 150,000, including four families of Roman Jews who claimed to be descendents of Jesus.

Sister Valerie Galizie, an Italian nun who was a member of the society of Saint-Vincent-de-Paul and who had for 40 years run an orphanage in West Jerusalem for Arab children, told me: "Incalculable numbers of prayers have been said for peace to come to Jerusalem, but those said here by John Paul II in the twilight of his days and at the heart of the conflict, prayers offered up on the banks of the river Jordan, are different: they resonate more widely, for they have opened men's hearts. This visit will be remembered not only by God, but by history too."

"Something wholly extraordinary and mysterious happened there," the Pope told his minister for culture, Cardinal Poupard, who related this to me upon his return.

At the next general audience on March 29, 2000, in Rome, where thousands of pilgrims had come to sing his praises, receive his blessing and hear him speak, the Bishop of Rome shared his joy at being able to perform his pilgrimage in Christ's footsteps. That morning, he spoke of the "inexpressible gratitude in my soul for this gift from the Lord that I desired so keenly."

Chapter Seven

CASTEL GANDOLFO AND THE ALPS: THE SACRED DUTY TO TAKE A BREAK

JOHN PAUL II TOOK HIS "DOWN" TIME AS seriously as his work. Despite his ascetic lifestyle, vacations were very important to him. He needed breaks every once in a while, the better to bear the mantle of his vocation—they were almost sacred to him, as I noticed at my expense on Wednesday, August 14, 1996.

Just before John Paul's trip to France, Cardinal Stanislaw Dziwisz had in theory arranged for me to have an audience with the Pontiff at his summer residence, Castel Gandolfo. With my usual optimism, I hoped to talk him into a sort of interview and exclusive photo report along the lines of "His Holiness on Holiday." The piece was timed to come out on the day he arrived in Paris. Msgr. Dziwisz had suggested going to see His Holiness on vacation. "You never know what's going through the Supreme Pontiff's mind—only God does," he said before hanging up.

Dressed all in black even though it was midsummer, I took the monsignor up on his offer. Of course, the Pope's private secretary had informed the security services of my visit. My name was slipped in among others, almost all of them Polish, on a ledger at the heavy front door. I was announced and went through the usual checks before being led into the main courtyard, where the Supreme Pontiff was planning to take his morning constitutional. From a distance, I saw him slowly walking forward. Father Dziwisz was whispering something in his ear that made both of them laugh. With a quick glance, Msgr. Dziwisz signaled that it was time for me to approach His Holiness.

No sooner had I respectfully curtseyed before John Paul II and kissed the pontifical ring than he said, "To make a long story short, you want to take advantage of the Pope's trip to your lovely country to write an article about him. But when the Pope is on vacation he is silent, and the French will have plenty of opportunities to see and hear him next month. All you have to do is wait!" Barely able to conceal my disappointment, I bit my lip, not imagining for an instant that the Holy Father would have spoken to me that way. After all, his personal secretary himself had more or less granted me this brief audience. He looked at me, noticed my frown and waved at Msgr. Dziwisz to take care of me. With his usual courtesy and inimitable savoir-faire, Msgr. Dziwisz patted my hand as if to console me as the Pope looked on with a bemused expression on his face. In a low voice and a confidential tone, the good priest told me, "Time does not have the same meaning here.

I know that at your magazine you think in terms of days, but I'm sure you can explain to them that we have been working differently for 2,000 years!"

That day I realized that the Holy Father considered vacations a sort of duty. (In fact, he was vacationing at Lake Spitding on January 13, 1964, when word came that he had just been appointed bishop of Krakow.) The Pope needed to recharge his batteries in order to continue his globetrotting ministry. Since the 1981 attempt on his life, John Paul II believed that the Mother of Christ was protecting him, but realized that he could not overdo it. He had faith in the Virgin, but did not expect her to perform miracles on his behalf forever.

One of John Paul II's acquaintances told me that he did not want to "tempt" God. The Pope knew that he had to take care of his old, careworn body and that, even though he was head of the Roman Catholic Church, he could not rely on divine privilege. So the Holy Father took real vacations as he had in the past, although the athletic days of playing soccer, kayaking and cycling were over. The Pope accepted the ailments of old age, but believed that by ignoring them and refusing to take a rest now and then he would fail to fulfill his duty.

John Paul II always enjoyed the mountains, where he felt like a new man, and he went there often, usually in July. Between July 1986 and July 2004, he traveled to Combes in the Val d'Aosta 10 times (the last time in July 2004), and to Lorenzago di Cadore in the Dolomites six times.

"Viva il papa! Viva il papa!" chanted the buoyant crowd. It was noon on a hot day in Lorenzago di Cadore, a mountain resort with a population of a few hundred in low season and several thousand in summer and winter. Happy children

(dressed in white and yellow for the occasion), Boy Scouts, old mountain dwellers and whole families gathered in the village square, jostling each other to touch, cheer, approach and surround John Paul II. "The man in white," whom they saw in lavish Vatican settings with heads of state, famous people and notable prelates year-round on television and in the papers, was suddenly right before their eyes. The villagers, and those vacationers who chose to forego crowding beneath umbrellas on Italian beaches on the Adriatic and Ligurian coasts, were rewarded with a treat: seeing the Pope taking a walk on vacation was not a common sight. The flock of faithful spontaneously waved handkerchiefs, scarves and little makeshift flags in the wind to honor him as he reached out and kissed children, made the sign of the cross on women's foreheads and took people's hands in his.

In July 1998, the outdoors-loving John Paul II came to this Dolomite Mountain village, which lies 1,000 meters above sea level between Venice and the Austrian border, for the last time, enjoying a two-week vacation far from lavish papal palaces. His cheeks were rosier than usual, and though he walked with a bamboo cane, he wore the same type of hiking boots that had served him well while backpacking in the Polish Carpathians. The Supreme Pontiff looked happy breathing in the pure air of mountain pastures—the only things missing were Heidi and the Von Trapp family singing, dressed in Tyrolean leather breeches.

Vacationers who dreamed of shaking the Holy Father's hand or meeting his gaze followed him from a distance. They knew from reading the press that the Pope received tributes from world leaders year-round, so they brought him what they could: flowers, cakes, honey, *bresaola* (a dried meat), baskets of blackberries, goat cheese and strong *grappa*. They could see that pain sometimes tightened his formerly bright smile, but the Pope emanated a soothing gentleness in this alpine atmosphere, as though he were merely a shepherd tending his flock.

The Pope was very relaxed that morning and, in almost accent-free Italian, he said, "The mountains forge character with courageous asceticism and soothe the spirit by putting it in touch with nature." Karol Wojtyla probably remembered the Polish song about the mountain dweller who left his home to earn a living in town, only to be overcome by homesickness. Although his voice was no longer as strong as in the early years of his papacy, when cadenced pauses and lively intonations marked a sharp contrast from his forerunners' brittle, droning tones, his words were still warm. John Paul II was so carried away by the cheerful mood that he nicknamed the prefect who had come to Lorenzago di Cadore to pay his respects "General." This senior civil servant, dressed in a very flattering blue uniform, bore the heavy burden of ensuring the Holy Father's security, in close cooperation with the Vatican police.

In fact, the Italian Republic was indulgent toward the Pope, putting its civil servants in charge of protecting him during his vacation. Such an arrangement would be unthinkable in France: if the president and the minister of the interior, who is also the minister of religious affairs, offered to fly Cardinal Lustiger in an official government aircraft or military helicopter from one point to another during his summer vacation at the taxpayers' expense, and provided his security as well, it would spark an uproar. (Article 1 of France's law on the separation of Church and State specifies that the minister of the interior has responsibility not only for the police but for religious freedom as well. When a French person is canonized or beatified, a French minister always attends the ceremony in person. For example, Jean-Pierre Raffarin went to the Pope's beatification of Mother Teresa on October 19, 2003, but that does not mean he fawns over the Princes of the Church.)

Italians, however, are so fond of the Bishop of Rome that nothing is too good for him. All Italian papers, even those that lean to the left, have a daily column about his comings and goings, and each major weekly has a Pope-watcher, some of them among the country's most notable editorial writers, including Luigi Accattoli *(Il Corriere della Sera),* Marco Politi *(La Repubblica),* Orazio Petrosillo *(Il Messagero),* Salvatore Mazza *(L'Avvenire),* Marco Tasatti *(La Stampa)* and Bruno Bartoloni (AFP), who was first to announce John XXIII's death. What's more, every Sunday the Italian public television station RAI broadcasts the Pope's blessing live on Channel One with commentary by Giuseppe De Carli, the famous religion correspondent for the TGI. So, in addition to the Swiss Guard, the Italian police—foreigners on Vatican soil!—protect the Supreme Pontiff. (The sturdy Swiss Guards, whose average height is 1.75 meters, are not considered foreigners because they are temporary citizens of the Holy See during their two years' minimum commitment.) Likewise, the Italian government courteously put an airplane at John Paul II's disposal for his vacation flights inside Italy. The Italian president loaned him his helicopter, which the Pope called "the big white dragonfly," to travel from Castel Gandolfo to Rome and back for the general Wednesday audience. That is just the way it was, and nobody dreamed of objecting. Italy's head of state acted somewhat like Napoleon, who referred to "My prefects, my bishops, my gendarmes!" when speaking of the imperial order.

In a moment of elation that morning at Lorenzago di Cadore, John Paul II nicknamed his worthy head of *vigilanza*—74-year-old Camillo Cibin, the man who had been running alongside his car since day one of his pontificate and always cleared the way in the most dangerous situations—his *commandatore*. He also appointed the village priest, Don Aldelardo da Prà, as *monsignore*. A letter bearing the apostolic signature and the Holy See's prestigious seal made the honor official, a worthy reward for Don Aldelardo, who, with few means, managed to make the parish look resplendent every time the Pope came and even, not without difficulty, to have the papal arms drawn on the campanile. Karol Wojtyla liked Don Aldelardo, who was 10 years his senior and resembled a typical Italian country priest. He had been shepherding the village flock for over half a century and nostalgically reminded the Pope of the brave Polish clergymen who often worked themselves nearly to death.

"I'm still looking for a priest who can preach the Gospel with the same fire as you!" the Pope told Father Aldelardo over a cup of coffee before enthusiastically elevating him to the rank of *monsignore*. This simple, 90-year-old man, who had devoted his long existence to the Lord, was so moved that he began to weep and started waving his hands in an attempt to regain his composure. This must have been the most beautiful day in his life. He was so moved that he ended up mislaying his black monsignor's robe with purple edging and buttons.

Holding a walking stick in his left hand and a rosary in his right, John Paul II was beaming. The Dolomites reminded him of the mountains in his native Poland. The program was always the same from one summer to the next, but since breaking his femur, rides in an unmarked SUV had replaced his long mountain hikes. However, once in a while the Pope, who spent his life climbing to eternity, took a few steps on forest trails to prove that he could still do it, though now a few meters felt like kilometers to him. Imagine the surprise of an old mountain dweller cleaning wild mushrooms in the doorway of his mountain pasture chalet when he suddenly saw a face that rang a bell but left him puzzled because the stranger was dressed in trousers, a sweater and a gray anorak instead of a white cassock. Leaping up from his little wooden chair he asked, "Are you the Pope? You look just like him!"

"Well, that's because I *am* him! And I apologize for causing such a stir everywhere I go," John Paul II told the rugged old mountain man who, stuttering with emotion, managed to say, "I would be very honored if you accepted my mushrooms and a glass of orangeade. You know, it's really a shame, my wife went down to the village to reserve a seat at the mass you're celebrating for the forest rangers on Sunday—meanwhile, you've climbed up to me!"

To console the dumbfounded man, the Pope took a little gift for his wife out of his pocket: a coveted rosary struck with the pontifical arms. Then he blessed him before walking away with a smile on his face, accompanied by the faithful Dziwisz and two bodyguards.

John Paul II would celebrate morning mass in the chalet where he was staying before he, his private secretary and his majordomo, occasionally accompanied by a guest, climbed into the Land Rover and drove off to enjoy a walk and a picnic on the banks of a stream or beneath the trees. Of course, that was when he still had at least some of his physical powers. The Holy Father sat in the shade of pine, fir and larch trees during his country breaks and would have a frugal meal of sardines, hard-boiled eggs that he sliced with a camping knife, and a bottle of local white wine cut with water from the gushing stream. He always wanted the big Russian sardines packed in oil found in the former Communist countries instead of the kind sold in luxury food shops. Sometimes he even had them served at Castel Gandolfo.

The Pope's chalet was a charming, postcard-perfect lime and wooden house with white walls and red geraniums in the window boxes, a private dwelling outside the village in the middle of Mirabello Park, sheltered by thick trees and tall hedges, which seemed desirable for his security. A climb of six steps revealed the kitchen on the left and the living room on the right. Upstairs were the Holy Father's office/living room and bedroom, whose simple decoration resembled the room Karol Wojtyla slept in when he was archbishop of Krakow. Its only contents were a dark wooden bed, a wooden crucifix above the headboard, a reproduction of the Black Virgin of Czestochowa, a few allegorical paintings, a photograph of mountains, a night table and a lamp with a straw shade. John Paul II always lived in spare surroundings. The chalet's dining room had a television set that he switched on now and then. Another room had been turned into a chapel. Sturdy handles and non-skid appliqués had been installed in the shower, since the Pope had become prone to falls. This little, unpretentious domain on the edge of a pine-scented forest belonged to the diocese of Belluno.

In the mountains, three sisters from a local community helped Sister Tobiana, who was always at the Holy Father's side. They performed all the household chores and prepared local, family-style meals, including soup, gnocchi, pasta, mushrooms, venison and pork stew, pungent mountain cheeses, yogurt, wild strawberries, raspberries and blackberry or blueberry pies.

To avoid offending the Italians, John Paul II took turns each year between the eastern and western Alps, splitting his vacations between the Dolomites and Combes in Val d'Aosta, 15 kilometers from Aosta in the commune of Introd.

He went to Combes for the ninth and last time in July 2001. The hamlet, which is 1,400 meters above sea level, has a population of approximately 50 during the low season and several thousand in summer (especially since John Paul II had started going there). Located 10 or so kilometers from the French border, it affords views of Mont Rose and Mont Blanc and served as John Paul II's home base for visiting villages in the valley. He enjoyed watching the fireworks in Savoy across the border in France on Bastille Day. The new chalet, which Salesian fathers had built for a winter vacation camp, came with an elevator—an important detail for the Pope, who was already having trouble climbing stairs. The two Polish nuns were housed there. The Pontiff's skeleton staff included the same people who accompanied him to Lorenzago: Msgr. Dziwisz, Angelo Gugel, Dr. Buzzonetti and, less often, his press secretary, Joaquin Navarro-Valls. Their quarters were in the lumberjacks' and forest rangers' summer school, which, like the chalet, was rented from the local diocese. The old stone oven had been put in working order for the distinguished guest, and everyone enjoyed lettuce, potatoes, leeks, beets and berries from the Salesian fathers' kitchen garden.

The village stood on the edge of Gran Paradiso National Park at the foot of the Sasso Croce. The locals respected the Holy Father's privacy and tried not to disturb him, but the more down-to-earth municipal government cleverly managed to make the most of his presence, building a small museum with pictures, papal medals and exotic souvenirs he had given them.

The Pope's stays in Combes and Lorenzago were strictly private, but to avoid letting down the faithful he recited the Sunday Angelus with them at least once during the 10 or so days he spent there. Up to 5,000 people crammed into cars as early as 7:30 A.M. in order to attend the service, and all the meadows became parking lots by noon. The Holy Father sat on a wooden platform as a choir of local children sang songs to welcome him. He always delivered a brief speech to thank the local officials and warmly mentioned the place with words such as, "Combes is a quiet spot where the body's strength is restored and the spirit can focus on reflection and contemplation" before voicing his usual compassion by saying something like, "I am thinking especially about those who cannot afford a vacation and had to stay home. I send my blessings to the sick, the elderly, prisoners and the lonely."

In 2000, 2001 and especially 2004, the ceremony was cut short and contact with the public reduced. A complex operation kept a close eye on John Paul II day and night: forest rangers, unmarked cars, police officers with dogs, plainclothes

Vatican agents (inevitably given away by their walkie-talkies), an ambulance for emergencies and an air force hospital helicopter stood by to deal with any eventuality.

In those summers, the Pope did not take rides in his big Mercedes or Range Rover but settled for very short walks in the mountains, which he reached by helicopter with his friend, theologian Tadeusz Styczen, who came to spend a few days with him.

On vacation the Pope celebrated mass at 8 A.M., prayed, read his breviary, said complines, napped in an armchair and, like Saint Francis of Assisi, listened to the song of nature. He also read works about history, philosophy and theology. The man who had once taught social ethics in the theology department at Jagiellonian University and the philosophical ethics of Saint Thomas Aquinas, Kant and Scheler in his "Act and Experience" classes at the Catholic University of Lublin took advantage of these moments of solitude and serenity to reflect on themes that would nurture his future speeches. He also wrote down his thoughts on projects he cared about, such as an upcoming bishop's synod, an important anniversary in Church history or a message to participants at an upcoming convention. The Popes, who seldom gave interviews, usually communicated with the faithful through universal messages in the form of encyclicals, bulls, apostolic letters and official speeches. John Paul II prepared such important texts in the quiet mountains, a place of intense meditation for him.

Msgr. Tadeusz Styczen is fond of telling the story about the time Karol Wojtyla, who was still archbishop of Krakow, asked him to accompany him to the Tatra Mountains. Msgr. Styczen spent the night on a train to join him before they left together, walking for hours in a religious silence that was almost unbearable for him; he had not seen the archbishop in a long time. Karol was so absorbed in his thoughts that they walked into Czechoslovakia without even realizing it before they were stopped by two stern, armed border guards, who had a hard time believing that the rugged man in gray mountaineering trousers was one of the Polish Church's highest dignitaries.

Even on vacation, the Supreme Pontiff filled every moment. "If he wasn't praying or studying," his friend Franciszek Cardinal Marcharski told me several times, "he had the feeling that he was wasting his time." In 1999, he taught a Christian ecology class to people from the Lorenzago area.

"I have pondered man's role in the cosmos," he said. "Humans have a special responsibility toward the environment not just for their day-to-day survival but for what they will leave future generations. The great foundations of ecology are to be found in the Bible. One day after the next, it is necessary not only to uphold and preserve earthly values, but also to ensure that that they develop harmoniously. The mountains are an admirable landscape and almost a school of life. You learn to tire yourself to reach halfway. Sometimes you help each other to overcome challenges and measure the relativity of one's being." The text was widely repeated and circulated afterwards.

Since the days when John Paul II was still in full possession of his physical powers, his breaks in the mountains and skiing holidays in the Alps and Apennines had made his love for the peaks familiar to the public. As the years went by, he convinced people that a Pope was also entitled to real vacations and that, believe it or not, he could wear something other than an immaculate cassock, a white caplet, a wide sash of the same color, thick socks and maroon slip-on shoes. The Holy Father had gradually reclaimed his freedom since his first getaway on July 16 and 17, 1984, when, in an anorak, black and white trousers, matching cap and red Nordica boots, he went up 3,035 meters to ski down a glacier. That break in the Trentino-Alto Adigio would probably have gone unnoticed. The Pope wanted to visit the Adamello-range glacier incognito, but the interior minister, not daring to assume the heavy responsibility for his safety alone, informed the head of state, Sandro Pertini. Karol Wojtyla was not just the Supreme Pontiff; he was also a head of state on foreign soil and therefore could not move about without the security forces' knowledge. The popular, 88-year-old Pertini decided to accompany the Pope and invited him to use the presidential plane, which brought the affair out into the open. They rode up to the top of the slopes in a snowcat to avoid the public's prying eyes.

Armed with amazing willpower, John Paul II blazed a new trail as Pope, even managing to have the Roman curia accept extraordinary new behavior that probably would have scandalized them just 20 years before. He also managed public opinion with matchless skill. Once, it would have been impossible to picture the head of the Roman Catholic Church on a pair of narrow Austrian skis, like Valéry Giscard d'Estaing or John F. Kennedy. His frail, pallid, out-of-breath forerunners moved with an implacable, majestic slowness, as though carrying the weight of the world on their shoulders required a pace of life incompatible with a minimum amount of exercise.

On August 26, 1979, shortly after his election, the Pope

went to Canale d'Agordo, his predecessor's hometown near Venice, to pay tribute to John Paul I and meet his family. Helmut Schmaltzl, the future coach of Italy's national ski team, gave him a daring, unusual gift: a superb pair of white skis, entirely handmade by a famous woodworker from Cortina d'Ampezzo. That morning, AFP Vatican correspondent Bruno Bartoloni told the coach that he should have given His Holiness flowers or a painting. How could he have pictured a Pope zooming down ski slopes surrounded by bodyguards?

Harboring the secret hope that John Paul II would pass the peculiar gift on to him, Bartoloni disingenuously asked the Supreme Pontiff, "Most Holy Father, do you think you will put on that pair of skis one day?"

"Every morning I pray to heaven to avoid that temptation," replied the 264th Bishop of Rome, who, to the journalist's great disappointment, kept the skis. The rest is history.

Shortly afterwards, Bartoloni did receive a gift from the Pope: a photograph, signed by the Pope, of Arturo Mari standing next to the Holy Father and holding his skis. This was not much of a consolation for the journalist, who said that the precious picture was enchanting but admitted he would have been even happier if the Pope had signed the skis themselves and given them to him.

John Paul II had won the right to regularly treat himself to a sporting break in the mountains. This new approach to papal vacations prompted a journalist to ask him whether he thought "the Vatican was like a gilded prison." The Pope replied, "It took that prison for me to appreciate my freedom better!"

Even in his later years, John Paul II enjoyed sneaking off.

For example, on April 4, 2000, no sooner was he back from a journey to the Holy Land when he disappeared for a day without telling anyone. At 5:30 A.M. he secretly escaped from Rome in a black BMW with tinted windows driven by his second chauffeur, Piero Cicchetti, a former bus driver who had been in charge of his "noble" garage, with Msgr. Dziwisz, Dr. Buzzonetti, Angelo Gugel and the head of the *vigilanza*, Camillo Cibin. Nobody knows where they went. Anybody who asked came up against a wall of silence. "There was a spot of personal freedom that we had no information about," they told me at the Vatican. The Holy Father often ran away like that. One of his bucolic escapades took place during a searing heat wave on July 14, 2003, when he managed to sneak away by car to an unknown destination without journalists or anyone at the Vatican finding out about it. By that time he was already confined to a wheelchair; these getaways made him feel as though he were just like anyone else.

Each summer, John Paul II took a more traditional vacation at the stately, 25-plus room papal villa in Castel Gandolfo, perched 380 meters above sea level on an extinct volcano's gently sloping hillside. Popes have been using this noble palace, located exactly 30 kilometers from the Campodoglio in Rome (distances to the capital have been measured from that spot since ancient times), for centuries. This was actually a semi-vacation, because the Pope flew back to the Vatican by helicopter every Wednesday for the general audience.

During his stay, which always lasted around two months, the Pope's entourage was limited to his inner circle: Msgr. Dziwisz, Angelo Gugel, Sister Tobiana, the Ursuline librarian Sister Emilia (the other sisters often went back to Poland on vacation), 10 or so Swiss Guards and gendarmes, and some 50 people who kept up the estate's 50-hectare grounds and model farm, which was run by Giuseppe Bellapadrona. The group included neither prelates nor *monsignori* from the Vatican staff.

Every year on about August 15, John Paul II entertained a few old friends from Poland at Castel Gandolfo, receiving them more casually than in Rome—the mood was much more relaxed than at the Vatican. The guests included Jerzy Kluger, various intellectuals and philosophers, old acquaintances and the Polish bishops with whom he reshaped the Catholic world. They arrived with gifts, including bags of irresistible, melt-in-your-mouth *Krowka Popularna* caramels and chocolates that the Holy Father handed out to young people who came to visit. These were the friends with whom he enjoyed joking and laughing. He often asked them to imitate various central European accents, especially Romanian and Russian, and to let him in on the latest jokes about Saint Peter and his famous keys. When a group of young Polish pilgrims came to visit in August 2000, he even imitated Charlie Chaplin, twirling his cane!

Apparently, the Poles are accustomed to this kind of humor, which can be quite crude at times. John Paul II was obviously happy to spend time with his countrymen. On July 10, 2003, Cardinal Poupard had lunch with him at Castel Gandolfo. "That day," he told me, "I said to the Pope, 'Most Holy Father, today there are just three things I would like to discuss with Your Holiness: Oslo, Nagasaki and Moscow.'"

"'Just three things?' the Pope replied. 'That's not much for a French cardinal! Aren't you feeling well today?'

"Another time, when I was the only non-Pole, the Supreme Pontiff appointed one of his guests to act as an interpreter for me. But once in a while he made a sign not to translate certain comments because they were too Slavic!"

Officially, John Paul II was on vacation at Castel Gandolfo and the curia's activities slowed down, but he nevertheless always rose early. The Pope, who enjoyed watching the sun come up, celebrated mass at 7:30 A.M., slightly different from the time he did so in Rome. Some 20 people, including his entourage and guests passing through, attended the services. By sheer providential coincidence, the chapel is dedicated to the Black Virgin of Czestochowa, so highly venerated by Poles. A reproduction of the icon hangs above the altar flanked by two windows with white and gold diamond panes. Art Nouveau frescoes on the right wall depict "the Miracle of the Vistula," honoring the Polish troops' defeat of the Red Army on August 14, 1920. In another coincidence, Pius XI, who was once the papal nuncio in Warsaw, had the chapel decorated the year Karol Wojtyla was born.

After mass, John Paul II often asked a few people from the congregation to stay for a copious breakfast of tea, coffee, fruit juice, milk from his farm, rolls, scrambled eggs with wild herbs, cheese, bacon, butter and jam made with fruit from the orchard, including peaches and apricots from Castel Gandolfo, which are famous for their size and flavor. Then the Pope would take leave of his guests to rest because of the hot, often muggy weather. Sometimes he walked alone on the terrace, where in June 2001 he greeted George W. Bush, the 43rd president of the United States and a Methodist who claims to read the Bible every day, and showed him the beautiful view of the lake. Sometimes he skimmed his breviary or books in the author's language. Even when he was on vacation, John Paul II read one and a half hours per day and almost always had a rosary in his hand. At his office in the pontifical palace or beneath the shade trees in the garden, he also immersed himself in his dossiers, consulting some for the first time and rereading others that he did not have enough time to focus on during the other 10 months of the year.

Every morning, Msgr. Dziwisz compiled a press review. If the Holy Father was in good form, he commented on what journalists had to say about him—something he never did in Rome. His secretary kept him abreast of world events, and every other year John Paul II gathered political scientists, clergymen, laymen and philosophers for a casual two-day seminar. Sometimes he invited writers, such as André Frossard. When this author and *Le Figaro* journalist went to see him at Easter one year at Castel Gandolfo with Patrick Poivre d'Arvor, who was making a documentary about the Holy Father, the following memorable dialogue took place:

"We're having lunch together on Wednesday, aren't we?" asked the Pope.

"Yes, Most Holy Father," replied Frossard. "As I have already told your secretary, my wife, Simone, will be coming with me."

"I'll be coming with Sister Emilia," replied John Paul II.

Who was this mysterious "insider" nun at the Pope's side? She was the Vatican archivist and librarian whom he had "loaned" to Frossard when he was writing *Dialogue With John Paul II* in 1982, earning her the nickname "Miss Frossard" in the Holy See at the time.

When John Paul II could still take long walks, there was no place on the 50-hectare estate—bigger than Vatican City—where one might not run into him. He enjoyed ambling along the avenues criss-crossing the 16 different flowerbeds. The Supreme Pontiff walked everywhere, from the Italian garden to the mirror garden, the citrus orchard and the Little Virgin grove surrounded by cypress trees. Sometimes he even went to the farm, which was laid out by Pius XI. At other times, he invited Boy Scouts, pilgrims, Catholic students, seminarians and groups of young people in for refreshments, although that happened with decreasing frequency as time went on. Often the guests were Polish, and he spoke to them in their native language. Early in his pontificate, the astonished staff thought he was talking to them in Latin!

During the 15th World Youth Days in August 2000, John Paul II hosted 15 young people from Italy, Canada, Tahiti, Guinea and Sri Lanka at the Castel Gandolfo estate. They had breakfast with him in the ochre palace and shared a typical Italian meal with ham, melon, pasta, cakes and red wine. The Pope sat at the head of a horseshoe-shaped table so that everyone could see him better. These meals, which were more casual than in Rome, let him keep in touch with young people and the outside world without forgetting that, as he liked to remind them, his most important function was as a priest.

Every year during Easter ceremonies, John Paul II secretly sat in one of Saint Peter's imposing, solid-oak confessionals like a simple, black-caped vicar to hear the confessions of 12 people (for the number of apostles) chosen at random. At Castel Gandolfo, he alternated between meditating, praying and working. Even on vacation, he still had to make decisions, write apostolic letters and plan journeys. And despite the odd, end-of-an-era mood of the last years, when newspapers were running "Who will succeed John Paul II?" headlines, he continued his spiritual exercises.

His office might have been a table in a shady corner of the garden or the little room next to his bedroom where he enjoyed the quiet and the view of Lake Albano. The massive palace's thick walls always kept it cool. The Pope, who was accustomed to Poland's icy lakes, disliked hot weather but could not bear air-conditioning, except in the Popemobile. That is one reason why he suffered so much from the heat wave just before his exhausting journey to Slovakia, September 11–14, 2003.

At Castel Gandolfo, John Paul II never had lunch at the same time: that material detail mattered less than spiritual and intellectual nourishment. He only drank half a glass of white wine, usually *castelli romani*, a dry local vintage, cut with water. The Pontiff ate more lightly than in the mountains because it was so hot. A typical lunch consisted of soup, vegetables, salad and fruit, followed by a short nap. He also relaxed by taking incognito strolls in the surrounding area. Or he would take the elevator leading directly to the garage, get into a navy blue, unmarked Lancia, Mercedes or BMW with the ever-present Dziwisz and Angelo Gugel and take a little ride in the hills. Toward the end he almost always used the big Mercedes because he could stay in his wheelchair, which was hoisted into the vehicle.

When John Paul II went to Rome for the Wednesday general audience, he first rode down an avenue thickly lined with admirably pruned oak and yew trees to the garden, where a beautiful blue and white helicopter was waiting for him next to the henhouse (the noise never disturbed their laying). Some 20 minutes later he landed in the Vatican gardens near Saint John's Tower, where a Fiat, Lancia Thesis or white Toyota SUV was waiting to drive him to Saint Peter's Square. (In the last two years of his life, the Pope no longer took the helicopter because it was less convenient: once his wheelchair was settled in the Mercedes he no longer had to move until reaching Saint Peter's, sparing him the anxiety and inconvenience of having to be transferred from the vehicle to the chopper.) John Paul II put on two "apostolic shows" a day for as long as he could, one inside the basilica, the other outside in the square. He had to satisfy the huge throng of pilgrims and tourists so eager to catch a glimpse of him. At around 1 P.M. the helicopter would whisk the Holy Father back to the pontifical villa, where all the local officials greeted him on his return.

Castel Gandolfo looks more like a Renaissance palace than a big vacation villa. The first-floor apartments, which Karol Wojtyla liked very much, were elegantly plain, but the second floor featured a series of interconnecting ceremonial suites, including the Consistory Room, Swiss Hall and many others with tall windows, harmonious pastel tones, frescoes and lavish multicolored marble floors—it almost resembles the Vatican. But the swimming pool that John Paul II had built, covered with a molded plastic dome to let in sunlight, could not be more contemporary. "How dare he have a modern pool dug in this majestic park instead of a noble stone one?" the Roman curia's senior prelates grumbled.

As early as the summer of 1979, John Paul II decided that, although he had to abide by the centuries-old rule of spending his vacation a few miles from the Vatican, nothing in the Bible or the four Gospels according to Saints Matthew, Mark, Luke and John forbids Saint Peter's successor from enjoying sports. Although Karol Wojtyla liked mountain climbing more than swimming, he nevertheless took a dip at Palidoro Beach, 15 kilometers from Fiumicino Airport, on October 15, 1978, the day before his election. The Institute of the Holy Spirit had created this seaside resort for cardinals, bishops and priests some 40 years previously. The future Pope enjoyed it so much that, almost immediately after his election, he questioned the permanent staff about the Vatican's sports facilities. The only thing, they firmly replied, was a rundown tennis court near the Vatican museums. John Paul II asked them to rehabilitate the court, which he never used for lack of time and partners. Nobody dared to play against him. The Italian cardinals waxed indignant at the idea that a Pole with an unpronounceable name, the first non-Italian Pope since Adrian VI in 1522, had the nerve to take an interest in sports just because he used to go skiing at Zakopane, mountain climbing in the Tatras and hiking and kayaking with students when he was a chaplain in Krakow. The idea seemed so daring and far-fetched that it nearly scandalized the Holy See's Italian hierarchy. Yet they had to get used to it, for the Pope is not only the spiritual leader of the world's Roman Catholics but also the temporal head of a sovereign state. His arms and portrait are everywhere in the Holy See, much as a picture of France's president hangs in every one of the country's town halls and many of its official buildings.

Why wouldn't this strong-willed head of state with the stubborn chin usher in a new, more relaxed style, with or without the curia's support? Fortunately, when a group of wealthy Canadian Catholics found out that a Pope in the prime of life—he was only 58—was disappointed at not being able to practice sports, they immediately donated funds for a swimming pool. But should it be built inside Vatican City or at Castel Gandolfo? John Paul II unhesitatingly chose his summer residence because, first, the grounds were more extensive than at the Vatican, and second, he could swim far from the prying eyes of grumbling prelates and the telephoto lenses of *paparazzi*.

The director-general of the Vatican's technical departments unsuccessfully tried to counter the plan. John Paul II simply told advisors who dared to criticize his decision that a swimming pool would be less expensive than another conclave. Of course, the Pope eventually took full advantage of the right to don his thick, black bathing trunks and do the breaststroke in his private, 16-meter-long, eight-meter-wide pool—swimming in an outdated style, people said. He stopped in 1994 after breaking his femur and, in another fall later that year, his collarbone, despite advice from Dr. Buzzonetti, who stressed how important exercise was in strengthening muscle tone after such accidents. From then on, the pool became the exclusive domain of the Swiss Guards and gendarmes. There again, John Paul II stood in sharp contrast to his forerunners by making Vatican facilities available for staff use.

At the Sunday Angelus, the Pope greeted pilgrims in his residence's huge inner courtyard, shielded from the heat by an elegant, oatmeal-colored canopy. Sometimes a young people's orchestra gave a little concert in his honor, which absolutely delighted him. But toward the end John Paul II's face betrayed pain and fatigue that could no longer be hidden from the public eye. When I was invited to Castel Gandolfo, without a photographer, in August 1996, I noticed how much the heat seemed to bother him. It was painful for me to see how much he suffered under all those layers of vestments, even though they were made of light fabric.

The pilgrims saw the Holy Father before he invited a lucky few to tour the grounds and admire the various buildings of the Villa Barberini, a noble, nearly 1-sq-km estate that has served as the Popes' summer residence since the 17th century. Before then, they rested in their cardinals' lavish palaces around Rome. The villa was named after Prince Barberini, the future Pope Urban VIII, who had his aristocratic family's residence built between 1624 and 1629, inaugurating the tradition of pontifical vacations in Castel Gandolfo. It stands on the ruins of one the Roman emperor Domitian's villas and is bordered by Lake Albano on one side and the Roman countryside on the other. Over 20 Popes have summered there, fleeing the heat of the Eternal City. The tradition was broken from 1878 to 1934: Pius IX, Leon XIII, Pius X, Benedict XV and Pius XI could not or would not leave the Vatican until the Lateran Accords were signed on February 11, 1929, by Cardinal Gaspari on behalf of Pope Pius XI and Mussolini on behalf of King Victor-Emmanuel III. By the terms of the agreement, the Holy See recognized the Italian state with Rome as its capital, and the Italian state recognized the Pope's sovereignty over the Vatican.

The Roman question was definitively settled and recognized by the concert of nations, and a tiny new state was born. John Paul II commemorated the historic event's 75th anniversary on

February 11, 2004, by saying, "These accords marked a positive turning point in the history of Church-State relations in Italy." On the eve of his 84th birthday, Karol Wojtyla, as politically minded as ever, took advantage of the occasion to respond to several small leftist parties that regularly demanded a referendum to abolish the Concordat between the state and the Roman Catholic Church. The Pope diplomatically reminded political leaders during an audience that "although the Lateran Treaty is and must remain untouchable, the Vatican is open to later revisions"—after he left the stage, of course.

Pius XII revived the reassuring, pleasant tradition of papal summering at Castel Gandolfo. He started out by tastefully restoring the palace and outbuildings that had remained abandoned for nearly half a century. The Pope had the gardens redesigned and planted with superb Mediterranean vegetation. Pius XII spent his first vacation at Castel Gandolfo and started going back on a regular basis in 1938, when he cleverly advanced his departure date to avoid being in Rome on the historic day when Hitler visited Mussolini. On August 24, 1939, the Pope delivered a message from Castel Gandolfo that he hoped would thwart the Second World War: "Nothing is lost with peace," he said. "Everything can be lost with war."

By war's end, Castel Gandolfo had housed up to 12,000 refugees and the Pope's apartment had been turned into a maternity hospital where 44 children were born. The harmonious crypt of the church designed by Bernini served as an air raid shelter, for bombs did not spare the Pope's residence, which suffered heavy damage after the Allies landed at Anzio.

The solitary, aristocratic Pius XII did not return until 1947 to the Villa Barberini, where he died on October 9, 1958, and

20 years later, on August 6, 1978, it was the shy Paul VI's turn. Both Pontiffs drafted their most important encyclicals in the shade of the papal estate's tall cypress trees.

State-of-the-art medical facilities were set up at Castel Gandolfo following the attempt on John Paul II's life; doctors had to keep a close eye on his shaky health. The two nearest hospitals were always on high alert when he was in residence. On August 4, 1996, the Holy Father was rushed to the one in Albano for an emergency scan. A military hospital helicopter with two pilots, a doctor and a nurse was always stationed a few hundred meters from the palace. Dr. Buzzonetti juggled the schedules of the eight doctors, who had the heavy responsibility of monitoring the world's most famous patient in shifts.

Twenty-four hours a day, seven days a week, a powerful radio antenna linked the police office in Castel Gandolfo with the Ministry of the Interior in Rome.

John Paul II was a star, and the whole world was fascinated with his vacations. Pictures of his athletic exploits always sold for high prices. In 1979, a photograph of the new Pope skiing fetched the equivalent of €365,000, or around $470,000, before going around the world. From *Newsweek* to *Paris Match*, the most austere newspapers to the greatest international weeklies tried to outbid each other for pictures of him skiing in the Alps. After Italian press magnate Angelo Rizzoli paid about $774,000 for a few indiscreet pictures of the Pope swimming, he fell all over himself trying to get the Vatican to forgive him. Rizzoli, who was rumored to be involved in the murky P2 Masonic lodge scandal, gave the negatives to John Paul II's entourage in the hopes of buying himself a place in heaven, or at least shortening his stay in purgatory. The pictures were never published, but a few weeks later several famous magazines published photographs of Karol Wojtyla in black swim trunks, but they had been taken at Palidoro, the clergy's famous beach, on the day before he became Pope.

The shots of an athletic John Paul II were a far cry from the allegorical paintings of the past depicting pallid Pontiffs, stuffed into very heavy, gold-embroidered papal vestments encrusted with precious stones, riding in carts drawn by four white mules or coaches escorted by courtiers and soldiers on horseback as villagers bore them gifts in wicker baskets or red leather cases.

John Paul II, one of the 20th century's greatest performers, was never photographed with his donkey, which a humble Brazilian, Damiao Galdino da Silva, a driver at Brazil's senate, proudly gave him during a visit to his country in 1980. After much expense and trouble, the little ass that looked like something straight out of the Bible eventually reached the freight terminal at Fiumicino, Rome's international airport. The Holy Father donated the creature to a Franciscan community near the capital, surprising the Vatican, where everyone thought he would put it out to pasture at Castel Gandolfo. Later, a cardinal half-jokingly confided to me that the Pope had told him, "It's not worth keeping him; there are already enough asses at the Vatican!"

Chapter Eight

JOHN PAUL II, BISHOP OF ROME—THE THIRD SECRET OF FATIMA

On my many Vatican visits, I noticed John Paul II's fervent devotion to the Virgin of Fatima. Convinced that she had saved his life during the 1981 assassination attempt, he demonstrated his gratitude on numerous occasions. What's more, the Pope thought that the famous third message of Fatima was a prophetic warning of the attempt on his life.

On June 26, 2000, the Vatican astounded the Christian world by disclosing the third message that the Virgin had given three Portuguese shepherd children at Fatima on May 13, 1917. The first two were about the First World War and the "conversion" of Russia. In the third message, which several Popes had kept secret, Mary predicted, "A bishop dressed in white would be shot."

Many people saw a link with the attempt on John Paul II's life during the Wednesday audience in Saint Peter's Square at 5:17 P.M. on May 13, 1981.

The Holy Father saw the connection almost immediately. He was convinced that the Virgin had deflected the bullets fired by Ali Agca, a professional killer according to the Vatican, telling the faithful gathered in Saint Peter's Square a few weeks later, "Divine Providence, by the intercession of the Very Holy Mother, saved the Pope's life."

When John Paul II visited Agca in prison on December 27, 1983, the Turkish terrorist, who considered himself an infallible sharpshooter, told the Pope that he was amazed at not having killed him despite firing two lead-filled hollow-point bullets from a 9-mm Browning at almost point-blank range—less than six meters. The shot was so loud that it sent the startled pigeons in Saint Peter's Square fluttering into the sky. In what could only be called a miracle, the bullets missed the Pope's vital organs by less than a centimeter.

Not a minute was wasted to save John Paul II's life. The office of the Prefect of the Congregation of Bishops was just above Saint Peter's Square on the second floor, the nuns' apartment on the first. They screamed so loudly that the prefect immediately alerted all the emergency services. The ambulance quickly reached the Gemelli Polyclinic, where an operating room had just been prepped for a Juventus soccer player who had suffered a stomach injury but could wait a few hours because his life was not in danger. The Pope was immediately rushed into the operating room.

From 6 P.M. to 11:25 P.M., surgeons operated on the Pontiff's intestines, right elbow and left index finger. Msgr.

Dziwisz, to whom John Paul II managed to mutter, "My stomach hurts," as he was being wheeled through the clinic's courtyard, was the first person to point out the amazing coincidence between the shooting's date, May 13, 1981, and the date of the Virgin's first appearance to the little shepherds of Fatima on May 13, 1917.

John Paul II asked Msgr. Dziwisz to bring him the third message delivered by the Virgin to Francesco and Jacinta Marto, which had been in the Vatican archives since April 4, 1957, but which none of his predecessors had ever revealed. The Pope received two envelopes, one yellow, the other white. The yellow one contained the third secret, which the little shepherd girl Lucia Dos Santos wrote in Portuguese at her bishop's request. The white one contained the Italian translation. John Paul II unsealed it and read the following lines: "A bishop dressed in white, whom we had the feeling was the Pope, and various other bishops, priests and monks . . . climbed to the top of a steep mountain, where there was a cross . . . The Holy Father, afflicted by pain and suffering . . . prayed for the souls of the victims he found on the way. When he reached the top, a group of soldiers shot him to death."

When John Paul II read this prophetic text, he started associating the Virgin's apparitions at Fatima with the date of the assassination attempt. The Pope spoke with increasing frequency of the miraculous healing that the Madonna of Fatima had made possible. There was no longer any doubt in his mind: he was the bishop dressed in white, but he survived—the Virgin had saved his life. Later, the Pontiff pointed out that the attack had played a providential role in his life because, he said, "Throughout my long days of suffering, I gave much thought to what it meant, to this mysterious sign that came to me like a gift from heaven."

By the time of the attack's first anniversary, John Paul II was convinced that an invisible power had protected him. That is why he went to Fatima to thank the Virgin. On March 25, 1983, the Feast of the Annunciation, the Pope had the statue of Mary that commemorated the apparitions at Fatima brought to Rome and exhibited for 48 hours for the veneration of the faithful, first in Saint Peter's Basilica and then in Saint John Lateran, the cathedral of the Bishop of Rome. Two days later, the Bishop of Leiria, Msgr. Alberto Cosme do Amaral, escorted it back to Fatima along with a small chest bearing the Pope's coat of arms that contained one of the bullets Ali Agca fired. Later, the bullet was set among the precious stones in the Virgin's golden crown; in another amazing coincidence, the hole was just the right size.

On May 13, 1991, John Paul II returned to Fatima for the attack's 10th anniversary. In May 2000, he went back again to beatify two of the Portuguese children, Francisco and Jacinta Marto. (The third child, Lucia Dos Santos, a nun in Coimbra, was still alive. In February 2005 she passed away in her convent at the age of 97. Portugal observed a day of national mourning to honor Sister Lucia, the last surviving shepherd child who had seen the Virgin in 1917.) During the pilgrimage, he repeated his profession of faith: "One hand fired the shot, another deflected the bullet." He was referring to the third secret, which the Vatican fully disclosed six weeks later, adding, "The other secrets of Fatima involved the 'conversion' of Russia, which is what happened with the fall of the Soviet Union and is unmistakably a miracle."

The Virgin Mary had always had a special place in Karol

Wojtyla's heart: at 15, he was already a member of Poland's Marial Society. John Paul II did not devote his arms to Mary for aesthetic or heraldic reasons, as many of his predecessors had done. Like every Pope, he had to choose a motto and blazon expressing his calling. He kept the ones he had adopted upon becoming Bishop of Krakow in 1964: *Totus tuus ego sum et omnia mea tua sunt* ("I am completely yours, and everything that is mine is yours") and a cross with the letter "M" signifying his devotion to Christ through Mary, for she was the road that led Karol Wojtyla to Him; she remained standing at the foot of the cross. The Holy Father's faith in her was so steadfast that his doctors at the Gemelli Polyclinic, many of whom were fervent believers and strictly observant Christians, sought to convince him to take it easy and not rely on any more miracles. They had all the trouble in the world trying to talk him into lightening his workload and focusing only on major events. Trusting in the Virgin, whom he venerated more than ever, the Pope serenely and stubbornly refused to curtail the efforts he devoted to his pastoral mission, except for his vacations. The Virgin, he thought, had been shielding him from harm ever since he had decided to devote his life to her. He ceaselessly displayed his gratitude, making 108 visits in 26 years to shrines dedicated to her, from Guadalupe, Mexico, to Czestochowa and Kalwarià Zebrzydowska, Poland; Fatima, Portugal; Pompeii, Italy; Lourdes, France, in August 2004; and Loreto, Italy, a month later. For a long time, these visits were physical feats, but then they actually became ordeals. In October 2003, the Holy Father returned from his second journey to Slovakia (his first was in October 1979). As soon as he was back in Rome, the exhausted Pope went to pray at the shrine of the Virgin at the archaeological site of Pompeii, a short day trip to conclude the Year of the Rosary.

Not everyone at the Vatican shared John Paul II's faith in the Virgin's apparition at Fatima. His predecessors John XXIII and Paul VI voiced doubts about the "miracle."

At a June 2000 press conference, Joseph Cardinal Ratzinger, prefect of the Congregation for the Doctrine of the Faith—which once bore the evocative name of the Holy Office—dean of the Sacred College and future Pope Benedict XVI, said that "the revelations of visions such as those that have occurred at Fatima and Lourdes are a message that can be a genuine help in understanding the Gospel and living it in a better way at a particular moment in time; therefore, it should not be disregarded. It is a help that is offered, but that one is not obliged to use. The criterion for the truth and value of a private revelation is therefore its orientation to Christ himself."

The wording is somewhat elliptical, but what Cardinal Ratzinger meant is that every believer has the right to interpret these "miracles" as he or she sees fit. Nowadays, however, the event in question must overcome a series of hurdles in order to be certified a proper miracle. First, the phenomenon is submitted to the scrutiny of a scientific committee, including agnostics, before being approved by the prelates belonging to the Congregation for the Causes of Saints and, subsequently, the cardinals of that institution meeting in the presence of the Pope, who signs the decree authenticating it.

John Paul II created more saints and declared more people blessed than any other Pope in history. He beatified 1,338 individuals and canonized 482 of the 800 saints proclaimed by the Pontiffs who had preceded him since the late 16th century. Pius X (1903–1914) celebrated two canonizations and 13 beatifications; Benedict XV (1914–1922) two and seven, respectively; Pius XI (1922–1939) 14 and 15; Pius XII (1939–1958) 21 and 52; John XXIII (1958–1963) seven and five; Paul VI (1963–1978) 20 and 30. The unlucky John Paul I's reign was so short that he had no time to canonize or beatify anyone. Prior to the 16th century, the saints were proclaimed by popular vote. Pope Paul VI removed from the list a dozen who had never existed, including Saint Christopher; others, such as Saint George, were eliminated from the Roman calendar.

John Paul II regularly made pilgrimages to Marial shrines, including Beauraing, Belgium; Kevelaer, Germany; Ta'Pinu, Malta; Maastricht, the Netherlands; and Marierzell, Austria, which is also an important place of prayer for Hungarians, Slovaks, Slovenians, Croats and Czechs. Talking about John Paul II's visit to Marierzell on September 13, 1983, the Cardinal of Vienna, Christopher Schönborn, said, "The Holy Father looked as though he never stopped praying. I never saw anyone so constantly immersed in union with Christ and God, as though it were a permanent state that led him to submit everything he did into the Lord's hands. His attentiveness to others, his gestures, words and readings—everything he did was bathed in prayer, like the great mystics."

John Paul II sent the wide, white, bloodstained waistband that he was wearing when he was shot to the shrine of the Black Virgin in Czestochowa. When I went there in August 2000, I was unable to see the garment because the Pauline brothers kept it under wraps in the keen expectation of receiving specific instructions from the Pope one day.

With fervent but secret patriotism, Karol Wojtyla had always venerated the shrine of the Black Virgin of Czestochowa, which lies approximately 100 kilometers northwest of Krakow. The site is an object of immeasurable devotion in Poland, where 92% of the people are baptized Catholics and 50% are regular churchgoers. The Church hierarchy and the faithful alike consider her Poland's patron saint and queen. Hundreds of thousands of pilgrims make their way to Czestochowa to celebrate a mass in her honor several times a year. A monk in Jasna Gora monastery says that the throngs that gather for the Feast of the Virgin Mary hail not only from all over Poland, but also from neighboring countries. When *Solidarnosc* (the Solidarity movement) came into being, the Black Virgin became such an important rallying point for the trade unions that Lech Walesa even wore a pin with her image on his jacket lapel. She is still a symbol of hope for the deeply religious Poles. Her image always figures prominently on floral crosses that people lay anonymously at the foot of religious monuments. The Madonna of Czestochowa means much more to Poles than the Virgin of Lourdes does to the French, who do not consider her a symbol of the nation.

I was surprised during my visit to the shrine. Poland is a still a deeply impoverished country, yet the basilica is flamboyant, lavish and luxurious. In fact, so are most Polish churches, which are usually packed for mass three times a day. Most striking is the pilgrims' youth and fervor. I saw dozens of Karol Wojtylas in the making: little blond-haired, blue-eyed boys lighting candles with ecstatic expressions on their faces. Pilgrims of all ages walk, cycle and even ride horses hundred of kilometers to reach the shrine. I saw thanksgiving plaques from sailors, former Resistance fighters and Solidarity activists. Belarussians, Czechs, Lithuanians, Latvians, Ukrainians and Slovaks who cannot afford a journey to Rome travel to Czestochowa, accounting for many of the 5 million pilgrims who make the trip there each year.

In 1957, when Stefan Cardinal Wyszynski—the primate of the Polish episcopate, leader of the Church's spiritual resistance in his country, and a great religious figure in his own right—wanted to have the Black Virgin circulate throughout Poland, the Communists sequestered the portrait for six years. Only the empty frame, with a lit candle symbolically flickering in the middle, traveled from village to village, visiting 10,000 parishes in nine years.

The pious Poles pamper their places of worship. Consequently, museums have always been bursting at the seams with gifts from various other museums. The poorest farmers have given their only precious possession (usually a gold watch), Marie Curie gave her rosary and Prince Radziwill his 16th-century rock-crystal rosary.

In November 2003, Cardinal Jozef Glemp, the primate of Poland, visited Paris to meet the members of the Polish mission in France: 122 priests in charge of 72 Polish communities throughout the country. He announced that a Church of the Sacred Heart would be built in Warsaw to fulfill a vow dating back to the late 18th century. "Since that time," he said, "our country's stormy history has kept us from satisfying that vow, but now that we are free and at peace, we can. The future Church of Divine Providence, which is rising in a new part of Warsaw thanks to donations from France, is a sort of replica of Sacré-Cœur Basilica in Montmartre. The first mass will be celebrated when the church is finished on May 2, 2004, the day after Poland joins the European Union."

More recently, wealthy Poles in the United States have given Czestochowa a ciborium set with rubies, emeralds and diamonds. Ingenious Sicilian farmers arrived with a mosaic in pieces that they preferred putting together on-site to avoid difficulties at customs. John XXIII had sent a superb monstrance decorated with precious stones. And the white and gold throne reserved for Karol Wojtyla still sits in a corner of the monastery near the sacristy. A special entrance—a black marble portal surmounted by his arms carved in gold and the papal tiara—was built in his honor.

The Poles' incredible veneration of the Black Virgin stems from the belief that she has always revived their faith and saved Poland from moral shipwreck during its darkest hours. For Polish believers, the icon stands for hope, perseverance and faith in the victorious outcome of an entire people's struggle for freedom. In 1655, it was responsible for a "miracle." Sweden's armies were overrunning Poland's plains, and the country seemed lost—nothing appeared able to save it. Just then, the Pauline order's prior-general, valiant Father Augustine Foredeck, rallied his countrymen beneath the banner of the Black Virgin, and the Poles drove the invaders out of the country. Wounded but victorious, Poland rose from the ashes, and the precious icon has been the emblem of resistance to occupation ever since. The Pauline brothers, Catholic missionaries under the patronage of Saint Paul, jealously guard the portrait, which depicts the Virgin Mary holding the Infant Jesus in her right arm. There are two scars on her right cheek, the work of brigands who looted the monastery in the 15th century. Legend has it that when one of them trampled on the icon and slashed it with a saber, blood gushed from his face and he dropped dead on the floor. The period's finest artists tried to repair the scars, but they always reappeared beneath the coats of paint.

The icon's origins remain shrouded in mystery. Some say the evangelist Saint Luke painted it. Others believe it is a sixth-century Byzantine work. One thing is beyond doubt: Prince Gladiolas of Poole found the portrait in Ruthenium (the western part of present-day Ukraine) and brought it to Czestochowa in the 14th century.

On August 15, 1955, the eve of the "little October Revolution," over 1 million faithful gathered before the monastery where the icon is kept to beseech the Virgin for the release of Cardinal Wyszynski, Karol Wojtyla's spiritual father, from Poland's Stalinist prisons. Their prayers were answered: a year later, the impressive, imposing cardinal was free. This made a deep impression on the young Wojtyla, who harbored deep respect and unfailing admiration for his superior despite occasional personality clashes due to his character and to Wyszynski's authoritarian nature. It was partly due to his influence over the other cardinals, especially the German ones, and his tremendous prestige that John Paul II was elected Pope.

After Wyszynski's death, John Paul II, celebrating mass at the Gemelli Polyclinic, told Msgr. Dziwisz at the moment of the Eucharist, "I will miss him. A long friendship bound me to him. I needed his presence." In a tribute to Poland's primate and to thank Mary for continuing to protect him, on May 13, 2000, John Paul II laid a red leather box containing the ring that the cardinal had given him early in his papacy before the Virgin at Fatima. The ring symbolizes the union and reciprocal fidelity of spouses, who often lay a bouquet of flowers at the foot of a statue of Mary on their wedding day in a symbolic gesture entrusting their destiny to the Virgin. It means the same thing for bishops, and in Poland, thanking the Virgin at a shrine after a wish has been fulfilled or grace obtained is a tradition and a natural response. John Paul II laid the ring he had worn on his right hand, one that thousands of anonymous faithful and famous figures had kissed so many times, at the foot of the Portuguese Virgin. On the day he became Pope, Cardinal Wyszynski prophetically told John Paul II, "The Lord has called you. You must usher the Church into the third millennium"—and by and large, he succeeded.

John Paul II's symbolic, meaningful gesture at Fatima once again took his close entourage by surprise. Neither the secretary of state, Cardinal Sodano, nor the other Church dignitaries (except for Msgr. Dziwisz) were aware of his intentions.

The last time the Pope visited the shrine of Czestochowa was in June 1999. With 15,000 pilgrims in attendance, he knelt in front of the Black Virgin to once more entrust her with his papal mission, dedicate the Polish Church to her and ask her for the precious gifts of peace for humanity and brotherhood among all people. These were insistent repetitions in accordance with his Polish dialectic, whose style Valéry Giscard d'Estaing had understood early in his papacy, listening to him deliver a homily at the end of the mass he had co-celebrated on the huge podium in front of Notre Dame with the bishops of the Ile-de-France and 400 priests in attendance.

"I was struck," Giscard d'Estaing told me, "when, during the homily, he repeated the question Jesus asked the apostle Peter—'Do you love me?'—always going back to the beginning of his speech. It is a less formal, less deductive, more circular form of reasoning than ours. His way of developing his arguments was more classic and more emotional than ours. We go from point A to point B. His eloquence and logic, much more Slavic than Latin, does not draw on Cartesian reasoning. Karol Wojtyla went down side streets and led his people like a walking crowd that was always brought back to the same place."

One of John Paul II's close friends, Msgr. Marini, who was responsible for the liturgical ceremony (and also served as the titular bishop of Martirano), told me about a serious incident at the Vatican that convinced the Pope the Virgin was still protecting him. It was January 6, 1998. John Paul II suddenly had a dizzy spell and nearly collapsed in the Sistine Chapel, where, as he did on Epiphany every year, he was baptizing some 20 babies from various countries. He clutched his heavy silver pastoral cross and staggered, but Msgr. Marini, his reassuring shadow, was there to catch him in time. Once more, although less discreetly than usual because cameras were present, Marini broke his fall, with help from the Virgin Mary. Some 18 years after John Paul II had appointed him master of liturgical celebrations, the benevolent, athletic prelate was skillful enough to brilliantly manage the rest of the religious service while anticipating the Holy Father's every move and never letting him out of his sight.

Msgr. Marini always mentions those moments with tact and modesty, never dwelling on how he protected John Paul II. "At first," he told me, "my biggest concern was making sure the celebrations went off smoothly. But as the years went by, His Holiness became increasingly frail and I had to focus more of my attention on him. Eventually I stopped taking care of the ceremonies altogether. I looked after him with the same conscientiousness and tremendous respect that a family member might show when looking after a close relative. I opened his missal to the right page and showed him which chapter to read. The Pope was so thorough that he had the text read to him line by line prior to every celebration. Toward the end, I held the chalice during communion and made sure that the wind did not lift his liturgical vestments. That's all."

A few days after his fainting spell, the Holy Father stubbornly brushed aside his doctors' advice and visited Assisi to comfort its inhabitants after an earthquake struck the area. His health had visibly declined. John Paul II believed that he had survived the 1981 assassination attempt not only because of his reflexes, Msgr. Dziwisz's cool-headedness and the skills of the surgeon, doctors and hospital staff who had tended to him, but above all because of Divine Providence and the Virgin Mary's protection. "To you, Mary," he used to say, "I entrust the sick, the elderly and the lonely." He was so sure that she would support him until the end that, when his entourage tried to slow him down, he firmly, invariably replied, "If the word has not converted, the blood will."

Just before John Paul II died, a senior figure very close to him told me more about the discreet but historic meeting at Fatima between the Pope and Umberto II of Italy on May 13, 1982.

Umberto II was the king of Italy until June 2, 1946, when he abdicated after the referendum that established the Republic. He lived a good part of the year in Cascais, in southern Portugal, and went to the shrine on May 13, 1982, to assure John Paul II of his profound deference and admiration. The former monarch was quite ill and wanted to tell the Pope that at his death he would bequeath to him the famous Shroud of Turin. His family had owned the precious relic, which was kept in Turin Cathedral, since coming into its possession in 1453; it was their personal property but under the guardianship of the Archbishop of Turin. Umberto sought to both honor John Paul II and change the relic's hybrid status with a flourish. However, he did not want to embarrass the Pope and put him in a situation where he would have to thank him, so he decided not to bring up the subject with the Holy Father and talked to his entourage about it instead. But after King Umberto died in a Geneva hospital on March 18, 1983, his heir and only son, Prince Victor Emmanuel III of Savoy, was in no hurry to inform John Paul II of the donation.

Why did he suddenly feel he had to hasten the transfer of ownership of the relic, which had already passed through so many hands over the centuries? In 1453, Marguerite de Charny (how she came into possession of it is a mystery) gave the precious shroud to Louis of Savoy in return for two castles and his protection. The relic was on display at the Sainte-Chapelle in Chambéry before being moved in 1578 to Turin, the Savoy dukes' new capital, where it has remained near the royal palace ever since, exhibited now and then on notable occasions.

One day in 1984, the Holy See's press office spokesman officially announced that John Paul II would visit Switzerland from June 12 to 17 of the same year. Victor Emmanuel III took the opportunity to discreetly let the Pope know that he wished to meet him on Swiss soil—which clearly meant being photographed beside the Supreme Pontiff by Arturo Mari. The secretary of state drafted an ambiguous, diplomatic response, telling the prince that the Pope might see him at Fribourg, which would be a unique opportunity to discuss the holy shroud.

Victor Emmanuel immediately understood that, contrary to what he thought, John Paul II was already aware of the section in his father's will concerning the shroud. What mattered most was saving face before Saint Peter's successor. The Pope saw him in Fribourg on June 13, 1984. The former king's son assured him that by the end of the year, his sisters, Princess Marie Gabrielle of Savoy and Princess Maria Pia of Bourbon-Parma, would officially give him the relic, since he himself was banned from setting foot on Italian soil. Appearing next to the Pope at last was well equal to a mass in Turin. It was a small price to pay to wipe away the Roman curia's bitter memories of the Savoy family's ties to Mussolini. Everyone knew that Umberto disapproved of il Duce's and the fascists' seizure of power, but he dared not oppose his father, King Victor Emmanuel II (1869–1947).

As promised, Prince Victor Emmanuel's sisters solemnly handed the holy shroud's title of ownership to John Paul II at a ceremony in Turin Cathedral, and the relic has belonged to the Vatican ever since. It was a royal present—and an opportunity for the House of Savoy to make an important gift to the Pope, as it had once before done by signing the Lateran Treaty in order to settle the long dispute after the reunification of Italy.

Prince Victor Emmanuel actually wanted the Pope to invite him to the Vatican because no male member of the Savoy family had been allowed to set foot on Italian soil since the 1946 law that sent the king into exile (a law Italy repealed 57 years later). After so many years of banishment, such an invitation would have meant a sort of rehabilitation for Prince Victor Emmanuel, if not outright recognition for his family. Born in 1937, he was in no way responsible for the painful past.

John Paul II perfectly understood how the heir of the Italian crown might have felt. He invited him to the Vatican just before Christmas 2002. The Pope greeted Victor Emmanuel, his wife Marina, and their son, Emmanuel Philibert, in the famous Vatican library on the second floor with all the honors due their rank. They returned in October 2003, when the Pontiff invited them to a concert in the Nervi Room celebrating the 25th anniversary of his papacy.

In 2002, the prince was on crutches, suffering from the after-effects of a car crash in Egypt. Despite that slight handicap, Victor Emmanuel was beaming, so thrilled that the Holy Father had at last invited him to his native soil. The moving visit also revealed the Pontiff's respect for the royal families that had once been an integral part of Europe's history. In Poland, the clergy and nobility elected the kings. According to one cardinal, a friend of John Paul II, he always seemed delighted to meet the descendents of the great European sovereigns who had shaped the Old World. The Pope, they said in Rome, was always impressed by the splendor, honors and pomp they displayed at home.

Chapter Nine

HIS LAST TWO SORROWS

JOHN PAUL II ARDENTLY HOPED TO SEE IN the new millennium and celebrate the Holy Year jubilee. The Pope's wish came true, but that was not enough to ease his bitter disappointment at having failed to fulfill his dream of uniting the Christian religions.

Armed with the feeling that Providence was on his side, the Holy Father nurtured elaborate plans: the reconciliation of the Roman Catholic Church with the Orthodox Christian Churches after 950 years of separation (since 1054), and the reunification of the official and underground Catholic Churches in China. Those were the Pope's last two goals after his pilgrimage to Israel, but the challenge was probably too daunting for an 85-year-old man. Age and poor health eventually got the better of him before he was able to make his ecumenical hopes come true.

God would have had to grant Karol Wojtyla a few more years of life for him to see those projects through to a successful conclusion. Reconciliation with the Orthodox Churches still seems a long way off. On Vladimir Putin's second visit to the Holy Father in November 2003, the Russian president did not repeat the invitation that Gorbachev had extended to him in December 1989.

The reason was the opposition of the Moscow Patriarch, Alexius II. On the few occasions, such as the day before Putin's trip to Rome, when the patriarch suggested that a papal visit would be possible, he ran afoul of the Holy Synod—in other words, the college of Russian Orthodox bishops. And clearly it would have been difficult for the Supreme Pontiff to visit Moscow without the Holy Synod's consent, even on an invitation from the Russian president. On that occasion, Putin said, "If the Pope came to Moscow without meeting the Patriarch, it would cause an uproar, which would surely not contribute to closer ties." A rather subtle man, John Paul II perfectly understood all that, especially since September 1996, when his attempt to meet with Alexius II during a trip to Hungary failed.

When John Paul II managed to visit Cuba and Israel, his *persona non grata* status in Russia, one of the world's biggest Christian countries, became unbearable to both the Slavic Pope and the Holy See's crafty diplomats. The rift between Orthodox Christianity and Roman Catholicism did not seem unbridgeable and, in this specific case, the reasons why the Pope received no invitation to Russia involved a highly complicated mix of politics, culture and dogma. One should probably never underestimate the complexity of issues with a Church that has so many branches, four old patriarchates—Constantinople (Istanbul), Alexandria, Antioch (the seat is in Damascus) and Jerusalem—and five new ones, in Russia,

Serbia, Romania, Bulgaria and Georgia, not to mention the Churches of Cyprus, Greece, Romania, Poland, Albania and the United States, which are not to be confused with the four patriarchal bishops of Venice, Lisbon, Goa and the East Indies, who bear the purely honorary title of Catholic.

The schism's roots are hard for today's believers to fathom. East and West clashed over the "procession" of the Holy Spirit: the Holy Spirit proceeds from the Father and the Son according to Rome, but from the Father only according to Constantinople. The rift arose when the Western Church introduced the Latin word *filioque*, meaning "and from the Son," into the Creed, leading the Patriarch in Constantinople to cast anathema on the Pope in Rome and the Pontiff to reciprocate in 1054. What's more, the Eastern Patriarchs have never acknowledged the Bishop of Rome's primacy *(primus inter pares)*. Disagreements over whether or not purgatory exists deepened the split, which climaxed when the Crusaders sacked Constantinople in 1204, prompting the Byzantines to exclaim, "Better the turban than the tiara!" The passing of centuries did not improve matters.

From the czars to Stalin, the Orthodox Church has always been Russia's national religion (Orthodox bishops are always close to the government). When the Soviet Union collapsed and religious freedom returned, the faithful felt bullied by a large-scale Roman Catholic missionary offensive. That was not the only bone of contention, however. There is no denying that the papacy has habitually tried to gain ground in Russia since Pius XI by strengthening the Catholic hierarchy there. When Stalin ruled the Soviet Union, Pius XI secretly ordained Catholic bishops and asked them to clandestinely ordain Catholic priests in turn. The Russian Catholic Church has only about 100 priests, including a mere 10 or so Russians, whom Orthodox clergymen call "mass-stealers," and 1 million faithful, most of them descendents of Poles and Armenians deported by Stalin, but its proselytizing alarmed Alexius II.

Jacques Chirac shrewdly measured the Orthodox Church's political importance. When he visited the Soviet Union as prime minister in May 1987, the French leader insisted on attending a three-hour sung mass at the Church of the Transfiguration in Peredelkino, near Moscow. Then, taking up a suggestion by Prince Constantine Andronikof—theologian, deacon of the Russian Orthodox Church in Paris and Charles de Gaulle's former Russian and English interpreter—who accompanied him, he visited Boris Pasternak's gravesite nearby.

There are two more sources of strain. First, Stalin had wiped out the Russian Catholic Church, confiscating many of its churches and turning them over to Orthodox bishops, who, of course, have refused to offer restitution. Second is the 300-year-old Uniate quarrel, which is hard for Westerners to understand. During the Counter-Reformation, the Catholic leaders of Austria, Hungary and Poland persuaded some of the Orthodox Churches to recognize the Pope's primacy. That was the origin of the Uniate Church, which brought together Eastern, Byzantine-rite Christians who recognized the Pope's authority. Karol Wojtyla loved them and tried to protect them as long as he could because he knew how much hardship and persecution they had endured under Stalin. Today, however, Moscow considers the renascent Ukrainian Uniate Church as the Vatican's fifth column.

In his short, 33-day papacy, John Paul I had tried to bypass

Patriarch Pimen, the head of the Russian Orthodox Church, by inviting Metropolitan Nicodim of Leningrad, who was involved in the dialogue with Rome, to the Vatican. In 1978, Metropolitan Nicodim believed that Catholic support for the ROC was indispensable, telling Cardinal König, president of the Pontifical Council for Dialogue with Non-Believers, "We're lost without you." Unfortunately, on September 5, 1978, he dropped dead of a heart attack in the middle of an audience with John Paul I. Later, John Paul II said, "Either he died too early or I became Pope too late."

Alexius II, who has been Patriarch of Moscow since 1990 with the Russian government's support (after having been metropolitan of Leningrad), stood up to John Paul II while having an ambiguous attitude toward him. In January 2005, he said that Vladimir Putin was willing to invite the Pope anytime and that there were no problems in the relationship between Russia and the Vatican, but that a visit would be pointless unless the ROC and the Holy See settled the issues between them. This meant that the state and the world's largest Orthodox Church, which, he stressed, had been celebrating the mass on Russian soil for over 1,000 years, had to extend an invitation to visit Russia. But the Patriarch of Moscow opposed the Pope's visit, accusing him of openly trying to win converts on Orthodox soil. "The reproaches we have expressed to the Vatican are still the same," he said, "and no effort to end the contradictions has been made." Alexius II added that the Holy See was pursuing its proselytizing work, primarily in Russia, the Ukraine and Belarus.

The Orthodox Church is a precious element of stability in Russia, a huge country where the State has been administratively and politically weak since the fall of Communism. As soon as Vladimir Putin was sworn in as president of the Russian Federation on March 26, 2000, he proclaimed that he was a practicing believer (he often attends religious ceremonies). "The Orthodox Church," he said, "must return to its traditional mission of providing stability and unity for Russia based on shared moral values." After Boris Yeltsin underwent quintuple bypass surgery in 1997, he had his five grandchildren baptized. At the time, Russia's former ambassador to the Holy See, Viacheslav Kostilov, said, "Boris Yeltsin's religious sensibility has grown and perhaps God has moved into him."

In another meaningful gesture demonstrating the official favor that the Orthodox Church enjoys, in the 1990s the mayor of Moscow, Yuri Luzhkov, who was also baptized late in life, ordered and generously funded the reconstruction of the world's biggest Orthodox cathedral, Christ the Savior, which Stalin had destroyed in 1931. Its golden onion domes have risen from the ashes and once again overlook the heart of the city. Seen from the opposite bank of the Moscow River, the majestic cathedral's impressive proportions and imposing beauty beckon Muscovites to revive their faith in Orthodox Christianity. Czar Alexander I had the cathedral built to commemorate Napoleon's 1812 retreat from Russia. Taking over half a century to construct, Christ the Savior was inaugurated in 1883, only to be dynamited on Stalin's orders less than 50 years later. That was when Russians realized that Communism was going to last for a very long time. Stalin had planned to replace the cathedral with a huge Palace of the Supreme Soviet, but the project was too grandiose even for him and an Olympic-sized outdoor swimming pool was built in its place.

In 1990, Alexius II obtained permission to demolish the pool and rebuild an exact replica of Christ the Savior using private funds. Two years later, on January 7, 1996, the Patriarch celebrated his first mass in the cathedral, wearing ceremonial dress and a heavy gold tiara encrusted with pearls and precious stones, surrounded by the mayor of Moscow and the new local notables. On September 4, 1997, the landmark was officially inaugurated for Moscow's 850th anniversary.

The lavish, flamboyant cathedral cost 1 billion francs to build. Magnificently decorated with gilding, frescoes, marble, bronze, mosaics and icons of Saint John the Baptist, Saint Nicholas of Myra, Saint George, Saint Dimitri, Saint Peter and Saint Paul—paintings intended for veneration and reflecting upon the beauty of God and the saints—it can accommodate 23,000 worshippers. The cathedral is a very impressive symbol of faith, with 13 bronze doors, 24 massive bells, 3,000 candles and incredible luxury, where a host of long-bearded metropolitans and bishops—dressed in chasubles richly embroidered with gold and silver thread and covered with icons and glittering crosses of precious stones and pearls—celebrate mass every day and share the honor of receiving President Putin to mark Holy Russia's major religious events.

Despite his poor health, Alexius II, an imposing figure who walks with a snake-shaped crosier, is besieged by throngs of old, bearded bishops and monks who consider themselves a bulwark against ecumenicalism, lambasting it as "an unhealthy idea from the West." Supported by the strength of their Church and its 128 dioceses, 17,500 priests, 2,300 deacons and 480 monasteries, these clergymen dream of reviving the old Russian Messianism and turning Moscow into the third

Rome, after Constantinople. They do nothing to promote good relations with the Vatican. Just back from Russia, a high-ranking prelate with the Holy See described the situation of Catholic priests in Moscow to John Paul II. "I went to Moscow in the dead of winter when it was minus 25°C," he told me. "Of course I found this debilitating, because I'm accustomed to Rome's temperate climate. I was so cold, and my teeth were chattering so much that I could hardly speak."

John Paul II probably made some tactical mistakes. For example, the Vatican was the first state to recognize the independence of Slovenia and Croatia, which are Catholic, arousing anger not only in Serbia but also in other Orthodox countries, including Greece, Romania and, of course, Russia. And on a 1998 visit to Zagreb, the Pope threw fuel on the fire by beatifying Cardinal Stepinac. The Serbs say he was an accomplice of the pro-Nazi Ustashis, who massacred thousands of their countrymen during the Second World War (which, the 20,000 pages of the beatification process seem to show, is inaccurate).

On top of everything else, many Orthodox Churches are poverty-stricken or even bankrupt, and are envious of the Roman Church's wealth.

John Paul II relied on Christoph Cardinal Schönborn, the Archbishop of Vienna, to approach and try to charm the Orthodox Church. The Pope had met him shortly after the 1981 attempt on his life, when he was appointed to the International Theological Commission. Schönborn was thoroughly familiar with the Orthodox Churches; he exercised his ministry "at the gates of the Orient," wrote his lectorate dissertation on "The Image of Christ in the Icon," and had many contacts with

Eastern Christians. The diocese of Vienna kept up a long tradition of relations with the Orthodox patriarchate of Moscow and was a center of ecumenical encounters with the Eastern Churches. In 1964, Cardinal König (a humble son of German farmers who spoke 12 languages and skillfully reconciled the Austrian left with the Catholic Church, he was the last surviving cardinal appointed by John XXIII, dying in March 2004 at the age of 98) founded Pro Oriente in Vienna and was very involved in dialogue with Eastern Christians, discreetly enabling Schönborn to regularly meet with Orthodox Patriarchs far from official eyes. The Pope hoped that his efforts might revive talks with the "stray sheep." In June 1998, I saw John Paul II and Schönborn together in Vienna when the cardinal became president of Austria's Conference of Bishops (there is no official separation of church and state in Austria, but rather a long tradition of cooperation institutionalized by a concordat). I was struck by how close they seemed to each other. The Austrian primate had many points in common with the Pontiff. He, too, was born in the east, in Skalskò, a part of Bohemia that is now Czech. At the end of the Second World War, his aristocratic parents decided to start a new life and moved to Vorarlberg, a rural area in the Alps, where, like Karol Wojtyla, he developed a love for mountains and skiing. The Pope was fond of the robust Dominican and his trust in him was obvious and touching. The elegant, distinguished-looking Schönborn is related to the heirs to the French throne, and two of his ancestors were cardinals. A descendent of high Middle European nobility, he, like the Pope, speaks six languages.

At the age of 18, Schönborn entered a Dominican seminary in Westphalia. Later, he taught theology for 16 years at the University of Fribourg, Switzerland, before John Paul II appointed him to replace Cardinal Groër, who was forced to step down after allegations of pedophilia proved true. That is when John Paul II started to appreciate Schönborn for his knowledge, intellectual turn of mind and work as a theologian. In 1997, he asked the cardinal to preach at the Roman curia's Lenten retreat, an event that left a deep impression on the Austrian prelate's religious life. "At first it was a bit traumatizing because I found out that I was to preach at the Holy Father's and the curia's retreat only two months in advance," he recalled. "The prospect of nurturing the Holy Father's meditation for five days straight was petrifying. The Pope and Msgr. Dziwisz were in a little room on the second floor of the palace, adjoining the Matilde Chapel (now called the Redemptoris Mater Chapel). I was the only person who could see them. Some 50 members of the Roman curia also followed the 22 meditations. I think John Paul II was happy then. He said nothing until after the last sermon, when he spoke some very kind words to me and gave me a cross that I wear all the time as a sign of communion with him." The Pope's gift was a token of trust and a highly coveted privilege in the Sacred College.

Cardinal Schönborn's gift of the gab and scholarly rigor appealed to John Paul II. Although the Pope was a Slav and his manner was more brisk, he viewed this man, whom he made a cardinal on February 21, 1998, as the prophetic ambassador who just might manage to reestablish ties between the Western and Eastern Churches.

I have always found one detail amusing. For many years,

Msgr. Schönbrun, who was the main author of the Catholic Church's catechism between 1987 and 1992, often stayed with the Dominicans on Via Cassia when in Rome. He, too, was a protégé of Sister Marie Johannes, the mother superior whom I admired so much when I attended the Dominican school in Rome. In 1980, this charismatic, powerful woman was President Giscard d'Estaing's guest in Rome. He invited her to dinner because people had told him that she did justice to French culture. The sister was also Jean-Pierre Raffarin's guest in October 2003 at the French embassy to the Holy See, where I introduced my former teacher to the prime minister and Mrs. Chirac as a "cardinal-maker." These were a few moments of levity at an austere occasion. But let us now return to the challenges facing John Paul II.

Hoping to bring the Pope and Alexius II together for a meeting, the Archbishop of Turin, Msgr. Severino Poletto, acting on an idea from Cardinal Sodano, went to Moscow in March 2000 with a delegation from his diocese. He met the Patriarch and invited him to Turin to see the holy shroud, but Alexius II refused.

Meanwhile, John Paul II continued his efforts with other Orthodox Patriarchs. The first was Bartholomeos I, the ecumenical Patriarch of Constantinople. Rome recognized his historical primacy, but the Russian Orthodox Church objected. "The Patriarch of Constantinople has 200,000 faithful," Alexius II protested. "I have 70 million!" The Russian also insinuated that the wealthy Greek diaspora funded Bartholomeos I, even loaning him a private jet on a regular basis.

The Vatican paid the Constantinople Patriarch's tuition at the French seminary in Rome and always showered him with honors and gifts. The seminary, which is almost across the street from the Pope's tailor on ViaSanta Chiara, on the ruins of the baths of Agrippa behind the Pantheon, enrolls 52 students a year, or approximately 4,600 seminarians since opening in 1853. Its alumni include four French cardinals—Garrone, Billé, Etchegaray and Tauran—as well as other foreigners and Orthodox Romanians, Bulgarians, Armenians and Greeks. The most famous is Bartholomeos I, who graduated in 1965.

John Paul II was very courteous and generous with the Patriarch, who—like him but exactly six years later, in January 2004—went to Cuba for the inauguration of Saint Nicholas' Orthodox Cathedral in Havana, built under Fidel Castro's auspices. However, these niceties had no practical effects. What's more, the very demanding, rather ungrateful Bartholomeos I distanced himself from the Vatican, even calling the "summary conception" of the papacy into question and vaunting the Orthodox Church's flexibility compared to what he called Roman Catholicism's "heavy" centralism. Yet the Holy See has always been indulgent with the Patriarch. His Paris host was Cardinal Lustiger, who co-celebrated Orthodox vespers at Notre Dame for the first time with him. Previously, Bartholomeos I had marked the 100th anniversary of Saint Stephen's Greek Orthodox Cathedral with a five-hour ceremony. Then, the 3,000 Greek Orthodox believers in Marseille welcomed him with open arms. The Orthodox authorities in Moscow took a dim view of these festivities.

With his long gray beard, earnest intensity and metal-rimmed glasses, Bartholomeos I intrigued me. In March 1993, before having the pleasure of meeting John Paul II, I had had a long talk with him at a private dinner party at the home of

Herbert von Karajan's widow, Eliette, in Salzburg. He was incognito that night, and I was unaware of his identity until we had coffee, when the Patriarch took off his long black coat because he wanted to sit next to the fireplace. Suddenly I spotted a magnificent icon sparkling on his chest and an Orthodox cross hanging on a long gold chain around his neck. The jewelry captivated me so much that I asked him, "You wouldn't happen to be a metropolitan, would you?"

"You've almost got it, madame, you're burning hot!"

"Do you mean you're the Patriarch of Constantinople, the primate of world Orthodoxy?"

I could not believe it. I was so awestruck at having spent the past five hours next to "His Beatitude" without suspecting it in the least that the idea of apologizing for my gaffe did not even occur to me. Instead, I asked him what he was doing in Austria. The Patriarch told me that the purpose of his journey was to make contact with the Orthodox community in neighboring Hungary and to lay the groundwork in that country, where everyone was free to practice the religion of his or her choice since the fall of the Berlin Wall. He explained that Cardinal König, John Paul II's great elector, had opened up a dialogue with the Orthodox community, and that he had promoted ecumenical relations between the Roman Catholic Church and the pre-Chalcedonian and pre-Ephesian Orthodox Churches. I was fascinated, despite having no idea what he was talking about. The Orthodox metropolitan of Vienna was accompanying him. When I told Bartholomeos that I was Catholic, he responded in perfect French (like the Holy Father, he speaks six languages) by praising the Pope and ecumenicalism, but implied that Orthodoxy and Catholicism were openly competing with each other in Hungary and that time was of the essence.

The patriarch had visited Herbert von Karajan's grave on the previous day. Before leaving, he handed me his business card, on which was printed, "H. H. Patriarch Bartholomeos, Rum Patrikhanesi, 34220 H. Fener, Istanbul, Türkei." I was dumbfounded that such a figure would have made that kind of gesture. I have trouble picturing the Pope slipping a business card, with a religious image printed on one side, to a guest, much less a woman. At the time, I told myself, "If you're lucky enough to have spent a long evening with the Patriarch of Constantinople, perhaps one day you might meet the Pope." The next day, Bartholomeos flew to Budapest in a private jet that a wealthy Greek industrialist, Dimitri Pappas, had loaned him.

Shortly before his death, Msgr. Jean-François Arrighi, the rector of Trinité-des-Monts Church (and brother of the former National Front deputy Pascal Arrighi), who was at the secretariat for the Pontifical Council for Promoting Christian Unity, philosophically told me, "You cannot heal centuries of discord in a single pontificate, even with highly talented, more-or-less official ambassadors." He was probably referring not only to Cardinal Schönborn, but also to the French Cardinal Roger Etchegaray, who on several occasions had been the Pope's special envoy to the Orthodox Churches, as well as to Israel, but with more success.

The Patriarch of the Romanian Orthodox Church, His Beatitude Teoctist, a highly controversial figure because of his involvement with Ceausescu's Communist regime, invited John Paul II to Romania in May 1999. The Holy Father's trip yielded no results in terms of closer ties between the two branches of Christianity, but it was a hugely popular success. Some 200,000 people attended an outdoor mass in front of Ceausescu's outsized palace, holding up portraits of the Pope and Patriarch Teoctist and waving little white and yellow flags. Young people flocked to catch a glimpse of "the man who toppled the wall," and many Romanians prayed for him to "come back to the true faith." But John Paul II had also received a slap in the face: as a condition for his visit, the synod of the Romanian Orthodox Church had demanded that he stay in Bucharest, preventing him from visiting Transylvania in the north, home to most of the country's Eastern-rite Catholics, who were not any more successful than their Ukrainian counterparts in recovering their churches, which Ceausescu had confiscated. Many of Transylvania's Catholics are of Hungarian stock.

Two months later, in November 1999, John Paul II went to Georgia, where the results were also disappointing. The patriarchate demanded that the Pope celebrate mass in Tbilisi indoors instead of outside in a square. Patriarch Ilya II, who attended two ceremonies, cautiously refrained from uttering the word "ecumenicalism" when the Pope made a vibrant appeal for Christian unity. No common prayer was possible between the heir of the apostle Peter and the successor of the apostle Andrew, who, according to tradition, evangelized Georgia. The country's president, Eduard Shevardnadze, a great admirer of John Paul II, even had to twist Ilya II's arm to meet the Pope, who received a chilly welcome. A cardinal told me that the Pontiff had said to him, "Governments make eyes at me more than Orthodox priests do." To a Russian minister, who had welcomed him with the words "Christ is risen!" the Pope commented, "I'd rather be awaited in churches than in official palaces."

On John Paul II's March 2000 visit to Cairo, he and Pope Shenouda III, the Patriarch of 6 million Orthodox Copts, lavished praise on one another and solemnly exchanged Latin and Coptic crosses, but steered clear of all the issues keeping them apart, from the existence of purgatory to the procession of the Holy Spirit. The deepest rift still involves the Roman Church's primacy. Saint Mark evangelized Egypt, so the Copts do not see why they should obey the successor of another apostle, Peter. The Vatican-Coptic Church committee, which was created to smooth over doctrinal differences, has not met for over 10 years.

To make matters worse, the Orthodox monks at the famous Saint Catherine's monastery on Mount Sinai gave John Paul II a halfhearted reception, to put it mildly. Guided by their superior, Msgr. Damianos, some 10 monks dressed all in black, with long beards and distrustful looks, huddled in a corner speaking among themselves as though nothing were happening, while a few feet away John Paul II presided over a religious ceremony before thousands of people. In his welcome speech, Msgr. Damianos urged the Pope "to humbly return to the true faith." All the monks remained silent when the Holy Father and his entourage prayed aloud. However, that has been the custom since the Great Schism.

John Paul II's June 2001 trip to the Ukraine was no more successful. The country's president, Leonid Kuchma, welcomed the Pope as a head of state with a 21-gun salute, but the Orthodox Patriarch of Kiev, faithful to Moscow, did not attend the reception in his honor at the Philharmonic concert hall. More disappointments were to come. The Pontiff's first mass in Kiev, where few Catholics live, drew just 50,000 people, half the expected number. President Kuchma deployed almost as many police officers—one every 10 meters—to control the crowd, and people along the Pope's route had to shut their windows. These measures probably intimidated the faithful, who might have feared a terrorist attack. John Paul II's many attempts to forge closer ties with the Orthodox Church ended in failure. His pastoral trips to Orthodox countries ringing Russia—from Romania to Ukraine, Armenia, Kazakhstan and Bulgaria—to meet these once-oppressed peoples and preach Christ's word to them, only further annoyed the Patriarch of Moscow.

The Pope was no more successful in China. In 1949, Mao Tse-tung expelled or imprisoned foreign Catholic priests, and in 1958, he broke diplomatic relations with the Holy See. Since then, China's Catholic Church has been torn in half. The Communist authorities set up an official Catholic Church to keep a close eye on the faithful. The Patriotic Catholic Association, which was founded in 1957 and put under strict Party control, appoints bishops without consulting the Pope. Meanwhile, the underground Catholic Church has remained faithful to the Pope and has undergone persecution. According to the Holy See, China has approximately 10 million Catholics, traditional and official combined. Exact figures for each branch are hard to come by because they vary depending on the province, diocese, religious figure and local politics.

Fearing a repeat of the events that occurred in Tiananmen Square, China's leaders wanted to keep John Paul II out of the country; that is also why they have never conceded any freedom to Chinese Catholics. Even today, Chinese bishops cannot exercise their ministries in China, and they are often arrested. One of them, Msgr. Tan, a Jesuit, paid "the price of his faith," as he puts it, spending 18 years in prison and nine in a reeducation camp. "Being a bishop in China isn't easy," he says. "You constantly have to fight the government. I was ordained in 1945. I am perfectly aware that you cannot do anything without the state's permission. Life was a real ordeal for many Christians, who were once not even allowed to pray for the Pope! I have paid such a high price for my religious beliefs that I often thought it was worse than purgatory."

As a result, this man of conviction, who cautiously decided not to be listed in the Vatican's directory and changed his name several times, belongs to both the Chinese Patriotic Church and the Roman Church, while considering himself "a dissident bishop."

Mao closed every house of worship in China and relentlessly persecuted, imprisoned and tortured Christians. By the end of his reign, those who could flee China did so. While the government officially eased up on its repression 20 years ago, surveillance is still effective and ever-present. Spies keep a close eye on everything and there is precious little room to maneuver. Theoretically, believers can pray and meditate in churches as long as they keep their mouths shut. "Journalists can freely criticize Communism," says Msgr. Tan, "but we experience it from the inside. We're constantly being watched. I try to criticize the system in a 'friendly' way. I always speak as though I'm talking to Communists because I know that informers are everywhere." According to Father Bernard Cervellera, the editor-in-chief of the Catholic Asia News agency, a somewhat discouraged Msgr. Tan recently asked the Vatican if he could rejoin the Church of Rome, or at least be considered openly faithful to the Supreme Pontiff.

The number of imprisoned and tortured priests is still shrouded in mystery, and rumor has it that some have even been killed. Human rights groups say that approximately 60 "underground" Catholics, including a bishop over 75 years of age, are in jail. Allegiance to the Roman Catholic Church is treated as an anti-patriotic crime in the service of a foreign power. Mainland China was officially absent from the August 2000 World Youth Days, but slightly more than 100 Chinese Catholic students took advantage of their studies in Europe to discreetly travel to Rome and take part in the event. Official and underground Catholics make pilgrimages side-by-side to the shrine of the Virgin of She Shan, where Mary is said to have appeared in 1910. Chinese Catholics also secretly worship Theresa of Lisieux, the patron saint of missions, on October 1, the day of mainland China's national holiday.

John Paul II worked for years to normalize the Holy See's relations with Communist China, where the number of Catholics has doubled from 6 to 12 million in a short time. Local Catholics heed Bishop of Xian and moral authority Antoine Li Duan, but the country is still without a bishop's conference. As a result, the claims of both parties are hard to reconcile. Of course, the Pope asks for bishops' appointments to be subject to his approval, but Beijing demands that the Holy See recognize the bishops chosen by the Patriotic Catholic Association and break off its relations with Taiwan.

Several negotiators were involved in the Vatican's difficult talks with the Chinese, including Msgr. Celli, Cardinal Sodano and Father Shi, a Chinese Jesuit who teaches at Gregorian University in Rome and is Radio Vatican's director of Chinese programming. On January 6, 2000, Beijing named five Chinese bishops without consulting the Pope, who on the same day consecrated 12 foreign bishops in Saint Peter's Basilica. It was the new millennium's first solemn ceremony, with the Sacred College, diplomats and senior Italian officials in attendance. Beijing obviously chose the date with the goal of annoying the Vatican. Even so, the Holy See's negotiators repeatedly told the Communist Chinese government that the Vatican would welcome a concordat similar to the one reached with Vietnam, where the Pope now appoints bishops, although they are subject to Hanoi's approval. But would a concordat with the world's most populous country be enough to reunite the official and underground Catholic Churches?

On June 30, 1979, John Paul II appointed a Chinese cardinal *in pectore*, which means "close to the chest" or "in secret." According to a very old tradition, Popes can create cardinals, in general for political reasons, and keep their names secret in order to avoid reprisals against them in their home countries. If the situation changes and becomes less critical, the Pontiff can officially divulge their names and their seniority dates back to when the secret appointment took place. Twelve years later, during the consistory of June 28, 1991, the Holy See, hoping for a thaw in its relations with China, disclosed that the cardinal was Kung Pin-Mei Ignatius, who has since died at the age of 99. But it was whispered at the Vatican that John Paul II had created another Chinese cardinal *in pectore*. Of course, nobody knows the mysterious prelate's name. The "official"

Bishop of Shanghai, Jin Luxian, whom the underground Church considers a "collaborator," intimates that he has the Pope's ear and that he would be happy to act as an intermediary between Beijing and the Vatican.

Unfortunately, Beijing's unexpected appointment of five new bishops put the negotiations on hold again. "The Chinese authorities and the Holy Father were on the verge of renewing ties," Msgr. Joseph Zen, the coadjutor Bishop of Hong Kong cautiously said. "We could do plenty of things without diplomatic relations, such as invite priests and seminarians to Hong Kong and organize pastoral training courses . . . Everybody is welcome, although a resumption of diplomatic ties between the Holy See and Beijing is impossible right now."

In his own way, John Paul II wanted to revisit China's history. The Middle Kingdom has gone through periods of great Christian fervor since it was evangelized in the 17th century. The Pope paid tribute to Matteo Ricci, an Italian Jesuit who arrived in China in 1582, in order to honor that past. Father Ricci and the Jesuits who accompanied him visited Macao before going to Beijing in 1601 with the goal of converting China to Christianity—quite a tall order! With their usual skill, the Jesuits became as integrated into Chinese society as Buddhist monks, whom the literate classes had considered a foreign import and viewed with suspicion. The Jesuits quickly realized that they had to adapt their customs, manners and rites in order to win over China's elites—to become Chinese, in effect. What's more, the Chinese admired them for their learning. The Jesuits translated books on trigonometry, astronomy, mathematics and hydraulics into Chinese and explained highly complex clock mechanisms to them. They also improved the Chinese calendar's accuracy, which was very important because the emperor told the farmers when to sow. Last but not least, they published a world atlas.

Today, despite the ups and downs of recent history, Jesuits such as Msgr. Luxian and other members of the Association of Patriotic Bishops are welcome to resume training priests, teaching in seminaries and commenting on Vatican II texts. However, in spite of the Jesuits' best efforts, the Chinese elites have always considered the Bible a jumble of incomprehensible legends and it is hard for them to join a religion whose representative on Earth underwent death by crucifixion. Conversions were few and far between. Despite protection under Emperor Kangxi (1662–1723), the Christian faith never won over more than a tiny minority of senior civil servants.

In 1705, the papacy, which was closely monitoring the Jesuits' work in China, sent Msgr. de Tournon to ask Chinese Christians to stop practicing ancestor worship, which the Jesuits tolerated, and to obey the Vatican's orders. Those instructions annoyed the next two emperors, who protested by saying that if they sent bones to Europe, the reigning princes would be up in arms. The Vatican's clumsy steps were the main reason why Christianity failed to spread in 18th-century China, leading to the end of the Jesuits' cross-cultural "experiment." In the 19th century, the Opium Wars and the West's dismemberment of China were the final blows, and only a handful of Protestant missionaries remained in the country.

In the 20th century, the fact that Chiang Kai-shek was a Christian helped fuel the growth of the Catholic and Protestant Churches somewhat. Rome was able to name bishops in China until 1949, when Mao Tse-tung broke off relations.

When Beijing appointed the five bishops in January 2000, the Pope's trip to China, which, after long and complicated negotiations, had been taken for granted a year before, was postponed indefinitely. The Chinese's sudden turnaround clearly showed that party hard-liners, who considered the Catholic Church the Trojan horse of capitalism, had gained the upper hand. A few months later, officials furiously protested against John Paul II's canonization of 120 Chinese Catholics who were martyred between the 17th and 20th centuries, and whom the government considered "the running dogs of imperialism." Their anger ran especially high because the canonization took place on the People's Republic of China's national holiday. This was not a good sign.

John Paul II was hurt by his failure in China. Despite his tireless efforts, the only chance of establishing positive relations during the waning years of his papacy was through Msgr. Joseph Zen, the Catholic Bishop of Hong Kong and a member of the Pontifical Council for Justice and Peace. In November 2004, he went to Rome to participate in his organization's activities. Bishop Zen, who could move about freely in China, also hoped to gently advance the thorny issue of the Chinese Catholic Church, even though the Chinese are apparently alarmed at its seemingly runaway growth and at the rise of religious activity in general.

Whenever John Paul II was asked about these ecumenical challenges, he replied, as if to ward off bad luck, "We'll see next year, if I'm still alive." But he never lost hope. On November 18, 2003, the Pope had an audience with Paul Cardinal Kuoshi, the Bishop of Kaohsiung, Taiwan; His Beatitude Cardinal Ignatius I; and Raissa I Daoud, the prefect of the

Congregation of Eastern Churches, to take up the two thorny issues he still cared so much about.

For those who, like me, observed Karol Wojtyla with fascination for years, what seemed most striking with this extraordinary man was, in this area as in others, his ability to never give up, to always bounce back and share his contagious enthusiasm. Just when you thought John Paul II seemed too exhausted to even speak, he would utter something as puzzling as it was unpredictable. Until the end, the Pope believed that he would achieve his last two goals through his political skill, his sense of diplomacy and the power of prayer.

It will probably be up to Saint Peter's next successor to heal the rift between the Western and Eastern Churches, which John Paul II called his "last challenge."

Chapter Ten

THE DAY HE TOLD ME, "*SONO UN VECCHIO PAPA*"

JOHN PAUL II'S ENTOURAGE WAS CONSTANTLY worried about his health during his papacy's later years, but the Holy Father was stoic and trusted in God. He seemed detached from physical hardship, even joking about it now and then.

One morning in late 1999, I was in John Paul II's private apartments, where Msgr. Dziwisz had invited me in order to plan a brief photo shoot for our magazine. By a kind of grace from heaven, I had earned the affection of the Pope's private secretary, who along with Joaquin Navarro-Valls was rather happy to control Karol Wojtyla's image. The Polish prelate advised me to come and see His Holiness with previous copies of *Paris Match* to convince him to agree to another photo session. But nothing is simple at the Vatican and you must play it by ear, making things up as you go along while giving the Pope the reassuring impression that everything has been thoroughly thought out and is under control. Msgr. Dziwisz asked me to carefully lay our previous issues out on the big table in the library/living room and I briefly, very politely explained to the Holy Father that pictures taken just before his jubilee would look wonderful in our magazine. Holding my breath, I anxiously awaited John Paul II's reaction. He leaned over the table and carefully scanned each picture before smiling, looking at me and saying with a mischievous grin, *"Sono un vecchio papa!"* ("I am an old Pope!"). I realized that I had embarrassed him, and he waited for me to react. I stammered in Italian, "No, you aren't, Very Holy Father, your date of birth has nothing to do with it. Your Holiness's energy is not only very impressive, it's also . . ." He cut me off and said laughing, "Let's say that with you there's an excellent professional to photograph an old Pope!"

Angelo Gugel, who was standing just behind him, gave me a big smile. He was as delighted as Msgr. Dziwisz that I had dared to courteously contradict the Pope.

John Paul II really did impress me with his bravery and determination. But like everyone who followed him, I could not help worrying about the obvious deterioration of his health. What a difference from the alert Pope of 1978 who energetically strode through the Vatican's corridors with big steps, far ahead of elderly prelates and out-of-breath *monsignori*. He was perfectly aware of the change and tried to share his trust in Providence with others. Every year, the Pontiff did his best in front of the diplomatic corps, but since 2004 (after discontinuing regular dinners with guests, which some rarely invited members of the curia called "holding open table," slightly less than a year before) he had done away with the annual Sistine

Chapel ceremony on January 6 for ordaining new bishops and celebrating baptisms.

Four years earlier, on January 12, 2000, John Paul II had received, in accordance with protocol, the ambassadors of the 178 countries accredited by the Holy See for the New Year's greetings ceremony in the Royal Room on the second floor of the apostolic palace. They sat in alphabetical order, with the ambassador of Andorra first. The Holy Father knew that they were scrutinizing his every move to gauge his state of health before sending diplomatic cables to their respective countries. In a few sentences, he said that he had confidence in his future and tried to reassure the Christian world about his declining health. He mentioned that, supported by prayer and generous Providence, he was able to make his dream of ushering the Church into the third millennium come true despite physical disability. As time went on, those words took on greater meaning: nothing could stop John Paul II, who had a clear mind and a brave heart. On October 16, 2003, he celebrated his papacy's 25th anniversary and on March 14, 2004, he reached the 9,280-day mark, surpassing Leon XIII. That day, John Paul II's papacy became the third-longest in history after those of Peter (according to Church tradition) and Pius IX (1846–1878). Karol Wojtyla, the record-breaking Pope, rose to that challenge as well.

John Paul II was not the least bit embarrassed to admit his limits and have his picture taken just as he was, for example with President George W. Bush in the Vatican library on May 11, 2004, and Pakistan's President Pervez Musharaf a few months later, among others. Week after week, he kept his commitments despite his declining strength, not even canceling his August 2004 pilgrimage to Lourdes despite a stifling heat wave. In his later years, he also insisted on continuing to regularly visit Rome's parishes on Sundays. The last mass he celebrated at a local church in the Italian capital was on February 14, 2002, at San Enrico. Until then he had visited 301 of the city's 334 parishes, but afterwards priests came to him instead of the other way around. He always enjoyed surprising them by saying a few words in Roman dialect. As the weeks went by he continued, although at an increasingly slow pace, to greet figures in the Clementine Room, such as those who participated in the plenary meeting of the Pontifical Commission for Latin America on January 21, 2005, not to mention archbishops, ministers of foreign affairs and their retinues, ambassadors to the Holy See and their spouses, and members of various bishops' organizations.

However, for two years John Paul II no longer read his own speeches at the Wednesday general audience. Sitting in his papal armchair on wheels, he barely managed to bless the few people lucky enough to be led to him. When civil and religious officials came to call, the visits were increasingly short. The secretary of state, Cardinal Sodano, solemnly handed over the speech that the Holy Father was no longer strong enough to deliver. On New Year's Eve of 2000, he started using a mobile platform to move around Saint Peter's Basilica and the Paul VI Room. The next year, he started using a specially designed elevator to board and disembark from his plane. Toward the end, the Holy Father was very weak and could only move through the apostolic palace's endless, slippery marble corridors in a wheelchair. If he was in a good mood, he would joke, "Everyone else has a mobile phone. I have a mobile chair!"

In his private apartment, he used a walker. Those who saw him up close on a regular basis were always astounded that, despite these drastic changes, John Paul II still had a passion for accomplishing what he had set out to do. Sometimes his face would turn sullen when a member of his entourage tried to help him grab a sheet of paper or hand him a Bible before he himself asked for it with precise, willful signs. For many years, perhaps until October 16, 2003, the 25th anniversary of his papacy, the Pope only courteously pretended to listen to his doctors and did as he pleased. The only one whose advice he heeded was Dr. Buzzonetti, his personal physician.

One day a neurologist close to John Paul II told me, "Renato Buzzonetti didn't have prestigious diplomas, but he possessed remarkable common sense and knew the Pope better than anyone else. He used tact and savoir-faire with his famous patient, and was flexible enough to keep his trust. Amidst all those professors giving their opinions, his psychologically savvy family doctor knew exactly how to get him to accept a higher dose of medicine, take his pills or undergo a test, all under the watchful gaze of Msgr. Dziwisz, who kept a close eye on events and directed everything. I have a great deal of esteem for Renato Buzzonetti, who devoted himself heart and soul to the task. I was always fascinated by his patient, because he took about as much interest in how I intended to treat him as he did in, say, the world of ants. One of the most complicated things that a doctor treating him had to understand was that he had the last word on the 'miracle' prescriptions and advice that arrived from all kinds of doctors and even 'healers' from every corner of the globe. Not knowing which way to turn, his entourage was tempted to lend all of them an ear, falling under their influence without really differentiating between them. None of that kept John Paul II from remaining intellectually strong right up until the end. He had an incredible zest for life. He was totally mystical and didn't wonder about his health. He preferred not to know."

And as soon as the Pope started feeling better after a bad spell, he wanted to speed up the pace of his daily life.

John Paul II was hospitalized at the Gemelli Polyclinic eight times. The doctors there will always remember him telling them, "If the Pope is sick, he stays; if he is better, he leaves." That attitude was catching. Several people in his entourage from the same generation, including Dr. Buzzonetti, who formerly practiced at San Camillo hospital, and his security chief, Camillo Cibin, were so fond of him and so impressed by his ability to overcome obstacles that the idea of retiring never crossed their minds for a second. How would they manage it, anyway? The Pope always had fresh travel plans. He had become very weak and regularly implored the sick to offer their suffering to him and his mission as the universal pastor of Christians. His faith sustained him through extraordinary physical hardship. "Christ on the cross had no crown so he wears this crown of thorns day after day," one of John Paul II's close collaborators told me a few weeks before his death. His words left a lasting impression on me.

Almost until the end, John Paul II's workload stretched his weakened body's natural limits to the breaking point. His face looked tired, but his stooped body reflected his secret habit of regularly accomplishing the 14 Stations of the Cross. He gave suffering a mystical value. "I am here to serve the Church and all of humanity," the Pontiff reminded the faithful in

January 2005 when he was in the Gemelli Polyclinic for acute respiratory distress. To him, the ideal Christian is the martyr. I saw him praying with his eyes half-closed and his face glowing with serenity so often that I quickly realized how much his faith sustained him. Everyone who saw John Paul II on a regular basis envied his inner strength, which was a real miracle. He stoically stood up to his Parkinson's disease, which made his left hand increasingly shaky and, toward the end, not only caused his speech to be slurred but also brought about severe respiratory problems. These ailments only compounded the after-effects of the assassination attempt and numerous operations.

Professor Bruno Dubois, a neurologist at Pitié-Salpêtrière Hospital in Paris who specializes in Parkinson's disease, told me that the malady affects 1% of the population over 65 but, when properly treated, patients can lead an almost normal life. "The brain is affected by a shortage of dopamine, a hormone that decreases the limbs' motor skills," he explained. "That deficiency leads to the characteristic shaking, which goes away during voluntary movements, and an abnormal stiffness of the limbs, which may become almost helpless, but in 90% of cases, intellectual ability remains completely intact. Treatment consists of replacing dopamine with L-dopa, a neuromediator. But L-dopa wears off after a little while, which means that the patient must take a dose every three to four hours. Otherwise, disorders such as blockages that suddenly lead to a total loss of speech will quickly reappear."

Of course, Dr. Dubois's description leaves out the countless other health problems afflicting the Holy Father since 1944, when 23-year-old Karol Wojtyla was hit by a truck while walking out of a Solvay plant; he spent 12 days in the hospital with a concussion and a broken arm. After the 1981 assassination attempt, John Paul II underwent five hours and 20 minutes of surgery on his abdomen, elbow and index finger and subsequently required two more operations because of the after-effects. In 1982, he underwent surgery to remove a tumor from his colon, and in October 1986 he had surgery performed on his intestines and a few adhesions. That is when his right hand started shaking, his voice became slightly more monotonous and his face a little less mobile. People at the Vatican were whispering that he had Parkinson's. In July 1992, he underwent surgery to remove part of his intestines after histological tests revealed the presence of a benign tumor. On November 11, 1993, doctors operated on him to repair a broken right shoulder after he had slipped during an audience and tripped over his cassock. He wanted to stand up on his own and continue. Pain seemed to have little effect on him.

When someone close to the Holy Father described his stoicism to me, I thought of the evening in March 1983 when I accompanied Valéry Giscard d'Estaing on a ski trip to Courchevel. The former president fell and broke his foot, but kept on skiing to the bottom of the slope because he did not wish anyone to know he was in pain until the next morning. Giscard d'Estaing did not want to have a cast put on his foot because two days later he was scheduled to meet the mayor of Lyon, Francisque Colomb. Despite his extraordinary determination, he had no choice and eventually relented.

On April 24, 1994, John Paul II slipped in the shower and broke his femur. Doctors operated on him to replace the fractured thighbone with a rod, and from that time on he walked with a limp. Like Jacques Chirac, he always refused physical therapy. On August 10, 1996, he had an appendectomy.

The Pope underwent seven operations with general anesthesia in 26 years. Good Friday 2000 was the last time he walked the Via Crucis, the 14 Stations of the Cross at the Coliseum, which he had done every year since becoming Pope. Afterwards, he was unable to do so because of shooting pains in his knee caused by arthritis.

John Paul II brushed off these ordeals, saying, "The Church is governed with the head, not the legs!" When doctors advised him to save his strength, he often lost his temper. Sometimes he was almost provocative with cardinals who seemed to be counting his days, telling them a person is as old as his soul, not his arteries.

The Holy Father was under the constant care of specialists from Rome's Gemelli Polyclinic, a sprawling university medical center five kilometers from the Vatican with 1,800 beds, 39 wards, 58 diagnostic and treatment departments and a heliport. The hospital, which belongs to the Italian bishops under the aegis of the Sacred Heart Catholic University, has a staff of 660 doctors and 1,600 nurses.

The Pope's doctors at the Gemelli Polyclinic coordinated with his two personal physicians. The most notable, Dr. Renato Buzzonetti, who has a degree in gastroenterology and hematology, ran the Vatican's health services, administered its health insurance system and was at the Holy Father's side from the beginning of his papacy. He ran a dispensary behind the Vatican's walls with approximately 50 doctors in almost every medical specialty except gynecology. This little hospital had signed conventions with Rome's best medical centers. The Pope's other personal physician, Dr. Patrizio Polisca, a cardiologist and specialist in pre-operative hemodynamics (the forces that the heart has to develop to pump blood through the cardiovascular system), is nearly 20 years younger than Dr. Buzzonetti.

A French team famous for its work with Parkinson's patients, as well an American team, also took part in caring for the Pope's health, but very discreetly and unofficially in order to avoid offending the Italians, especially since the world's oldest medical school is in Padua and the Agostino Gemelli Polyclinic's school of medicine and surgery has a fine reputation. The facility was inaugurated in November 1961 with Pope John XXIII and Giovanni Battista Montini, the bishop of Milan and the future Pope Paul VI, in attendance.

In addition, Sister Tobiana, a physician, constantly looked after the Pope at the Vatican and abroad.

The Pope had a small, three-room suite on the 10th floor of the Gemelli Polyclinic permanently set aside for him. The bedroom had a bed, armchair, desk, sofa and two imitation leather chairs, with a simple cross and a reproduction of the Black Virgin of Czestochowa on the wall and a radio on the night table. An altar was set up in the room next door so that John Paul II could celebrate or co-celebrate mass, as he did in February 2005 after doctors had to perform an emergency tracheotomy under light anesthesia to help the Holy Father breathe better and provide him with "adequate ventilation" to reduce his laryngitis. This visit brought the number of his hospital stays to 10. The third room was turned into a spare bedroom for the Pope's private secretary. As John Paul II said one day on his way to the hospital, "I'm starting to know the Gemelli Polyclinic very well!"

The Polyclinic's history started in 1934, when Pope Pius XI donated a 37-hectare plot of land in northern Rome's Montemario quarter to the Giuseppe Tonioso Institute for a medical school, which John XXIII inaugurated in 1961. The hospital has two chapels: one for staff and the other for patients.

Despite all this, did John Paul II receive good treatment? A high-ranking prelate and friend of the Pope's told me, "Generally, senior figures are treated by what you might call a 'medical brotherhood,' in other words, an inner circle of doctors who are not always chosen on scientific grounds alone . . . and who might be reluctant to seek other medical opinions or assessments that might help them see the patient in a different light." Sharing knowledge would have been rather incompatible with the confidentiality desired.

An emergency unit with a kind of hospital room was also set up in John Paul II's apartment next to the apostolic palace's antechamber/office. It included an intensive-care bed, oxygen, a defibrillator, artificial respiration equipment with a laryngoscope, a non-invasive, positive-pressure ventilation kit, a pulse monitor, blood-pressure and respiration-reading devices, an electrocardiograph with 12 settings, a hemodialysis device, equipment to perform minor surgery and a gastric aspiration system. The unit also had a full-range pharmacy with various adrenaline-type cardiovascular restoratives, digitalis, Isuprel, calcium, anti-arrhythmia drugs such as amiodarone, anticoagulants like heparin, and modern antithrombitic drugs, antiallergic drugs including cortisone, diuretics such as furosemide to prevent pulmonary edema, neurological drugs, intravenous pumps and blood and plasma reserves. It was a veritable hospital emergency room. Physical therapy equipment and a massage table were in a room next door. In his last years, John Paul II had to have physical therapy almost every day because his muscles were so stiff, and speech therapy to improve his diction and to teach him how to position his tongue to avoid choking.

In spite of all that, no ordeal was enough to wear down the Pope's courage. Perhaps that is because his harsh youth as an orphan, full of physical and emotional hardships, inured him to suffering at a very early age. After he was hit by a truck in front of the Solvay plant in Krakow, no one close to him came to see him in the hospital because he was already alone in the world. The accident left him with a small scar on his left ear, which he showed workers during a visit to the Solvay plant in Tuscany 38 years later. (The plant in Krakow no longer exists; a Carrefour supermarket has replaced it.)

In a 16th-century sonnet about Rome, Joachim de Bellay wrote, "Tell me, if you will, news of the Pope and rumors of the city." That would take several volumes today. Yet even in those distant times, when neither television nor telephoto lenses existed to zoom in on the Pope's suffering, people scrutinized his smile, commented on his gait and took a keen, continuous interest in his health.

Four centuries later, Rome is still the same. In Roman taxicabs, and at Gilberto's, Da Arlu's and the Hotel Columbus (which belongs to the Order of the Holy Sepulcher), the three restaurants in the Borgo Pio (the neighborhood adjacent to Saint Peter's Square) where Vatican insiders fill the seats every day, John Paul II's slightest move was as much a topic of conversation as soccer.

With nonchalant hypocrisy, diners gossiped about the Pope's

latest sufferings at the Eau Vive, a restaurant—also known by Romans as "The Bishop's Rest"—belonging to nuns on the Via Monterone. Popular with senior Vatican prelates and pious tourists alike, this singular, vaulted restaurant, decorated with Renaissance frescoes, is owned by the "working missionaries" of the Immaculate Conception, who start singing "Ave Maria" in the middle of serving you spaghetti. Its muffled ambience is conducive to telling secrets. Everything about John Paul II, including his health, surprised people. He always swam against the tide and broke the law of silence. This might be explained by the fact that Karol Wojtyla had endured censorship in Poland for so long that he wanted none of it in Rome. In his papacy's earliest days, he decided to keep no information about his health from the public, an attitude that only intensified after the assassination attempt.

When John Paul II appeared in public during the last years of his papacy, his back was stooped, his face wracked by pain and his voice weak if not inaudible. Sometimes an assistant had to read out his homilies for him. Yet he had no fear of looking like a worn-out man fiercely fighting against old age and illness. The Pope was often unable to walk and had to be literally carried to an elevator when boarding a plane. Whether in Cuba, Nazareth, Bratislava or elsewhere, it hardly mattered to him if he looked exhausted; he showed the people of God his true condition. During his next-to-the-last trip to Poland in June 1999, the Holy Father fell at the Nunciature and required three stitches, yet he did not hesitate to appear in public with a small bandage on his temple. John Paul II cared so much about transparency that, despite his stooped back and immobile face, he let himself be photographed for the 2003 pontifical directory, the Vatican's cross between the Social Register and Who's Who. His hearing problems increased his tendency to cock his ear toward his guests, which sometimes made it difficult for Arturo Mari to photograph him when he was turned three-quarters toward the person he was greeting.

Being seen clutching his pastoral silver crosier, which once belonged to Paul VI, or apparently dozing off sometimes during ceremonies, did not lessen John Paul II's popularity. People loved and admired him as much as ever, even though his eyes had lost their alertness and cortisone had turned that handsome Slavic face with high cheekbones into a puffy mask. In any case, young or old, in sickness and in health, the Supreme Pontiff is the pride of every Roman.

John Paul II was indignant at the hypocrisy and scheming that goes on behind the backs of many political leaders and heads of state, whose press offices release glowing reports about their health even though they are knocking on death's door. That is one reason why he opted for as much transparency as possible. During my first assignments at the Vatican, I was amazed to see how meticulously health bulletins jointly signed by various doctors, complete with sketches, described the slightest detail of his operations at press conferences. Depending on the ailment, the reports specified whether or not his intestines were functioning normally again, gave detailed results of his latest electrocardiogram, disclosed the exact number of stitches he had received, described what he had swallowed, divulged his blood pressure, revealed his heart and breathing rates and more. The press office released pictures of a drawn-looking John Paul II in white pajamas with bandages around his arms and catheters in his hands. He also appeared at his hospital window to bless thousands of kneeling well-wishers gathered below. Emotions ran very high on these occasions, especially when he told them, "Societies are judged by the help and respect they give their weakest members." The world followed his recovery live after the dramatic shooting in Saint Peter's Square and his many accidents and illnesses. The only departure came toward the end, when the health bulletins no longer emanated from the Pope's doctors but from the talented, effective Joaquin Navarro-Valls, the Holy See's persuasive spokesman, who even in the darkest moments tried to make us believe that the Holy Father would soon embark on another journey.

John Paul II's attitude contrasted sharply with that of his predecessors. Pious XI had an operating room built at the Vatican to avoid going to the hospital, which would have been unthinkable then. John XXIII hid his stomach cancer as long as possible. Paul VI secretly underwent prostate surgery behind the Vatican's thick walls. John Paul I, Saint Peter's 263rd successor, was Pope for only 33 days and passed away before anyone could even start thinking about his health; however, though he was already weak and under terrible stress because of his difficult task, his death gave rise to sinister rumors and conspiracy theories. That must have shocked John Paul II, who immediately set out to establish a sort of contract of confidence and transparency with the faithful at every moment—not that this ever prevented gossip about his health from spreading and providing the press with plenty of grist for the rumor mill for a quarter-century, the chapters of an endless novel where fiction was often stranger than truth.

As soon as he became Pope, John Paul II realized how

symbolically important the Pope's physical presence was for the world's Roman Catholics. Unlike other religions, he represented the Church's universality in the flesh: "*Ubi papa ibi Ecclesia*" *("The Church is where the Pope is")*. This is also what prompted him to lead his life in the public eye. He often spoke openly about his health during the Wednesday general audience, entrusting his operations and ailments to the prayers of the planet's 1 billion Catholics. Four days after the shooting in Saint Peter's Square, John Paul II sent them a message from the hospital: "I know that you are with me," he said. "I offer my suffering for the Church and for the world."

The Poles, who live in a deeply Christian country where faith and its practice are innate, never stopped lighting candles and saying rosaries on their knees for their Pope. Italians and passing pilgrims left best wishes, flowers and sweets at the Gemelli Polyclinic every time John Paul II was in the hospital, praying and singing beneath his windows. The president of the truffle association sent him huge white Alba truffles, the most expensive in the world. The Italian community in Geneva gave him a state-of-the-art hospital bed. Every Roman knew the now famous hospital's address. Angelo, the Pope's faithful butler, had no idea what to do with all the medical and orthopedic equipment the faithful sent from around the world, especially the countless white-lacquered electric armchairs.

When his health allowed, John Paul II went to the hospital in his huge black Mercedes with the papal arms on the side doors instead of in an ambulance. There were two reasons for this: he wanted to avoid photographers and he did not want his state of health to be shrouded in mystery.

With biting humor, the Holy Father sometimes disarmed "caring" cardinals who inquired too eagerly about the evolution of his Parkinson's disease. The Pope's shaking and even his slightest yawns alarmed his entourage and were reported by the international press and analyzed by countless ministries of foreign affairs, day after day. The media interest only intensified with time, especially in February 2005 when Cardinal Sodano mentioned a "possible resignation," long an off-limits topic at the Vatican. This was the first time that the Pope's "prime minister" brought the subject up in public.

Hasty speculation about the Holy Father's imminent death was rife. This was nothing new: true and false rumors about the Popes' health have always been common. On August 19, 1914, the popular *Giornale d'Italia*, a bestselling newspaper at the time, published a front-page article reporting that Pius X, his face contorted with pain, was unable to stand up at the end of a meeting. The next day, an editorial in *L'Osservatore Romano* vehemently denied the news, asserting that the Pope was only suffering from a bad cold. Some 24 hours later, he was dead.

There was nothing surprising about this because, until Pius XII, the Vatican controlled everything through the doctor in charge of treating the Pope, who had the title *archiatra pontificio*, or primary pontifical physician. The Holy See did away with that solemn position after the scandal involving Dr. Galeazzi-Lisi, who sold photographs of Pius XII on his deathbed that were published in several magazines, including *Paris Match*, as well as other pictures of the Pope undergoing treatment. The famous doctor was actually only an ophthalmologist. He had managed to become the Pope's physician through his cousin, the engineer and architect Galeazzi-Lisi, who designed the apostolic palace and was a friend of Cardinal Pacelli's. In John Paul II's time, Dr. Buzzonetti belonged to the *famiglia pontifica*, but nothing was ever put in writing to indicate that he was the Pope's official doctor.

In the somber, tumultuous end-of-an-era atmosphere of John Paul II's last years, he was perfectly aware that his potential successors—and there were many of them—were engaged in intense, Machiavellian, behind-the-scenes maneuvering. The Pope always splendidly ignored their scheming, even though it sharpened his liking for challenges. During his last consistory, on November 21, 2003, he could be seen indifferently, even mockingly, observing the cardinals who kept a sneakily close eye on his every move. After all, during his papacy he had canceled only three trips and two Wednesday general audiences—on September 25, 2003, and February 2, 2005—because of ill health. However, in 2002 Msgr. Dziwisz forced him to curtail their number and duration as well as to wholly give up mingling with the crowd.

In the interest of transparency and to avoid false rumors about his medical condition from spreading after the assassination attempt, after five hours and 25 minutes of surgery the director of the Gemelli Polyclinic, Dr. Luigi Candia, published a very clear press release as the clock struck midnight on May 13, 1981. "The Holy Father's surgery was unavoidable because of the multiple visceral lesions caused by the bullet, which was lodged in the sacro-abdominal region, leading to, among other things, a massive intra-abdominal hemorrhage," the report said. "The Supreme Pontiff also sustained wounds in the right forearm and the left index finger, with a fracture of the second and third phalanges, which were also operated on. The multiple abdominal visceral lesions have been repaired and a temporary colostomy performed. This extensive surgery was performed under general anesthesia with continuous monitoring of vital signs. The cardiovascular balance was rigorously maintained during the entire operation, in particular with transfusions of three liters of blood combined with the various drugs habitually used in intensive care. After surgery, the august patient gradually awakened, breathing on his own, and his cardiovascular condition has remained normal and stable. Kidney function has been preserved and the Holy Father has come out of the operation with relatively minimal after-effects, provided there are no peritoneal septic complications."

A few days later, John Paul II wanted the public to know that, in addition to Italian doctors' advice, he had seen several leading foreign experts on the digestive tract and internal surgery for their points of view, including Dr. Welch of Harvard Medical School, another American, a German, a Spaniard, a Pole and a Frenchman, Jean Loygue, professor of internal surgery at Saint-Antoine Hospital in Paris, who had once operated on President Jacques Chirac's mother. They had a positive opinion of the Holy Father's condition and of the administration of treatment.

Despite his health bulletins' transparency, each of the Pope's hospital stays prompted increasingly alarming, if not fanciful, commentaries and news reports. Just before his 1980 visit to France, an Italian newspaper even announced that John Paul II had leukemia. On World AIDS Day in 1993, the host of one of Italy's most popular television shows, on Canale

5, coldly declared that the Pope had contracted the disease following the attempt on his life. In fact, after the shooting the Pontiff had fallen victim to cytomegalovirus, which caused bouts of fever. What's more, the CMV contamination was never a secret or a scoop and John Paul II recovered from it shortly afterwards. He probably contracted the bug from a blood transfusion. The Pope had a rare blood type, AB negative, which is shared by only 3% of the population. It was vital to immediately find donors with the same blood group among the surgeons on the ninth-floor operating room, who unhesitatingly gave their blood to save the Holy Father. The situation was so alarming that at one point Dr. Buzzonetti asked Msgr. Dziwisz to administer last rites, which he did. The Pope's blood pressure had plummeted and his pulse was imperceptible. A transfusion was necessary before the extremely complicated operation could begin at a few minutes before 6 P.M. Dr. Crucitti and Dr. Castiglioni led the 11-member surgical team, comprising Drs. Salgarello, Viel-Martin, Zucchetti, Manni, Beccia, Sabato, Fiaschetti, Pelosi and Manzoli under the anxious gazes of Dr. Buzzonetti and Msgr. Elio Sgreccia, the Catholic University Medical School's spiritual advisor.

In September 2004, a phone call woke several cardinals in the middle of the night. Tearful voices told them that John Paul II had just died. The entire Vatican was grief-stricken. France's ambassador, Jean-Louis Lucet, immediately informed the ministry of foreign affairs in Paris. Shortly before dawn, the sacristy of Saint Peter's Basilica received instructions to say requiem masses all day. Then everyone found out it was an extremely tasteless practical joke.

In addition, every time the Pope underwent surgery it gave rise to rumors that he had cancer.

John Paul II's poor health had an effect on the Vatican's functioning. The administrative departments were paralyzed for five years because he had made almost no decisions and did not even answer notes from various congregations and dicasteries asking him to settle one issue or another. Those close to the Holy Father could no longer talk to him on the phone because his entourage blocked their calls. In any case, he had difficulty picking up and holding the receiver and, despite a few eye-catching pictures, never used a mobile phone. His staff left the letters that reached his desk unanswered. Msgr. Dziwisz seemed to try to avoid questions by asking those surprised at the Pope's silence, "Are you sure this is where you actually sent the letter you're talking about? The Holy See is so big!"

How could things have been otherwise? After being rushed to the hospital in February 2005, the 85-year-old Pope was a nearly helpless, extremely frail old man. His doctors feared that an internal hemorrhage, phlebitic event or a pulmonary embolism would occur at any moment. It was increasingly difficult for John Paul II to catch his breath during his rare public speeches: the main cause of death among those with Parkinson's disease is choking and congested lungs.

Unlike François Mitterand, however, who seemed fascinated by cemeteries, perhaps because he loved history, John Paul II was apparently indifferent to them. He preferred shrines. That is probably because he serenely looked death straight in the eye, which is perhaps not surprising for someone who has been familiar with it from a very early age, who comes from a country that lost 6 million people during the

Second World War, a nation whose territory was tainted by the Sobibor, Treblinka and Auschwitz extermination camps.

John Paul II was terribly familiar with death. On February 16, 1981, he nearly fell victim to a terrorist attack in Pakistan: 20 minutes before he was due to arrive at a Karachi stadium to celebrate mass, an explosion occurred some 40 meters from the altar. The attacker was killed when the grenade in his pocket blew up. On May 13, 1982, a Spanish fundamentalist priest tried to stab the Supreme Pontiff at Fatima. A year later, the police arrested a fellow Pole armed with a knife waiting for the Pope on the route he was scheduled to take, and 14 months later, a young Korean armed with a gun (which turned out to be a toy) tried to threaten him in Seoul. At a reception in his honor in Toronto on September 17, 1984, the police arrested a man armed with a knife and a stolen invitation. And there were countless plots hatched in Venezuela, Austria (by Turks), Ivory Coast and even Poland, where General Zenon Platek, who was in charge of religious affairs at the interior ministry, revealed that an assassination attempt had been foiled (information that was later denied, however).

Many unbalanced people tried to get close to the Pope both in Rome and abroad. On his 104 pastoral journeys outside Italy, he received innumerable threats as well as letters with skulls on them, which he did not want hidden from him. None of this ever upset him. "All precautions are futile," he used to say. "When I go out dressed in white I'm a sitting duck."

Nor did he fear old age. A few days before celebrating his 84th birthday at Fatima, John Paul II said, "You must never stop being on the front lines, even when you feel old in mind and body, tested by illness and suffering. If you know the eternal love that created you, you are also aware that you have an immortal soul. Life has four seasons and winter is not the last because spring always follows—the spring of the Resurrection. Your life is not limited to the confines of the Earth. Heaven is also there . . ." Msgr. Stanislaw Rylko, the secretary of the Pontifical Council for the Laity, said, "The Pope experiences his 'four score years' as something completely natural. He is not afraid of everyone seeing the limitations and frailty caused by age and does nothing to hide them. He looks far ahead into the future with the enthusiasm of the only youth that does not fade, the youth of the spirit. He has kept his intact."

In one of his *Letters to the Elderly,* John Paul II issued an appeal to "welcome and value the aged instead of relegating them to the margins of society." He wrote that in some parts of the world, especially Africa, "the elderly are rightly thought of as living libraries." The Pope also firmly condemned euthanasia, "which is considered a 'gentle' death that has gradually lost the connotation of horror it should naturally arouse in anyone who is sensitive to respect for life," but he reiterated that, in hopeless cases, palliative treatment without taking extraordinary measures to prolong life at all costs is morally permissible. As usual, John Paul II spoke clearly and truthfully, aware that he was addressing members of his generation, setting an example with his active faith. "I still enjoy life in spite of the limitations that have come with age," he wrote.

In the spring of 2001 I was asked to give John Paul II the Polish translation of my previous book. "Of course I have aged since that picture was taken," he told me, referring to the cover photograph. "But I'm still here, even if I'm no longer the Pope you once knew. I still have plenty of things to do!"

As he spoke, his face lit up and I was so moved that this time it was my hands that were shaking, not his, when I gave him the book.

In the eyes of the world's political leaders, John Paul II, an extraordinary example of human courage, remained one of the most notable figures of his time until his last moments. The proof is the many official telegrams he received to wish him a happy 80th and 85th birthday, the latter when he was in the hospital. Messages poured in not only from Italian President Carlo Azeglio Ciampi, of course, but also from George W. Bush, Gerhard Schröder, Morocco's King Muhammad VI, Vladimir Putin and even Alexius II, the Patriarch of Moscow. Both world leaders and countless citizens of humble means sent him gifts. On October 16, 2003, VIPs from around the globe were in Rome to celebrate his 25th anniversary as Pope. President Ciampi, the presidents of Italy's two legislative chambers, and many ministers were there, as well as Polish President Alexander Kwasniewski, Lech Walesa and countless other major international figures. The world's 192 Roman Catholic cardinals chipped in to give the Pope 1 million euros, which he immediately donated to Christians in the Holy Land.

On October 19, 2003, three days after beatifying Mother Teresa, John Paul II invited me and a handful of other laypeople to a classical music concert by the Mitteldeutscher Rundfunk in the Paul VI Room. Looking at him closely, I realized what an "old Pope" he had become, as he had told me a short time before. In this poignant atmosphere, all the world's cardinals and notable prelates, as well as nuns and priests at the head of congregations with mother houses in Rome, fervently thronged around John Paul II, as though they had the sad feeling that this might be one of the last times they would all see him alive.

During the concert that evening, I could not help thinking that this man, one of the 20th century's most notable historical figures, had terribly changed. He had been the traveling companion of several generations and was, along with Fidel Castro, one of the last survivors of another age. He had also been a kind of father figure, a guardian angel and a voice of moral authority for us. We will all be orphans when he goes, I thought. An essential chapter in contemporary world history will be closed and a part of our daily lives will fade away.

Chapter Eleven

THE LAST TWO JOURNEYS OF HIS HEART: POLAND AND POMPEII

JOHN PAUL II'S EIGHTH JOURNEY TO POLAND, in August 2002, was not his last trip abroad, but it must have been one of his dearest because that is when he delivered his testament-cum-message to humanity.

The Supreme Pontiff's countrymen sensed that he was visiting his native soil, "the source of my life and faith" in his own words, for the last time. His health had severely deteriorated, and the Poles, who had seen him on television, thought he was almost helpless. They believed that Karol Wojtyla would come home to retire after his 98th trip in August 2001. A contemporary survey had confirmed that 86% thought that this latest journey was an important event in their lives. When John Paul II arrived, the Catholics of Gdansk could not conceal their anxiety. The Pope's four-day stay was indeed his last trip to Poland, but instead of saying, "Goodbye, my brothers," he reminded them of Christ's doctrine for all Christians. Because of the political circumstances at that moment, the Holy Father's gesture again had an exceptional impact. After he helped the Poles win their freedom from Communist dictatorship, they looked to him for clues, at least spiritual ones, on how to get out of the quagmire in which they had been bogged down ever since. "The Polish people want to hear words that will guide them in the coming years," Poland's president, Alexander Kwasniewski, a former Communist, solemnly said the day before John Paul II's arrival. With nearly 19% unemployment, rampant corruption, rising crime and fierce debates over whether or not to join the European Union, the country was in disorder. "For Poles," wrote *Gazeta Krakowska*—the nation's biggest daily—that same day, "the Pope has always been a miracle-worker. In 1979, he beseeched God to defend Poland. A year later, the Solidarity trade union initiated its major strikes. Today, the entire nation needs him. Demoralized by unemployment, disheartened by political scandals and worried about the 'commercialization' of life and culture, we are in a state of uncertainty."

John Paul II knew how decisive this trip was for his home country and tried to deliver a message of hope, but he also wanted the whole world to hear his powerful words, steeped as they were in the love of God and the charity of Christ. The Pope sought to express a bright, reassuring guide to Christian thought that meant something not only to Poland but also to all humanity at the dawn of the 21st century. Of course, he spoke later on other trips, but never as forcefully as during this journey, when his words echoed throughout the Christian world.

The Poles sensed that John Paul II was once more coming to their rescue when, barely off the plane, he repeated three famous words—"Have no fear!"—to the 15,000 people who thronged the tarmac waving Polish and Vatican flags. Two children in traditional dress gave him a dish containing Polish soil. The Pope leaned forward to brush his lips against it: for years his health had prevented him from kneeling and kissing the ground. Then, as a prelude to a message he delivered two days later at a high mass in Krakow, he said, "I openly criticize a system that claims to govern the contemporary world according to a materialistic vision of humanity . . . No happy future can be built on the poverty, injustice and suffering of a brother."

In a few words, he said it all—or almost.

As soon as the local radio and television stations broadcast these words, a huge outburst of faith and hope gripped Poland.

"For us, this trip is a veritable celebration, a moment of high emotion," said President Kwasniewski, who had come to greet the Holy Father. "Everyone in Poland, believers and non-believers, young and old, admires Your Holiness' words and deeds."

The president hoped that John Paul II would soon speak his mind about Poland's membership in the European Union, an issue that had sparked lively debate among politicians, bishops and the entire clergy. The Pope addressed this issue just before leaving in order to give his words more weight. All the Polish people needed to hear, however, was "Have no fear, God is with you!" and they were reassured. Karol Wojtyla had repeated the powerful words he had so forcefully uttered on the day he was elected to Saint Peter's throne 23 years earlier on October 16, 1978—slow words that he repeated on his first trip to Poland, June 2–10, 1979, to urge his countrymen to shrug off their fear of Communist totalitarianism. They were etched in the memory of the Polish people, who had been repeating them ever since. "The Pope tells us, 'Have no fear,'" said Poland's Prime Minister, Leszek Miller, also a former Communist. "We will manage. We are already on the right track. With a little optimism, we can do everything it takes to have a brighter future."

John Paul II's message galvanized his countrymen. The next day, millions of them showed him their overflowing enthusiasm in Krakow when he once more voiced his thoughts, which were intended not only for them but for the rest of the world as well. His magnificent homily met with a fervent welcome that is hard to imagine anywhere outside Poland. To his fellow citizens, the first Slavic Pope in history was a gift from God and Providence. His election gave them the sense of avenging the terrible betrayal of the West, which had spinelessly abandoned them to the Soviet sphere.

Hospitals, schools and hospices in many Polish towns had already been named after John Paul II; so had Krakow's international airport, a distinction that was not bestowed on Charles de Gaulle in France and John F. Kennedy in the United States until after their deaths. Countless monuments were erected in the Pope's honor. In Krakow, John Paul II Street leads to the bleak, drab workers' city of Nowa Huta, where a huge sculpture of Karol Wojtyla, the biggest one in Poland, replaced Lenin's imposing statue. More bucolic and ecology-minded are the trails that have been created in the mountains on the paths where the athletic Pope once hiked. Kayak trips on lakes and rivers have been dubbed "In the Wake of John Paul II." And then there is the papal walking trail in Krakow. The Polish people worshipped the Pope, and his image had been a major source of zlotys (income) since he was elected. Henceforth, it will be a windfall, because John Paul II was a national hero even before he died.

In nearly every home in Poland, a portrait of John Paul II hangs prominently on the wall next to pictures of Christ or the Virgin Mary. Each of his trips back home made front-page headlines, filled entire pages in newspapers and monopolized magazine covers. Every speech he delivered in his native land had an amazing impact.

John Paul II was perfectly aware of all this, which is why he decided to issue an exceptional appeal exhorting the world to follow Christ's example of charity at the mass he celebrated before 2 million people in Krakow on Sunday, August 18, 2002. (One of the Pope's oldest friends told me that, in his constant desire to assert himself, the Pontiff always sought to leave his mark. This was all part of his extremely upright character. "The Pope can be humble," the friend told me, "perhaps because the 20th century, notwithstanding some obvious successes, was particularly tragic. We've entered the third millennium with a legacy of good but also of evil. Man often lives as though God does not exist. He sometimes puts himself in God's place. He claims the right to be the Creator and interferes in the mystery of human life [a reference to genetic manipulation, abortion and euthanasia], and wants to leave God out of culture and human consciousness." John Paul II recalled the need for charity in an age of unemployment and precariousness before affirming his conviction that "only Christ's message can save the world.")

Those fervent, passionate words rang out from the grandstand and resounded as an appeal that many Poles took to be an expression of the Holy Father's last wishes. They inspired the archbishop of Krakow, Cardinal Macharski, to comment, "The Pope came to Poland to tell us again that God exists and that, after the September 11 terrorist attacks in the United States, the world is in jeopardy if it does not integrate the dimension of divine mercy. He also wanted to recall that fighting terrorism is not enough: it is impossible to rebuild on spiritual ruins." On the same day, John Paul II condemned "the false ideology of freedom and the noisy propaganda of free-market capitalism that is gaining ground in our country as well."

That message, still relevant in a world beset by the challenges of globalization, remains etched forever in the hearts of Poles (many of whom spent the night praying and confessing in Krakow's churches). A human tide overran the former royal capital's Blonias Park, where the Holy Father celebrated a three-hour mass beneath a gigantic portrait of the merciful Christ.

The city was almost completely deserted; houses were empty except for dogs barking in windows. After John Paul II's 40-minute homily, the crowd chanted incessantly, "Stay with us! Stay with us!" Many Poles hoped he would step down as Pope and move into the ecclesiastical retirement home in Zakopane, where an apartment had been set aside for him. When the Holy Father responded, "Do you want to keep me from going back to Rome?" millions of voices broke into the refrain of a song that is very famous in Poland, "The Hymn of Catholic Youth," which speaks of leaving one's "boat on the riverbank" to go with God. "But I have never abandoned my boat in all these years!" replied the Pope solemnly.

Everyone felt at one with Karol Wojtyla during this moment of intense, astonishing emotion. Later, they found out that the Pope had never planned to resign, for he intended to live out Christ's Passion to the end.

John Paul II took time out on his trip to visit Krakow's Wawel Cathedral, a sacred place where, after secretly studying for the priesthood under Nazi occupation, he was ordained in 1946 and spent many great moments during his 14-year tenure as archbishop. Later, his helicopter flew over Wadowice, his hometown.

On Sunday afternoon, the anniversary of his father's death, John Paul II visited Rakowicki Cemetery, where his parents lie alongside his brother, Edmund, a doctor who died of scarlet fever at the age of 27 after contracting it while treating victims during an outbreak. Next, he traveled 45 kilometers from Krakow to pray at the Kalwaria Zebrzydowska Shrine, which a Polish prince had founded 400 years earlier in memory of Christ's Calvary. The area has approximately 40 chapels and churches on less than 300 hectares. Karol Wojtyla emotionally recalled his father taking him there on a pilgrimage, as well as the times he came to pray as a seminarian, bishop and cardinal. Rosary in hand, he always took the same paths he had trod as a young man.

"This is where," he said, "praying with the faithful, I learned the faith that guided me to Saint Peter's throne."

On Monday, August 19, John Paul II celebrated mass at

Kalwaria Zebrzydowska, which is Poland's second-largest shrine after the one dedicated to the Black Virgin of Czestochowa. He offered Our Lady of the Calvary a very moving prayer for the poor and for the Polish Church. The standing crowd listened to the prayer with tears in their eyes:

Our Lady full of grace,
Turn your eyes towards these people:
They have remained faithful to you and to your Son for centuries.
Turn your eyes towards this nation.
It has always rested its hopes in the palm of your Mother's love.
Turn your merciful eyes towards us.
Grant your children what they need most.
Open the hearts of the wealthy to the needs of the poor and suffering.
Help those who are jobless to find an employer.
Help those who sleep outdoors to find a home.
Give families the love they need to overcome all their problems.
Very Holy Mother, Our Lady of the Calvary,
Bring me the strength of body and mind to fulfill the mission that your resurrected Son has allotted to me.
To you I submit all the fruits of my life and of my ministry.
To you I entrust my nation.
In you I trust and to you I declare once more:
Totus Tuus, Maria! [All is yours, Mary!]
Totus Tuus.
Amen.

The day before, John Paul II had inaugurated the Lagiewniki Church. "The invocation of mercy seems to be rising from the most profound depths of human suffering on every continent," he said. "Where hatred and the thirst for revenge dominate, where war brings pain and the death of innocents, the power of mercy is needed to calm hearts and minds and bring forth peace."

These moving words referred to the tragic Israeli-Palestinian conflict and echoed the sentiments expressed by John Paul II on his trip to the Holy Land.

During the farewell ceremony at Krakow's airport before taking off for Rome, John Paul II at last uttered the words that President Kwasniewski and everyone in Poland had been so eager to hear.

"Polish society, which has been part of Europe for centuries, will find its place in the structures of the European Union," he said. "Poland will not lose her identity but, on the contrary, she will enrich the continent and the whole world with her traditions." After living in Rome as Pope for 24 years, Karol Wojtyla was still Polish to the bottom of his soul.

The Pontiff's words convinced those bishops who were still undecided about whether Poland should join the European Union, given that the European Constitution drafted under Valéry Giscard d'Estaing's leadership made no mention of the continent's Christian heritage. In his speeches and homilies, however, John Paul II had said that Poland's "traditions" were above all Christian, and that he hoped they would enhance Europe, which he feared was straying from God's ways and Christ's message.

For more clarity I turn now to the words of Cardinal Poupard, the first person who decoded the Vatican's secrets for me. In his book *Au Coeur du Vatican (In the Heart of the Vatican),* published by Perrin-Mame, he elaborated on John Paul II's thoughts:

In 2003, the debate over Europe's Christian roots was in full swing, but for John Paul II it was always clear that Christianity had shaped Europe. He finds Europe so unsure of its identity today that some people want to erase Christianity from its memory. The Pope reacted to this temptation very early on. At the outset of his papacy, on November 9, 1982, he launched an appeal to Europe from Santiago de Compostella: "Find yourself, be yourself, discover your origins, revive your roots, go back to those genuine values that made your history glorious and your presence on other continents beneficial." The Pope could not accept, as many Christians had, a secularized society that relegated religion to the private sphere, a society where the Church is no longer present and materialism reigns. Denying Christianity's legacy, presence and fruits in Europe made no sense to him.

On October 7, 2003, a few weeks after returning to Rome from his last journey to Poland, John Paul II went to Pompeii. The purpose of the trip was to solemnly entrust the world to the Blessed Virgin and to close the Year of the Rosary—which he had proclaimed in October 2002 in order to revive the dying practice—at the Marial Shrine, an important pilgrimage site.

"John Paul II wants to pray for world peace at this famous shrine," said the Vatican's official press release. "The Middle East and the conflicts tearing Africa apart were the focus of his prayers."

This was John Paul II's second trip to Pompeii. The first took place in 1979, hardly a year after he became Pope. He was deeply devoted to this shrine dedicated to the Virgin Mary.

The Pontiff traveled to Naples by helicopter in order to save his strength. A small lift hoisted his wheelchair up to the aircraft. Italian officials had put four local hospitals on alert so that he could receive immediate treatment in the event of the slightest emergency. Of course, medical staff also accompanied him. The Pope was clear-minded but exhausted: the medication that kept him in relatively good condition wore off every three hours. He arrived in Pompeii at 9 A.M. and left two hours later.

Despite the fact that his "protégé," Cardinal Schönborn, had described John Paul II as "near death" just a week earlier, and although his voice was weak, he insisted on setting two goals that were essential to him: "The peace that always helps to rebuild, and the re-Christianization of a modern society threatened by atheism."

Pompeii was important to John Paul II for a reason beyond the sacred nature of the shrine dedicated to the Virgin Mary, who was so dear to him. It is a highly symbolic place, and the ruins spoke to him. "They bear witness," he said, "to a great culture from which not only enlightening answers but also disturbing questions have sprung."

Then John Paul II caught his breath and clarified what he meant. "Today, as in the days of Pompeii," the Pope said, "it is necessary to proclaim Christ to a society that has strayed from Christian values and is losing its memory of them."

These words summed up the message he had delivered in Krakow in 2002, but now the Holy Father no longer had the strength to elaborate upon them: he could only repeat the main ideas.

Tens of thousands of pilgrims from around the world had come to hear him. Many thought that this was the last time he would ever leave the Vatican. His final words as a traveling Pope seemed like an irrevocable farewell to his pastoral mission. "Thank you, Pompeii, for your warm welcome," he said. "Thank you, young people, for your enthusiasm. Thank you, everyone. Pray for me at this shrine, today and forever after." The Pope uttered these words, perhaps the deepest and most prophetic he had ever spoken, before representatives of five continents, dressed in traditional garb, who lit five candles in front of the Virgin's portrait. "May the light of the Marial prayer of the Rosary shine the light of Christ on all the conflicts, tensions and tragedies of all continents," he said.

Karol Wojtyla had already commended humanity to the Virgin's open arms at Fatima. In Pompeii, he renewed this promise, his last symbolic gesture before making a pilgrimage to Lourdes in August 2004.

It was the last message of hope that John Paul II left behind. His words struck a chord with a great Italian Vatican expert, journalist Bruno Bartolini, whose father was an eminent professional at the Holy See's press office, then located at *L'Osservatore Romano*. "The first time I ever saw a Pope die was in 1958," he told me shortly after John Paul II's death. "That was Pius XII. I was an 18-year-old journalist. I have very intense memories of that historic event, which was marred by the scandal of a corrupt entourage. The deaths of the Popes who succeeded him—John XXIII, Paul VI and even John Paul I, whom I knew well personally and interviewed the day after his election—always left a mark on me. But when John Paul II died, I felt a real emptiness. Despite my often critical attitude toward him for professional reasons, as the years went by in my eyes he had become, because of his spiritual, moral and human stature, if not a father, then at least an old, wise, sometimes stubborn uncle who was always full of stimulating ideas. I saw him every day for over a quarter century. I watched him topple the feet-of-clay Soviet colossus, reach out to non-Christians, meet Jews and Muslims, help Catholics make the transition to the 21st century, mingle with crowds around the world, relentlessly but unsuccessfully try to obtain invitations to Moscow and Beijing and harshly chastise all those who could, in his opinion, threaten marriage and the family. One thing is certain: Karol Wojtyla was the last great worldwide star of our times. We will miss him."

Chapter Twelve

THANK YOU, VERY HOLY FATHER

THE MAIN REASON I WROTE THIS BOOK WAS TO share the feelings that my times with John Paul II, a veritable saint, inspired in me. Until I made his acquaintance, religious figures were just terrifying symbols of religious history to me. John Paul II fascinated me well before I ever met him personally. After becoming a journalist, I formed a goal to see him in Rome, accompany him on his trips and become part of his inner circle.

I wanted to understand how this luminous man in white, who seemed to live outside time, could be a mystic, a great politician, a media star and an intellectual all in the same day. His ability to easily move from one role to another always amazed me. When I followed the Holy Father, I never cared about theology, the celibacy of priests or birth control. Nor did I take any interest in Vatican rumors, scandals and intrigue, or in that tiny state that mints euro coins, issues postage stamps and strikes gold and silver medals with images of the Pope on them. Others have already covered that ground, sometimes in a fictionalized way and with wit and talent. The man, Karol Wojtyla, and his singular personality are what fascinated me.

After many years as a political reporter, familiar with the corridors of power and their antechambers, facts and anecdotes no longer had the power to captivate me. In this book my goal was to take a different approach: to not only describe a holy man's inner workings, but also to reveal the details of his daily life. This indomitable Slav who bore the Catholic Church on his sturdy shoulders for over a quarter century outlasted every US president from Jimmy Carter to Ronald Reagan, George H. W. Bush and Bill Clinton, up to George W. Bush.

Because I was a woman and, according to the Vatican's centuries-old rules, seemed unclassifiable, but especially because I managed to make him laugh, the Pope almost irrationally opened the doors of the world's most secret place to me. He probably thought that this mysterious celestial enclave would seem less intimidating to the faithful if they could see it through my eyes. My testimonial is therefore meant as a respectful epitaph to the memory of John Paul II and his role in history. Early in his papacy, Cardinal Marcharski told me, "In their sermons, Polish priests proclaim, 'Our Church is like a boat sailing on the Red Sea but soon the waters will be less red.'" Father Sukiennik, a priest in Niegowic, Karol Wojtyla's first parish, echoed these words: "Our Pope," he said, "is rowing his boat towards endless riverbanks before leaving it one day to embark for eternity with God." I kept my eyes on that boat until the final moment.

At first, I could not understand why John Paul II received

so much applause everywhere he went, including from journalists, which was contrary to custom. As time went on and I got to know him better, I discovered his incredible charisma and contagious serenity. I saw the Pope over 150 times before writing this book: in his private chapel, on his jet, in little churches, at huge show-masses around the world, in the Sistine Chapel baptizing babies, in Saint Peter's celebrating the jubilee of his priesthood surrounded by hundreds of priests from his generation, in the Paul VI Room, where he invited me as recently as October 2003 to the concert celebrating his papacy's 25th anniversary, and before thousands of pilgrims from the four corners of the globe. I was never able to contain my emotions in his presence; sometimes I was even moved to tears. He held me in his thrall, even in a crowd, because I always had the thrilling, magical feeling of being alone with him. Of course Saint Peter's successor had a sovereign aura, which the Vatican's dazzling yet solemn décor made even more enthralling, but above all he had the mysterious glow of an exceptional being buoyed by faith. I am lucky enough to have seen the head of the Roman Catholic Church up close, but I doubted whether I could ever portray all the intensity and magnetism emanating from him—but would it be possible for anyone?

John Paul II patiently, generously put up with my presence countless times, as though there were no such thing as protocol. I never perceived the least bit of annoyance on his part when I took out my pen and started taking notes. What's more, on many occasions he agreed with exquisite courtesy to have his picture taken by the photographer who accompanied me. Thanks to the indulgence of his entourage and the limitless support of Msgr. Dziwisz, I always had an insider's view of his lifestyle, which seemed outside time.

Karol Wojtyla blessed me so many times that he must have given me the strength I needed to write this book. After nine and a half years of painstaking work, I embarked upon this task in Cap d'Antibes across from the Garoupe shrine where I regularly hear hymns rising heavenward. With my enthusiasm, my doubts, and perhaps my subjectivity, I have tried to describe the admiration that this very great Pontiff's radiance inspired in me. Over the years, Karol Wojtyla became my hero and that of my daughters, Marina and Cosima, who talk about him almost as though he were a member of our family.

I have many memories, and they are etched in my mind forever. The most moving one is the first time I met John Paul II. It was in January 1996, when, looking me straight in the eyes with a gaze that radiated infinite goodness, he clasped my hands in his for the first time.

ACKNOWLEDGMENTS

Of course, my main thanks must go to His Holiness Pope John Paul II, not only because this book is about him, but also because he taught me to look at time and existence in a different way.

I would like to thank Malcy Ozannat, my editor, for her encouraging, motivating words. Her ideas gave me constant support.

I would like to express my endless gratitude to Philippe de Baleine—his tireless support and excellent and enlightening advice was of the utmost use to me in writing this book—as well as to Alain Genestar for his constructive friendship and the time he granted me, to Sylvain Maupu for producing the two covers and to Roger Thérond, who was the first to put his faith in my quest to approach John Paul II and followed the book's development with supportive friendship.

My thanks to Jean Cavé for his useful comments, to Marc Brincourt, Guillaume Clavières, Jérôme Huffer, Romain Lacroix, Didier Rapaud (for his gracious iconographic help); at *Paris Match* to Guy Trillat, Pierre Vergnol and Françoise Bretenneau, Patrick Jarnoux, Pierre Reynes, Fernande Ricordeau and Michel Sola and to the Hachette Filipacchi Associés research department.

In Rome, my thanks go to Cardinal Poupard, who opened up the Vatican's doors to me; Cardinal Deskur, for his storytelling skills and his sense of humor; Cardinal Glemp, primate of Poland; Cardinal Tucci, for his subtle observations, generous sharing of knowledge, clarity of expression and vivid memory; Msgr. Dziwisz for the invaluable trust he always gave me; Cardinal Schönborn; Bruno Bartolini for his faultless memory, ideas and sense of humor; and all the religious figures who wish to remain nameless.

In Poland, Cardinal Macharski, Marcin Krasicki for his skillful interpreting, Father Sukiennik and a great many other people of the Church—you know who you are.

In France, I would like to thank Kheira Alabouch, Cyrille Brenot, Alain Carron de la Carrière, Paula Dantas, Madeleine Delvaque Van Woerkom, Omar Fawzy, Jaques François, Yves Grosgogeat, Simone Huriot, Roland de L'Espée, Hubert and Isabelle d'Ornano, Eric Patenötre, Christian Potier, Princess Marie-Gabrielle de Savoie, Jacques Saulnier, Andrée Socquet-Clerc, Marc Taïeb as well as Arturo Mari, Sophie Pigozzi, Dennis Redmont, Joseph Vandrisse and Marjorie Weeke.

Many thanks to Christian Cairoche, Anselmo Castelli, Hugues de Giorgis, Arlette Gonthier, Jean-Marie Guénois, Marcel Landré, Nicole Lentier, Roger Lentier, Annie Moreau, Nadia Radovan, Claude Sanguszko, Cyrille Sialkowshi, Andrée Socquet-Clerc and Dino Vitale, and, last but not least, my eternal gratitude to Annette Rémond for her infinite patience in deciphering and typing this manuscript.

Special thanks to Marina and Cosima Sarno-Pigozzi for their endless patience.

I would like to conclude by expressing my gratitude to Muriel Lanceleur-Simottel for her speed and incomparable skill in editing the final draft.